Designing Interactive Worlds
With Words

PRINCIPLES OF WRITING
AS REPRESENTATIONAL COMPOSITION

Designing Interactive Worlds With Words

PRINCIPLES OF WRITING
AS REPRESENTATIONAL COMPOSITION

David S. Kaufer
Department of English
Carnegie Mellon University

Brian S. Butler
The Katz Graduate School of Business
The University of Pittsburgh

 LAWRENCE ERLBAUM ASSOCIATES, PUBLISHERS
2000   Mahwah, New Jersey   London

The fin.! camera copy for this work was prepared by the author, and therefore the publisher takes no responsibility for consistency or correctness of typographical style.

Lawrence Erlbaum Associates, Inc., Publishers
10 Industrial Avenue
Mahwah, NJ 07430

Cover design by Susan Hagan

Library of Congress Cataloging-in-Publication Data

Kaufer, David S.
Designing interactive worlds with words : a representational theory of writing / David S. Kaufer, Brian S. Butler
        p. cm.
Includes bibliographical references and indexes.
ISBN 0-8058-3423-0 -- ISBN 0-8058-3424-9 (pbk.)
1. English language--Rhetoric--Study and teaching. 2. Report writing--Study and teaching. 3. Representation (Philosophy) 4. Authors and readers. I. Butler, Brian S. II. Title.

PE1404.K38 2000
808'.042'07--dc21   99-054341
                                                    CIP

Books published by Lawrence Erlbaum Associates are printed on acid-free paper, and their bindings are chosen for strength and durability.

To Robert Simon, Role Model
– D. S. K.

To Michelle and Paul
– B. S. B.

Contents

Foreword

JOSEPH PETRAGLIA
TCU

For over a century, educators in disciplines across the academy have been in a rut. In our pursuit to create tasks and environments that facilitate student learning, most of our efforts have been directed at making learning cognitively "elegant," at reducing the complexity of problems to what is believed to be their barest bones. This reduction is carried out in the belief that pedagogically sound problems are simple problems. In the last decade, however, many psychologists and educators have begun to call into question these reductive assumptions. Bundling information into increasingly streamlined cognitive packages, they argue, does not appear to be the answer. Research such as that conducted by psychologist Mihaly Csikszentmihaly eloquently demonstrates what most teachers intuitively know: students cannot be made to learn if they are not motivated to learn and if they perceive school tasks as irrelevant. Moreover, other research suggests that students have good cause for doubting the relevance of much schooling: many of the assignments we give students are, in fact, academic in the worst sense of the word. For these reasons, I have long argued that a central problem that educators face is that of making tasks "real" or authentic to students.

Though my own work has tried to frame this problem in an original way, the problem itself is not new. Even before our present interest in authenticity, educators had been sensitized to issues of relevance. In fact, the progressivist movement, which placed the "active learner" at the center of the classroom, was inspired largely by Dewey's insistence on the connection of curricular and extra-curricular experiences. More recently, "constructivist" and "situated" theories of learning have identified the issue of authenticity as one that, along with technology in the classroom and school reform, poses the greatest challenge for American education.

Although, in the context of a foreword to a book on writing, the issue of authenticity may seem to be something of a digression, it is not. As David Kaufer and Brian Butler make clear in *Designing Interactive Worlds With Words: Principles of Writing as Representational Composition* (herein DIWW), the problem of authenticity is not solely a challenge for educators trying to reach students, but for writers trying to get their message across to readers. Readers, no less than students, are an audience requiring motivation; writers, no less than teachers, must engage their audience if they are to convince it that they are relating something authentic, something fundamentally true, about the world. Of course, DIWW starts from the premise that writing is always a substitute for real experience and interaction because it is mediated through a two-dimensional page or screen. It is always a compensation for the real thing. Kaufer and Butler argue that the skilled writer knows how to make the textual world appear genuine to readers by helping them overlook the mediated nature of their interaction with the writing. Accomplished writers have learned how to address readers and guide them through worlds of words for purposes of conveying information, supporting spatial tasks, or facilitating decision-making when the rhetorical situation calls for information, instruction, or argument.

Although we might readily understand DIWW as an expression of the "constructivist" learning theory mentioned above, Kaufer and Butler are, at the same time, resuscitating a classical belief in the power of language to shape our representations of the world. Though the authors' project is highly original, in inspiration it recalls the very old literary and rhetorical traditions of creating vivacity. For as long as we have had any record of human contemplation of communication, the word (oral and then written) has been presumed to possess an almost magical power. The sophist Gorgias (1993), for instance, supported his claim that language's force is supernatural by suggesting that "merging with opinion in the soul, the power of incantation is wont to beguile it and persuade it and alter it by witchcraft." Rhetoric's magic lies in its ability to trick listeners into believing that a real world is unfolding before them. Language cannot be other than deceptive, for, as the more theoretically astute sophists acknowledged, language is inescapably metaphoric. The consequence of such thoroughgoing metaphoricality,

Nietzsche (1989) wrote many centuries later, is that "Truths are illusions that we have forgotten are illusions . . . coins which have lost their embossing and are now considered as metal and no longer as coins." Removed from direct contact with reality, as listeners and readers we depend on the skillful communicator to put us in a mood, to breathe life into sounds and symbols and make them meaningful and immediate.

As we enter a new millennium, it is understandable that we are no longer in awe of writing's ability to beguile; the professionalization of the writing field and the "technologizing of the word" (to use Ong's memorable phrase) has ensured that whatever mystery writing held for the Ancients cannot be easily recovered. What Kaufer and Butler remind us, however, is that all really good writing is, in a sense, magical. Through the alchemy of words a writer can take inert symbols and electronic pulses and transform them into flesh-and-blood, into situations, and into actions having material consequences. Thus, what Kaufer and Butler are attempting here is, in part, the rehabilitation and recuperation of a tradition that looks at writing as creating a *sensorium* for the reader. DIWW does not reflect a sophistic mysticism, however, but a theoretically compelling and psychologically astute understanding of written language that admits magic while rejecting mystery. They provide an original explanation of how readers are led to experience texts interactively. What earlier proponents of vivacity in writing lacked was a nuanced understanding of why the creation of a world is critical to communication. They also lacked a representational theory of how to achieve those effects in a way that was systematic without being purely mimetic. Just as magic is dependent upon carefully crafted illusion, so written magic contains within it a method. In practical terms, DIWW is walking that fine and ancient line separating two definitions of effective writing: one as the mastery of a rule-governed art and the other as an intuition-governed sensitivity to the unique nature of rhetorical occasions.

And so Kaufer and Butler are wrestling with a paradox: On the one hand, those of us who claim expertise in writing accept that effective writing always connects a writer possessing complex purposes to embodied audiences living three-dimensional lives. Successful rhetorical performance is nothing if not contingent upon variables that shift from situation to situation. One who wishes to write well should be prepared for the hyper-contingency that characterizes writing situations as they exist in the "real world." On the other hand, in pedagogic terms this presents an enormous challenge, for the classroom is not the best place for hyper-contingency. Most of us persist in the belief that any instruction in writing (like instruction generally) must steer clear of the particularities and randomness that infuse everyday life. We continue to believe that students require structured and stable principles for learning and that, to provide them, teachers must offer guidance that simplifies the messiness of real-world situations. Yet we also know that it has been this very streamlining of complexity that has traditionally led to the reduction of writing to hoary rules-of-thumb and banal truisms about structure and process, thereby sucking the life out of what should be a lively and dialogic activity.

It is difficult to imagine that any instructor of writing or information design has not grappled with the paradox described above, but one finds little acknowledgment and even less engagement of this in contemporary books on writing instruction. Here is where I think DIWW distinguishes itself with what the authors call a representational focus on writing, a focus mediating writing as structure and genre. The principles of representational composition that they systematically lay out, chapter by chapter, are aimed at demonstrating how independent written elements combine to form complex rhetorical effects, effects that capture different elements of worlds designed for and felt by readers. Kaufer and Butler rightly note that the "hard" representational challenges they target for student practice are overlooked in theories of writing that depend either on overly specific rules about writing conventions or diffuse advice about writing contexts. Years of experience using a studio technique that bridges formal instruction with a kind of apprenticeship has presented the authors with a unique opportunity to develop assignments that avoid the excesses of rigidity and contingency. Pedagogically, the technique provides what I think of as "guided immersion." In practical terms, guided immersion entails providing the conceptual tools to mediate between the essential situatedness of all learning and the essentially heuristic nature of all explicit instruction. The book presumes writers, as designers of interactive worlds, need to understand, and importantly, practice, the art of balancing the appreciation of the uniqueness of situations and the acquisition of the rhetorical skills necessary to make them familiar and manageable.

And so I end where most forewords begin: with an attempt to identify what I see as DIWW's audience and purpose. DIWW is not a book of pure theory (at least not in a conventional sense), nor is it a textbook. And yet it may function as both. Kaufer and Butler propose a highly original theory of composition that first uncovers, and then exploits, a layer of representational composition too often obscured by narrow attention to either structure or genre. Their illustration of representational composition takes the form of pedagogically useful models of instruction that, in their words, provide learners with a "master palette" for confronting the challenge of creating virtual worlds for readers. Yet their larger goals are demonstrative and have clear theoretical import: to provide a systemic understanding of representational composition and its placement in a comprehensive theory of writing as a skilled activity.

The audiences for this book are as wide-ranging as its aims. Graduate students studying rhetoric or information design, undergraduates wishing to improve their own skills, or students in advanced or creative writing courses seeking to understand the elements of representation that both relate and differentiate genres—all these audiences will find much of value within these pages. But audiences for this book that are equally relevant are those instructors of rhetoric and writing, such as myself, who struggle to articulate the complexity of writing and who want to complement that articulation with practical guidance that does justice to the complexity without suppressing or retreating from it.

By allowing us to peer over the shoulders of writers in a studio setting as they create worlds with words, Kaufer and Butler guide readers in approaching the task of writing in a way that creates synergies among the current "best thinking" on rhetoric, writing, psychology and education. Balancing compositional wisdom with models and explicit directions for using those models, DIWW dispenses a great deal of wisdom in a very short space and, true to its own thesis, puts the reader in the shoes of writers as they work through problems of making the written word come to life. The reader comes away with an enriched sense of possibilities—and a clearer sense of the challenges—that good writing offers. Just as Kaufer and Butler guide their audience's immersion into a virtual world of writing and information design, so, in turn, can astute readers of DIWW become writers capable of guiding the immersion of their own audiences.

Preface

Elementary writing instruction begins with the notion that words combine to create clauses, sentences, and paragraphs. This is composition by structure, or structural composition. Advanced writing instruction begins with the notion that words and sentences address external situations and audiences to which the writer must respond. This is writing from genre, the writing that creates the résumé, the memo, and myriad other forms associated with the convergence of textual content, situational function, and historical context. This book addresses the know-how that marks a writer's development from elementary to advanced levels.

Writing from genre cannot succeed as a mature form if it is strictly formulaic. No two writing situations, no matter how similar, are exactly identical. The situation the writer finds herself in always departs, in small ways or large, from the situations she was trained to write for. The writer of genre must bring to every writing project a way of flexibly representing situations and audiences before rooting in the situation and readers at hand.

Where does the student learn about writing as flexible representation? Not from curricula within structural composition. Learning rules of sentence formation, however vital, does not scale to the construction of situations within texts. Not from the curricula dealing with genre. Writing in genres presupposes that writers, like painters, have learned to notice and deploy clusters within a text as local actions creating interactive worlds for readers. Yet, genre-based instruction, emphasizing distinctions between text types, typically omits the representational actions underlying types and blurring their boundaries. Genre instruction omits the craft know-how writers use to represent situations of writing generally, flexibly, and interactively within a text. Without representational know-how, students must fall back on formulas that over-specify what supple writing in virtually any genre is supposed to be.

The power of writing seems, foremost, a representational power. Mature writers have learned to blur the boundaries between words on the page and interactive worlds for the reader. Yet, writing instruction in the United States educational system has mostly failed to target this feature of well-constructed texts. The educational focus has remained, rather, on the before (i.e., structure) and after (i.e., genre) of acquiring this representational skill. This middle layer has been overlooked largely because the representational theories of writing that confer visibility to it have remained undeveloped.

By representational theories of writing, we mean theories that seek to isolate fundamental design elements, elements that work alone and in combination with other elements to create the feel of lived experience and the invitation to readers to learn from and act on that experience. These are the elements of a text that a writer designs to naturalize reading processes into everyday processes of experience, inference, and reasoning. They are the dimensions of writing that transform words into interactive worlds and conspire to make readers forget they are reading. Accomplished writers use their creative powers of textual design to create engaging experiences and interactive challenges for readers. They work this verbal magic because they have learned, tacitly, to deploy the elements of textual design to bring persons and environments to life for readers.

These elements of writing typically lie below the surface. They lie in the gap between the construal of words as entities without context (the emphasis of grammar) and words as context slots that close off, for a particular time and place, contextual variation (the emphasis of genre). This book seeks to fill the gap by presenting a systematic study of writing as flexible representation. It is a study of the know-how needed to compose words into interactive worlds.

Why have theories of the writer's representational know-how been missing? This know-how seems to have fallen in the cracks between two more visible and sometimes competing emphases in American writing instruction: rhetoric and composition. *Rhetoric and composition* is a curious conjunction because the practices of rhetoric, on the one hand, and composition, on the other, arise from different histories and traditions. Rhetoric originated in the ancient art of advocacy practiced by the privileged classes in Greece and Rome. As an ancient art, its primary focus was oratory with writing being a secondary focus. The ancient art stressed the speaker's invention of ideas along with their arrangement and style. Composition, by contrast, is largely a 19th century United State institution, still in place, devised to certify the writing skill of entry-level college students. Its traditional focus—certainly before 1970—was less in rhetoric than in what the ancients would have called the art of grammar, where words and clauses were taught as compositional units for sentences, paragraphs, and themes.

When we began collaborating several years ago, we noticed two curiosities about both traditions that implicated not only their different roots, but also some hidden dependencies. First, we noticed that, from the modern point of view, the ancient art of rhetoric did not take principles of composition with the same seriousness that they would come to be taken within the post-Enlightenment disciplines of the modern university. Modern research disciplines purport to provide closed grammars of knowledge. They show themselves built from concepts that compose themselves incrementally and cumulatively into tightly structured knowledge clusters. Ancient rhetoric was not a modern discipline in this strict compositional sense, but rather a loosely bundled set of practices used to train citizen orators. As Leff (1987) observes about rhetoric in the ancient sophistical tradition:

> So long as [ancient sophistical] rhetoric remained faithful to practice, it could not give a coherent theoretical account of itself. Thus sophistic veered away from a conception of the art as an ordered set of principles and stressed its function as the development of certain human capacities. Some theory was useful, but only as a place to begin, and once learned, theoretical principles became important mainly as points of reference that the mature orator would transcend and violate in response to the problem at hand. . . . This stress on performance betokened a thoroughly antimodernist attitude, and it was most clearly articulated by Quintilian when he came to classify rhetoric among the forms of art. Rhetoric, he maintained, had an affinity with the theoretical and productive arts, but it was first and foremost a performing art, more akin to dance than to metaphysics or sculpture. (pp. 25-26)

These very antimodernist assumptions about rhetoric had relegated rhetoric, we surmised, to a marginal discipline in the modern research university.

Second, we noticed that although the tradition of American composition took principles of composition seriously, relating smaller units of writing to larger, when it did so, it considered composition only within units of structure. The ancient art of rhetoric, by contrast, as opposed to the sister art of grammar, focused on principles above the sentence and above the structural properties of language proper. The rhetorical art focused on the speaker's representation of cultural situations into which audiences were invited for the purpose of judging or acting. The rhetorician's product was not sentences but rather interactive situations cast into sentences. The rhetor's product, to be sure, has a craft implementation in sentence structure. Yet to confuse the rhetor's art solely with the craft of the sentence would be to miss the cultural range of the representational art that is rhetoric.

Although allied in the phrase *rhetoric and composition*, and institutionally copresent within departments of English, the distinct approaches, we came to believe, were not yet intellectually allied in ways that might further benefit both. With respect to rhetoric's alienation from the modern research university, rhetoric seemed in need of a theory of composition to explain how the production of rhetoric can fit within a tight part-whole, or modular, organization of knowledge. With respect to composition's alienation from the representational focus of rhetoric, theories of writing seemed in need of a developed middle layer to account for the transition from structural and to flexible genre organizations of texts.

Rhetoric, thus, seemed, for various reasons, in need of composition. Composition, for parallel reasons, in need of rhetoric. We also determined that no single or short writing project could address both sets of concerns. Each would require a major writing project to tackle.

To address the first concern, we wrote *Rhetoric and the Arts of Design* (Kaufer & Butler, 1996). The purpose of that book was to show how rhetoric could be recast as an art of compositional design. By *compositional* we meant the property of being organized into modular building blocks that interact and combine in systematic ways toward systematic ends. The property of compositional organization captures a central feature of knowledge claiming to be tightly structured and fine-grained in the manner of disciplined or disciplinary knowledge. The alternative to a compositional framework is one that hangs only loosely together, like an unordered list of things to know. We offered that the handbook tradition of rhetoric, by missing the compositional element underlying complex rhetorical behavior, had inadvertently helped to distort rhetoric in the popular imagination to a lowly and loosely structured practical art. We demonstrated how rhetoric, in its underlying compositional intricacy and elegance, deserves a place alongside architecture, music, engineering, and other respected arts of design. We sought to show that the knowledge underlying the production of even popular rhetoric exhibits the organization and hidden complexity we associate with disciplinary knowledge.

The purpose of the present volume is to address the second concern. We seek to think through how the traditionally structural focus of textual composition, enumerating principles of how small units of text combine to form larger units, can be extended into the representational domain of rhetoric. Our aim is a theory of writing cast in terms of principles of representational composing. Although we did not intend to write a how-to textbook, we came to see that if we were to arrive at robust principles of representational composition for writing, we would need to follow closely the practice of individuals trying to compose interactive worlds for readers. Our theory could not evolve without studying practice. Yet, without theory, we could have no way to describe the practice we observed.

The main contribution of this volume is thus to present a theory of writing as rhetorical or, from our view equivalently, representational composition. Such a theory contrasts markedly with the structural theories of composing that continue to dominate writing classrooms in American primary and secondary education. A representational theory of written composition envisions texts not as words and clauses forming sentences and higher-level linguistic units but rather as words, forming into design elements stimulating imagery-rich narrative worlds and invitations for readers to interact with them. We believe that representational theories of written composition will become increasingly important in defining writing as the multimedia revolution follows its course.

Writing, trapped in an educational legacy stressing structure over representation, is made to seem an antiquated technology in the multimedia revolution. This misimpression says more about our restrictive theories of composition than about the reality of writing for which these theories seek to account. Professionals invested in the multimedia revolution may sense that writing remains relevant, but not likely because of their memories of freshman composition. The cutting-edge work in interactive narrative, involving digitized graphics and sound, tends to reduce language to a minor player. Nonfiction writing in general and informational writing, in particular, are widely perceived to pale as a representational medium in contrast to the newer visual media of representation.

To help correct this misimpression, we focus in this volume on the principles that underlie written composition as a representational art. In each chapter, we chronicle the principles by which writers produce challenging representational effects on readers. A central thesis throughout is that the representational writer, like the chariot driver bridling horses wanting to go in different directions, is constantly challenged to shape a text by combining representational effects that are fundamentally independent. Like a painter who must unify a variety of colors, strokes, and textures to effect an overall composition, a writer must make independent representational elements work effectively together to create a unified world and unified invitations for readers to explore it. Every chapter in this book seeks to document the relationship between a writer's achieving hard-won unifying representational effects and her managing to coordinate independent representational elements in the process of doing so.

We have arranged chapters so that they can be studied in a cumulative sequence. This means that the representational elements and effects presented in one chapter can benefit from and build on principles and effects introduced in earlier chapters. To illustrate the written principles and their effects, we have included the models produced by advanced students who have worked with us over a four year period in studio classrooms. These students were advanced undergraduates and masters candidates with a good deal of prior writing experience and a career interest in writing.

To signal our interest in theory more than textbook writing, we provide student models to illustrate principles; yet we offer no writing exercises or teacher's manual. To signal our concern for practice, we have written this book from the writer's perspective, the person who designs the text rather than the reader's, whose role is to follow the design. Our focus is thus not on formatted genres recognizable to readers in the marketplace. It is rather on the local actions that capture the hard representational challenges underlying writing in any genre, the challenges that writers at the highest level of mastery notice and address.

Throughout this book, we illustrate the interplay between theory and practice. Despite their experience, the student writers with whom we worked almost never produced satisfactory, much less optimal, texts in their early drafts. This was not a surprise. Learning any complex skill, like writing, involves getting some things wrong even as other things go right. We often refer to our students' early draft writing as writing that fails, for one or another reason, to instantiate the target principles and so to produce the representational and interactive effects the writer is after. For example, a writer may miss gross or subtle textual features that are needed to apply a given principle. Alternatively, the writer may inadvertently include unwanted features that destroy a desired effect, even if the principle is otherwise correctly grasped and applied. When we say a writer produces an imperfect draft, the failure pertains only to achieving a difficult effect on an early effort. In almost all cases, the writers we worked with who fell short in an early draft met with greater, often considerably greater, success in later attempts.

Finally, we employ various painting analogies (e.g., portraiture, landscapes, perspective) to go along with our understanding of a representational theory of writing. Our use of the analogy is limited to representational painting only. We do not mean to imply that all painting is or must be representational. Nonetheless, there is no controversy that paintings *can function representationally*. The same observation is more controversial for texts, especially for nonfiction and functional writing. Aside from the largely implicit master-apprentice workshop education of the creative writer, there are no schools of composition that advocate texts as explicitly representational. We will have made our case if readers come away from this book believing that representational composition furnishes a comprehensive, even if heretofore hidden, layer of writing know-how addressing how writers can use words to compose compelling interactive experiences for readers.

Acknowledgements

We wish to thank Susan Hagan, Cheryl Geisler, Chris Neuwirth, Davida Charney, Bev Sauer, David Fleming, Barbara Johnstone, Linda Flower, Richard Buchanan, Dan Boyarski, David Russell, Karen Schnakenberg, and Joseph Petraglia, for fruitful interactions and, in many cases, original research that have in one way or another influenced our thinking about the relationship between written composition, representation, and design. We wish to acknowledge Suguru Ishizaki and Kerry Ishizaki, gifted visual designers, for teaching us some of the underlying visual implications of thinking through writing as an art of representation. Their instruction to us is not immediately visible in this project, but it informs every page. Rob Chandhok, Geoff Wegner, and Paul Erion have also been instrumental in these efforts. Dan Kaufer, a neurologist with an interest in both the development and atrophy of writing skill in diseased minds, has been a ongoing resource. James Hirsch, a gifted writer, has mentored one of us over the years on the importance of creating mental pictures through words. The Carnegie Mellon Creative Writing Program, a distinguished and diverse collection of artists, continues that mentoring on a daily basis. We wish to acknowledge the stimulating environments in the Department of English at Carnegie Mellon University, the School of Design, and the Business School at the University of Pittsburgh. Without an interdisciplinary tradition in rhetoric to seed these various environments, this project would not exist. Linda Bathgate of Lawrence Erlbaum has been a supportive editor throughout. Debbie Ruel, also from Erlbaum, has been a true pleasure to work with. Julie Woodson is responsible for the layout and page design and has demonstrated a grace and patience under tight deadlines that complements her keen skill. Susan Hagan, a worthy theorist and designer in her own right, did the book cover and has supported this project in as many roles as one can assume short of co-authorship. We wish to thank our families, Barb, Aaron, and Mollie, Michelle and Paul, for their continued love and support. Finally, we save our longest applause for the many students, aspiring writers and visual designers, who worked in our writing studio and who gave their permission to make their work (especially their early and imperfect drafts!) available so that future generations of writers could benefit. In particular, we wish to acknowledge the writing of Michelle Bacigalupi, Eric Davis, Matthew Desantis, Jessica Flake, Laura Franz, Lauren Garcia, Susan Hagan, Randall Hechinger, Alyce Hoggan, Rick Hoobler, Aaron Jenkins, Ann Kim, Steve Kuhn, Beth Leber, Andrew McDermott, Christine McGuinness, Tammy Monk, Don Mulder, Hyunjung Kim, Kerry Ishizaki, Mary Quandt, Tim Richardson, Maria de los Angeles Stiteler, Cori Swinehart, Joy Sykes, Grace Tai, Holly Tait, Kenneth Toley, and Peter Wendel. We have found that the best way to learn about and to explain the principles of written composition as a representational art is to monitor the consequences, good and bad, that arise as good writers get better. This book is a result of observing that process with writers whom, in the end, taught us as much as we hoped, on our very best days, to have taught them.

Introduction: Writing and Representational Composition

From its inception, the English word *composition*, as old as the English language, has accommodated an unusual elasticity, ranging from high art to natural process. According to the *Oxford English Dictionary*, as early as 1682, a lecturer on plant anatomy acknowledged compositional principles both in human inventions, like words, and natural objects, like bodies: "The Composition of Atomes in Bodies is like that of Letters, in Words." From the 16th century on, principles of composition were finding their way into the natural laws of logic, math, physics, and chemistry. In the craft arts, Morley was tying composition to musical art and Dryden, a century later, to painting. Grammatical composition was also making its way into the English language, with Thomas Wilson's 1560 observation in *The Art of Rhetoric*: "Composicion . . . is an apte joynyng together of wordes in suche order, that neither the eare shal spie any jerre, nor yet any man shalbe dulled with overlong drawing out of a sentence" (original spellings preserved in the OED; edited and reprinted in Medine 1994, p. 192).

Sentence composition was one facet of rhetoric, though a facet the ancients would have known by the name grammar rather than rhetoric. What the ancients knew as rhetoric—the arts of speaking and writing leading to the creation of whole speeches and texts—was not to enjoy central cultural placement in the family of compositional arts. To the present day, the meaning of *written composition* is formulating words that assemble into sentences, sentences into paragraphs, and paragraphs into whole texts. This grammatical approach to writing contrasts starkly with rhetorical approaches, which focus on the whole text in its

1

context. When the focus shifts to contexts of writing, the strict meaning of *composition*—as the assembly of elemental parts into wholes—recedes. Rhetorical vocabularies rarely speak of part-whole principles whose combination results in the formation of texts. They rather emphasize the writer's purposes and the audience's expectations, aspects of the context that bring the writer and the reader together through language.

What underlies the dissonance between the ancient arts of speaking and writing (ars rhetorica) and the arts of grammar, music, the visual arts, and mathematics, the latter all seeming to adhere more exactingly than rhetoric to part-whole composition? We could simply repeat what many say, namely that rhetoric, unlike grammar, is too open-ended a knowledge and skill to pin down into formal part-whole elements. But that response overlooks the possibility that we can never notice what we are not encouraged to look for. The dissonance between rhetoric and the more familiar compositional arts is based largely, we suggest, on the absence of a cultural motivation to look for rhetoric's underlying compositional elements.

Rhetorical theorists and theorists of discourse in general have not been motivated to seek the elements underlying rhetorical composition, perhaps, because of the implicit standards of compositionality that rhetoric, on the surface, seems to fail. Arts worthy of the name "compositional" are linked to a process in nature. The art must be partly based in contingency and choice, but partly in natural law as well. At the very least, to credit an art as compositional, relying on the part-whole assembly of elements, requires one to be willing to include nature as well as art in the explanation of how parts fit to wholes. The master painter must learn excellent composition as a result of personal understanding and decision making. Yet these personal decisions also reflect tacit knowledge of the laws of geometry and human perception. The grammarian understands choice and variation in the formation of natural language sentences, affirmations to sentence composition as a flexible generative art. Yet the art is also deeply rooted in a knowledge of the natural laws of language that constrain choice and variation.

Rhetoric was a productive art that seems to have been denied a correlate in natural law. In the mind of the popular, if not elite or academic culture, rhetoric came to be stereotyped as an art that dared to compete with the natural laws of language and expression. The Platonic tradition of rhetoric was never deeply influential among elites who studied rhetoric as an academic subject. Yet, it won over, and continues to win over, a popular imagination that assigns rhetoric to a lowly craft of clever guile. Concerned to arrest charlatanry, Plato admonished that public speakers need to be masters of their subject matter, not just masters of the language used to reference it. On the Platonic standard of rhetoric, one had to pass mastery tests of the subject spoken or written about. To the extent these tests could be passed, the credit for the compositional art was assigned to the compositional principles (i.e., the balance of art and natural law) inhering in the subject matter. The expert biologist who communicated new truths about biology could credit her compositional skill to biology, not to rhetoric proper. The practitioners of rhetoric were put in a double bind. Without content mastery, they could not pass Plato's test as a compositional art. With content mastery, however, their effort to locate the seeds of a compositional art in rhetoric seemed an idle or redundant search, a search more reliably deferred in any case to subject matter experts on the occasion of presenting their knowledge to lay audiences. Rhetoric within the popular mind became either a lawless art or a superfluous one, an art, unlike the more familiar arts of composition, ungrounded in natural law.

By way of contrast, consider some of the subtle ways that more familiar, less controversial, compositional arts have passed the permeability test between art and natural law. The painter was understood to work back and forth between the tools of representation and the (represented) objects visibly emerging in the picture. Only through the oscillating reference between the picture in nature and the (emergent) picture in art could one realize Ruskin's definition of (representational) *composition* (cited in the OED) as relying on "everything in the picture [of nature]" to "help everything else [in the picture emerging]." Although the painter's mastery could lie in the real as well as the representational, representational mastery alone was sufficient to judge the art masterful. The painter could be credited as a master of the artistic depiction of plants without also mastering their natural anatomy.

The Platonic test for a true, grounded, and ethical rhetoric, by contrast, required the speaker to be able to see into the subject matter, not just into the words used to render it. Because no speaker can pass this test without substantive subject learning, the default was that speakers who could move audiences through words were not embodying natural laws unless they could claim substantive learning beyond the rhetorical art. Rhetoric lost the elasticity from the representational to the real. Unless proven otherwise, the practitioner of rhetoric was seen to control an art lacking a substrate in natural law.

Although composition in the United States since 1850 has a complex and increasingly studied history that is bringing out more variation than first believed (Brereton, 1995; Connors, 1997), the dominant traditions of this institution retained the elasticity of art and natural law in the manner of the culturally accepted compositional arts. The elasticity was achieved by limiting the mastery of the writer to the natural objects of language—words, sentences, paragraphs, thematically unified paragraphs. Composition in the United States offered to give students artistic control over these accretive objects of language. In accord with painting, music, and other forms of artistic composition, the American student could work seamlessly between language as the artistic rendering of expression and the "natural objects" explicitly seen and referenced in the art. A sentence could be represented by its visible structure on the page—the grammatical components that could be diagrammed on a blackboard or in a textbook. A sentence like "The settlers crossed the prairie in a covered wagon" was not a story about the American west but about how some verbs (viz., *cross*) can concatenate with a noun object (viz., *the prairie*) and a prepositional phrase (viz., *in a covered wagon*).

In the early to mid-20th century, the tradition of American composition relied on *themes* (e.g., love and hate) and *modes* (e.g., narrative, description, and argument) to prompt students to herd smaller units of structure into larger ones. *Themes*, such as love and justice, provided a unifying concept for the composition of paragraphs into whole texts. *Modes* provided a range of elaborative principles to fill in the slots holding together individual and multiple paragraphs. Scott and Denny (1893), popular textbook writers of the late century, for example, saw in description the opportunity for students to build a paragraph around a common noun (e.g., *a bridge, a human hand, a lawyer's office*). They saw in narrative the basis for student practice in developing paragraphs cued by generic event phrases (e.g., a *beggar's story, a visit to Bunker Hill Monument*). Finally, they saw in argument the occasion for students to elaborate paragraphs whose topic sentences were culturally contested propositions (e.g., *military schools should be encouraged; the assassination of Julius Caesar was justifiable*) (for a complete list of these exercises, see Brereton (1995, pp. 350-351).

By confining representation to visible language structure and its lawful variation, by making the units of language the subject of mastery as well as the target of artistic control, the dominant tradition of American composition embodied the elasticity of art and natural process that we are suggesting implicitly marked an art as compositional.

Yet, the focus on grammatical structure to establish the compositional nature of writing came at two high costs to the American tradition of writing instruction.

First, writing teachers in this tradition did not claim an expertise—the new term of mastery within the 19th century model of the German research university—beyond the structures of written expression. The American tradition of written composition thus isolated writing from regular subject matter learning. As Brereton (1995) has written in his recent historical study:

> To be sure, college teachers often took on a schoolmaster role when they
> taught subjects like languages, mathematics, or introductory sciences.
> But those courses also had the structure of an academic discipline to
> sustain them; students were being introduced, no matter how uncomfort-
> ably, to a subject. But composition had no subject; nothing lay behind it;
> the class was all there was to it. To most instructors it was a skill, similar
> to, though more private than, athletic prowess, rather than an academic
> subject. (p. 437)

A second, less obvious, cost was that writing, as a natural subject, came to be understood almost exclusively in terms of structural rather than more independently representational principles of composition. Freshman composition in the United States tradition reinforced that principles of writing could lawfully turn smaller structures into larger ones, words into clauses, clauses into sentences, and up the linguistic food chain. Yet no notion of written composition involving the representation of interactive experiences for readers was in the offing. In American composition, representational knowledge was eclipsed in favor of structural knowledge.

Our Purpose

Our focus in this book is on the fundamental elements that underlie texts as rhetorical compositions. Our primary thesis is that these basic elements are representational. A theory of rhetorical composition must be, in our view, a theory of representational composition. Our primary task is to present what we take to be the fundamental elements of representational composition and to inquire into their range of application as they combine to make increasingly complex textual tapestries.

We focus not on the world of texts in their full representational variety but on what we believe are the basic element patterns that the writer has available in the service of producing such variety. We seek to understand writing as an elastic merger of artful and natural representation in the senses of the familiar compositional arts. In representational paint-

ing, brush stroke and size, weight, texture, color, perspective, and placement present viewers with experiences of three-dimensional worlds of
objects, light, shading, shadow, and viewer angle. The institution of
American composition has offered no comparable nor comprehensive
notion of the written text as a representation composed from a perspective. Can we offer one?

Let us consider for a moment what it means to offer such a theory. It
means, first and foremost, to subsume rhetorical composition within
the family of other compositional arts. These arts include grammar, but
also visual and muscial composition as well. What unites these arts is a
focus on *elements* as the primitive unit of design. Elements are basic
constituents. They cannot be reduced further. At the same time, they
can be combined with other elements into larger patterns. Words and
their inherited syntactic properties are the elements of sentence composition. Lines, spatial relations, enclosed spaces, and negative (white)
space are among the elements of visual composition. Pitch and sequence
furnish some of the basic elements of musical composition. Compositional elements can be combined and unified within larger patterns. Single elements and patterns can retain an independent character even as
they do. While configured as parts of larger wholes, some elements can
command emphasis, can stand out above, other patterns.

Our task in this book is to describe the fundamental elements of
rhetorical composition. Because we maintain that these elements are
inherently representational, depicting interactive worlds for readers, we
choose to present elements of rhetorical composing through analogy
with the familiar categories of visual composition. Some elements of
rhetorical composing are elements we associate with portraiture, the
depiction of persons. Other elements are associated with landscapes,
the depiction of scenes and over-time events. Still other elements are
associated with the perspective of the reader looking into the text, what
we also call invitations to the reader. This is not a self-initiated perspective but one a writer assigns a reader.

To be sure, our project is not new in various of its facets. The
assumptions on which we launch it are old and well known. Writing as
a representational medium has been a tacit assumption of writing
systems for thousands of years (Olsen, 1994). Moreover, representational assumptions are taken for granted among fiction writers and
poets as a basis for their art.

However, significant conceptual barriers have impeded conceiving of
texts as, fundamentally, representational. Unlike the pure narrative of
the short story or novel, where the writer creates a world on the page
for an unacknowledged reader to engage, informational writing, often

at the center of freshman composition, seems functional without also seeming representational. For example, in informational writing, the writer's purpose in teaching the reader seems to override an interest in narrative representation. In instructional writing, the writer's interest in manually guiding a reader also seems foreign to representation. In argument, the writer's interest seems to feature action ahead of representation. Based on these considerations, representational composition may seem to be the wrong approach for describing textual composition from a unified perspective.

This skeptical thinking, although admirable in its caution, remains nonetheless wrong-headed. We can profitably understand even functional writing as relying on the representational notion of viewer (or, in the case of texts, reader) perspective. In the visual composition of painting, the use of linear perspective permits the projection of spatial depth and distance on a flat plane. It further provides that the artist can assign a subjective position to the viewer within the representation. In this way, visual composition made internal accommodations for the viewer standing outside the artifact peering in.

Literary scholars since Booth (1961) have appreciated that a work of literary art not designed for readers is as inconceivable as a representational painting not designed for viewers. Writing that fails, explicitly, to acknowledge a reader will still always leave traces of an implied reader's presence and involvement. Although all narrative implicitly accommodates a reader's keeping pace, functional writing simply makes explicit the terms of the reader's involvement. It raises to center visibility the writer's invitations to the reader, invitations that vary with the particular type of interaction the writer seeks to transact.

The writer's representational know-how, spanning narrative and information texts, involves making authentic, involved, and interactive worlds for readers. As an ensemble, these skills of representation create what Petraglia (1998) called *reality by design*. The skilled writer is able to replace the reader's here and now, the contrived experience of reading, with virtual lived experience. The skilled writer concerned with information, as well as experience, is able to help readers draw generalizations from a text with the same intensity and involvement they draw them from life.

To meet the challenge of building a representational theory of written composition, one must offer a theory that integrates representations and interactive assumptions across narrative and functional texts.

This is a challenge we set for ourselves. We address this challenge in the context of addressing two questions: How do writers design texts to create interactive worlds for readers? How do they do so under implicit reader contracts, where the effect of the writing is to make the reader a nonparticipant onlooker into a world that is mainly narrative representation? How do they do so under explicit functional contracts, where the effect is to make the reader a more engaged participant in the world of the text?

To make our theory and its pragmatic value as straightforward as possible, we have written it from the point of view of the composer. Readers, thus, get a chance to see the theory not only analytically, as the observer of a compositional system from the outside, but also from the inside point of view of the writer trying to build interactive worlds for readers.

So What?

At this juncture, one might raise the proverbial "so what" of representational theories of composing. Why is their absence not a mere footnote of importance? Our response is that the development of representational theories of writing is crucial to the future of writing, to how we define what writing is and how, or whether, we continue to value it in the wider culture.

In our cultural environment of increasingly visual and sensory-activated media, linear text has come, at a comparable increasing rate, to be devalued as a favored communication medium of professionals. The appeal of these newer media is their capacity to map structural to representational features of composition. Designers of new media learn how to manipulate the internals of the medium *in order to* manipulate the experience of reality the medium creates for the viewer. Composition theory in the American school tradition, tied to structure, divorced from representation, has lulled generations of students into thinking that texts pale as a representational medium in comparison to the "richer" visual and electronic media. Professionals in information design, who hunger after courses in multimedia, wonder why a writing course might have the slightest value to their future. Given that most of them have survived freshman composition somewhere, with a focus on structure over representation, their skepticism is not unwarranted and needs to be both addressed and repaired.

The alienation cuts deeper in the culture than the institution of freshman composition. It permeates professional practice and calls into question both the status and survival of professionals in the communication industry who see texts as their primary media and words as the tool of their trade. This is not to contest the importance and value of media other than writing. We harbor no misplaced nostalgia for the days when there were few alternatives to the written word as a culturally pervasive medium of representation. What we contest is the uncritical and creeping cultural prejudice that the newer media of representation have somehow won an undeclared war against writing. In the multimedia revolution, writers are often expected to take a back seat to the newer digital media. Writing too often gets classified solely as the filler content or copy for worlds that the newer media deliver. Writers are thought not to produce worlds, but only the post-visual annotations on a world delivered in media other than texts. This technological prejudice is implicit, but nonetheless pervasive in the professional world. We seem in our professional and work cultures, if not our literary and leisure ones, to have forgotten the fundamental visual-sensory powers of words, activating worlds through mental imagery. The result of this collective forgetting in the professional context is to reduce the professional writer to the annotator or caption creator for media specialists whose primary occupation is not texts.

These cultural trends are the sad legacy of entrusting writing education to a structural legacy of context-free (grammatical) and context-sensitive (specification-based) approaches that tend to obscure the representational powers of texts. These entrenched structural legacies for texts continue to dominate in a cultural environment where the newer media have—wisely and on behalf of their ever increasing cultural presence and power—been engineered precisely to map structure to representation.

Fortunately, texts constitute a medium more representationally sophisticated than the image cast by a century of structural composition. Virtual reality, a buzzword of the computer generation, refers to the use of multimedia technology to create artificial environments that envelop a user panoramically, simulating experience in the physical world. For designers of virtual reality systems, the challenge is to combine images and sound to create for users the illusion of stepping into the physical world. Creating virtual worlds is widely understood and promoted as a new, emerging art. Yet, the basic challenge was undertaken thousands of years ago with the development of our ability to tell stories. Narrative language, whether spoken or written, is also a form of virtual world design. Narrative brings a listener or reader into worlds that he didn't previously know. Functional discourse, whether spoken or written, is also a form of virtual world interaction, offering readers various invitations into textual worlds based on purposes to learn, do, or decide.

The sophisticated technology of virtual reality systems, the strange helmets, complex wiring, and other exotic paraphernalia, draw attention to the novelty of the art form. However, with narrative utterances and texts, the process of world design is so familiar that we have long ago forgotten to notice its strangeness. By telling stories or by writing static symbols on paper or electronic screens, we are able to bring complex, dynamic worlds to listeners and readers. This is possible even when the words of the text have no physical or even symbolic connection to the physical setting of the reader. The reader may sit at a desk reading under a dim light on a Tuesday evening, while the text can be prompting him to enter a world of another century and land.

Although we feel the effects of such displacement most visibly in imaginative literature, the effects are not limited to fictional texts. Nonfiction writers are world designers as well. Whether it is a historical account of the killing fields in Cambodia, a profile of a film star, the story of a company's history presented in an annual report, a technical manual, or a policy argument, writers prompt readers to move beyond their immediate context to engage new worlds. The virtual reality felt with digital technology is but an extension of the virtual reality listeners and readers have culturally known for millennia through texts.

The structural biases of composition in the United States tradition cannot mask the fact that texts are themselves a rich representational technology, a medium that compresses the tones, textures, and referential capacities of speech to fit the restrictions of the page. Managing this subtle compression without losing the timbre of a human voice and the effects of realism, reference, immediacy, and interactivity requires careful instrumentation and practice.

In standard writing curricula, the structural bias of freshman composition is typically superseded, in the higher curriculum, by practice in genre- or situational-based writing, which has received wide theoretical attention recently (Miller, 1984; Bazerman, 1988, Bazerman & Paradis, 1991; Yates & Orkikowski, 1992; Geisler, 1994; Orkikowski & Yates, 1994; Berkenkotter & Huckin, 1996; Russell, 1997). Training in writing that moves from structure to immersed genre is not new. It reflects training in writing even in the schools of ancient Greece and Rome (Murphy & Jerone, 1982).

In broad outline, we have no quarrel with this training sequence. Our caution is that, absent a representational account of composing, the leap from structure to genre is formidable and, in the worse case, unmotivated. How can the practice of paragraphs, themes, or specification templates pave the way for the dynamics of writing in immersive contexts? The former training maps simple onto more complex structure. The latter immerses the writer in true-to-life contingent situations where few prior generalizations transfer without significant dynamic adjustments.

The theoretical literature just cited has helped to establish genre as representational elements that have become (for specific times and in specific geographical locations) relatively settled and stable. Yet, when harnessed for the pedagogical market, genre approaches are frequently reduced to mere specification-writing, static guidelines and formulae for writing one type of standard text or another (e.g., a business letter vs. a literary essay). Such specification-based teaching, however practical within its own terms, merely extends structural composition from context-free into context-sensitive principles embodied as static templates. Yet genre is more accurately understood, as many genre theorists now understand it, as an historically emergent moving target that can temporarily stabilize in specific times and places and that must be artificially frozen and simplified for the classroom.

The educational paradox is that to truly acquire a genre, a student must recognize the limits of any static characterization. To grasp, beyond simple formulas, how a text can *historically* settle into a genre, writers must comprehend the design elements that a text makes available for settling. Training in genre fails if students cannot come to notice and, in their own practice, *feel* the gap between genres as fixed templates and as combinations of fluid representations. Understanding writing as representational composition can make this gap more apparent to students by exposing them to the elements of composition that assemble and settle in one or another genre.

Representational composition, addressing elements of texts and their combination into interactive worlds for readers, offers an important vantage for writers wishing to understand what's behind established and emerging genres. It engages students in interactive world-building with texts prior to immersing them in the exacting material (i.e., historical, cultural, sociological) specifications that cause a set of representations to settle into one kind of text or another. It further accommodates the fact that genres are themselves part of ongoing historical change and new genres involving texts, crossing multiple media, are being newly coined with dizzying speed. Significantly, nothing inherent within genre training provides for such quick retrofitting of a text to confront the shifting dynamics of the external context. No writer can be trained in exactly the situations in which he must eventually write, as no writing is exactly one pure type or another but a complex negotiation between the writer's take on the material situation and the local actions he musters to respond to it. Understanding written composition as a palette of local representational actions can help writers fit texts to a world of ever fluctuating external specifications.

In an ideal educational sequence for the writer, the writing student would receive the following training:

1. *Structural Composition*: Grammar, usage, diction, paragraphs, themes.

2. *Representational Composition*: Tying structure to the representational elements made possible through a text that can combine to make a seemingly infinite variety of depicted worlds, and invitations to readers to explore them. Only a small fraction from this variety historically settle into a named genre.

3. *Genres*: Learning the cultural, historical, and sociological specifications that have led to the settling in time and place of one or another family of representations as an object of sufficient recurrence and cultural visibility to be named (e.g., scientific report, résumé, memo, proposal, etc.).

Within Plato's skeptical framework toward rhetoric, the jump from structural composition to genre is well-motivated. Rhetoricians, as grammarians, can know the truth of the matter about language structure. However, to go beyond structure and retain their claim to expertise, they must turn to the empirical study of communication as it distributes itself across the culture. What Plato, and many contemporary educators overlook, is the rhetorician's expertise in language as an art of representational, not simply structural, part-whole patterning. The rhetorician's expertise here is not charlatanry. For the processes by which language represents interactive worlds for listeners and readers are based in the natural laws of how language connects with, configures, and prompts change in the social world. The rhetorician commands a great tacit understanding of the natural relationships between language and intersubjective reality and in this respect balances nature with artful discourse.

From the set of premises we have been establishing, our aim is to show that the writer's representational powers look no less worthy of the name *composition* than the powers displayed by the grammarian, musician or artist.

No writing textbooks have been developed to include representational composition as a middle step from structural composition to genre because the representational theories of written composition needed for this middle layer have yet to be adequately developed. This book presents a systematic exploration of this middle layer.

Our Work Within a Writing Design Studio

We have evolved principles of representational composition by issuing design challenges to advanced students in a writing studio course. Rather than asking for grammatical sentences and coherent paragraphs, we simply asked them to "make persons," "to make environments," and to make "invitations to readers" of various sorts for the page. In every case, we asked writers to create texts that make the reader believe he is experiencing reality rather than reading words on the page.

We marked and carefully documented students' misses at this effort as well as their achievements. Over the years of issuing these challenges, seven structured writing projects emerged: the self-portrait, the observer portrait, scenic writing, narrative history writing, information writing, instruction, and argument. These projects should not be mistaken for naturally-occurring genres. To be sure, their names bear a close connection to genres and not by accident. Our self-portrait project tried to capture some of the representational challenges underlying journals. Our observer portrait project tried to capture the challenge underlying personal profiles. The remaining projects also sought to capture hard representational challenges, about scenes, narrative history, exposition, popular explanation, instruction, or argument. Yet the projects we taught we considered prototypes rather than historical or contemporary genres.

Genres are complex amalgams of format, representation, and historical accident that don't provide a simple and pure look into the contribution of representational elements that language makes available. Consider that the genre commonly called the "profile" portrays persons in texts defined from the observer's vantage, from the outside looking in. Yet, if one surveys the actual texts falling under this official genre, one finds a wide variation of representational elements. *The New Yorker* publishes profiles, as do teen magazines. Were we to study the representational elements of the profile even from this cross sample, the demographic differences between the publications could obscure whatever similarities cause readers of both to become acquainted with persons as a result of their reading. Treating assignments as prototypes allowed us to isolate the design elements pertaining purely to representational challenges, without having to deal with the noise produced by contextual variations that, in our view, bore less firm evidence about representation.

What was important to us was that our prototype assignments fulfilled three requirements. First, the assignments, taken together, had to cover the range of representational challenges that confront a prose writer trying to design an interactive world for readers. A writer stepping through our assignments had to feel the cumulative effect of learning the wide palette of options available to any writer seeking to build interactive reality for a reader.

Second, each assignment, taken individually, had to be focused enough in the representational challenge offered so that students could understand the challenge and rise to it without being overwhelmed. The writer's representational palette is too vast to learn in one step. Each assignment had to represent an important, but manageable, cumulative step toward the whole of the writer's representational palette.

Third, each assignment had to embody a representational problem that was indeed a nontrivial challenge. To do well on the assignment, the student had to do well at the representational level of composition. Doing well at the representational level *on a first draft* had to be rare. This requirement forced us to develop an account of what makes representational challenges for the writer hard. As we will argue throughout this book, hard representational challenges require the alignment of *independent* design elements. What makes writing, or any representational art for that matter, challenging to learn, is the management of elements that are independent. Just as artists must employ unifying elements to bring independent local actions into a uniform composition, writers must find ways of unifying independent representational actions to give the reader a unified experience. The precise meaning of a unified experience for the reader becomes fully apparent only with concrete examples. We supply these examples in the course of our discussing, in every chapter, the hard-won challenges posed by each particular assignment.

Our writing assignments were continuously honed until we were satisfied that they fulfilled our three requirements. We thus, for instance, continued to refine the self-portrait assignment until we were convinced that it could be part of a cumulative theory of representational composition, and yet a focused and challenging assignment in its own right. The same was true of the other writing assignments. The seven writing assignments finally arrived at covered two broad classes of representational challenges: (a) designing the world of the text and (b) designing invitations to the reader to interact with that world in specific ways and toward specific ends.

Designing the World of the Text

The first group of writing assignments (self-portrait, observer portrait, scenic writing, and narrative history writing) relies on a cluster of representational elements and effects associated broadly with portraiture and landscaping. These elements are used to construct worlds that involve readers not as direct participants but as observers.

Portraiture covers the representational elements needed to portray persons in texts. The portrayal of a person can be accomplished by presenting persons either from a self or observer perspective. The *self-portrait* assignment introduces the central elements behind the writer's disclosing himself from the inside out. The *observer portrait* assignment introduces the elements behind the writer describing a third party from the outside in.

Landscaping comprises the elements used to represent environments in texts against which focal characters and objects persist, move, and change. From the reader's vantage, elements of landscaping affect the experience of staying within or shifting across scenes as the text unfolds. The *scenic writing* assignment introduces elements for sustaining spatial immediacy, motion, and contiguity, giving the reader the feel of spatial extension and shifts in spatial attention. The *narrative history* assignment introduces elements responsible for shifting scene and (more importantly) shifting time so that the world of the text feels palpably displaced in time and space from the world of the reader.

Designing Invitations to Readers Within That World

In this second group of assignments (information writing, instruction, argument), the reader becomes an element of the design—an acknowledged presence—rather than an offstage observer. All texts are implicitly interactive with readers. However, seeking greater control over the reader's response, writers can usefully make the reader's ties with and participation in the world of the text explicit. The textual representation across these assignments includes not only represented situations, but also cues that invite an acknowledged reader to engage in higher order cognitions (e.g., learning, doing and learning, deciding) with respect to interacting with, and in some cases acting on, the world of the text.

Our *information writing* assignment divides into different and nonexclusive representational challenges: exposition and popular explanation. Both exposition and popular explanation are prototypes organizing more basic elements of information writing. Both involve a reader in learning and generalization. They differ in the way they organize the elements of information as part of an interactive environment. In *exposition*, with a focus on imparting new knowledge, the writer develops the elements unfamiliar to the reader to rise above more familiar elements. In *popular explanation*, with a focus on familiarizing the seemingly inaccessible, the writer develops familiar elements to rise above and respond to the reader's prior expectation of unfamiliarity and inaccessibility.

Like the information writing assignment, the *instruction* and the *argument* grant visibility to the reader's perspective. However, beyond visibility, the instruction and argument grant the reader agency as well. The addressed reader is encouraged to change the material world either in the process of interacting with the text or as a result of that interaction. The *instruction* assignment invites readers to effect changes in the physical states of the immediate world simultaneous with their reading. The *argument* assignment invites the reader to arrive at a decision as a cumulative response to the interactive world presented.

In essence, this book examines seven distinct writing assignments as a family of related and different interactive worlds for readers to experience and explore. Were our aim solely to teach seven intact and standalone genres, our larger project would replicate hundreds of writing texts that have already been written. That is not our aim here. *Our focus is less on the different writing assignments and more on the collective and cumulative body of representational principles that underlie them.* We chronicle each of these writing assignments and students' paths through them as a stratagem to tease out a sophisticated and integrated body of representational principles. In their capacity as prototypes, each writing assignment brings to theoretical visibility a set of representational principles. The prototypes, as writing assignments, were designed to make the principles visible for sustained investigation.

We should not mistake thinking that the elements of representational composition introduced in different assignments are expressed only in the assignments that introduce them. All the compositional elements discussed in this book remain more or less active in any writing project. The self-portrait assignment, for example, brings to visibility the elements involved in making the writer's mind the center of the represented world. These self-portraying elements, however, do not vanish when the focus turns to less personal types of writing. They persist, although not as explicitly or in as unalloyed form. Written argument, for example, also depends upon elements of the writer's self-portrayal. Yet, in argument, elements of self-portraiture may share and be subordinate to other elements within the overall composition.

Every writing assignment is yet another prototype in exactly the above senses, opening a cumulative space of design elements that a comprehensive theory of representational composition must lay out, explore, and investigate, both as principles in isolation and in interaction with one another. Thus, each writing assignment does not stand on its own but rather serves to embody a subdomain of writing as representational composition. Each assignment, in sum, offers a different window on what we consider to be a unified representational theory of composing. By the time we cover all seven assignments, readers of this book should comprehend a diverse set of prototypes, covering a diversity of textual designs and invitations that nonetheless house a unified, interactive, and combinable set of representational principles for writing.

Taken together, the seven assignments comprehensively explore the representational space of the prose writer. They provide a systematic introduction to a master palette from which to render the kinds of interactive worlds that contemporary English prose is capable of rendering.

Learning the Building Blocks of Mature Composition versus Mature Composing

We close this section by cautioning against the confusion between a master palette and a masterpiece. Our concern in this project is the former, not the latter. Learning the building blocks of mature composition is perhaps necessary but never sufficient to produce full-blown masterpieces, that is, fully mature and original compositions. Like any art of design, once the designer knows the prototypes and the principles that are made available through them, the creativity of the design process becomes an emergent possibility, not a guaranteed outcome. This truth is general to principles of composition across all the arts of design. The purpose of compositional theory within design education—be it in music, architecture, graphics, engineering or writing—is to extend to the designer the building blocks on which creativity is based. The building blocks make creativity possible but they can never make it certain. Full maturation, including the aspiration to true creativity, involves making an assiduous study of how previous masters have deployed the building blocks in striking, affecting, and effective ways. It also requires a deep understanding of the subject matter and the context, both taught within the school setting and practiced long beyond it. Full maturation of the writer thus requires continuing education and practice, long beyond the time available for formal schooling. A representational approach to writing, taught within a school setting, can help insure that the student writer will be trained for change, will know, in response to external fluctuations, how to configure familiar building blocks into whatever new kinds of texts are required for new kinds of situations.

Although institutionalized in American education for only about 150 years, structural theories of written composition have been with us for millennia. They hold an important place in the education of the writer, but they do not scale to the representational complexities of natural genres. As a representational art of the highest sophistication, writing deserves representational theories of composing to capture the remarkable ways words combine to make interactive worlds. We reveal in the course of this book how student writers can be tutored in the primary building blocks of rhetorical composition and, in the process, acquire an image of themselves as artful designers of the reading experience.

I. Portraiture

1
Self-Portraiture

The premodernist, representationalist, understanding of portraiture conjures images of faces depicted on canvas with paint and oils. The images range from formal paintings of historic figures hanging in national galleries to charcoal caricatures of a walk-up customer sold at amusement parks. Whatever the image, the portrait portrays an individual in facial close-up, focusing on the subject's expressions and bringing out the contrastive detail required to reveal thoughts, attitudes, and moods. A well-done portrait will depict not only what is visible to the eye, but also some of the inner nature of the subject that can explain some features of the visual surface. Although visual portraits are perhaps most familiar to us, *portraiture* can be defined more generally as any attempt, in any medium, to represent people. Static images, film, and written text all can be used to construct portraits. However, while the design problem of representing people is common to various types of portraiture, the principles vary with the medium.

As with all the design elements explored in this book, elements of portraiture can dominate a text or remain a minor element in a tapestry of representational elements. If portraiture is the primary focus, the writer places people in close-up, in the foreground of the writing. The principles discussed in this chapter and the next become focal for the writing. If portraiture is not the dominant focus, these principles continue to apply, but with a clipped and more muted presence so that other representational elements stand ahead of them. Portraits of persons may still be evident, but against a wider panorama of space, time, and information that has the effect of pushing people into the background. In nature journals, for example, the writer may want to create mini portraits (perhaps of a bird watcher or mountain climber) to provide a point of human reference for readers. In narrative histories and chronicles, one may want mini portraits to breathe life into people who would otherwise disappear into the wallpaper of time past. In informational writing, the writer may wish to sketch a mini self-portrait to offer expert credentials or mini bios of others. In argument, mini profiles of advocates and opponents are routinely sketched in the course of leading readers to a decision.

The Role of Portraits in Written Text

Written portraiture turns on a set of representational elements that are seldom brought explicitly into the education of the writer. In the face-to-face world, most of us know how to put our best face forward when impressing a friend or a date. Yet, knowing how to manage a self-presence on paper is not a skill we readily pick up solely from knowing how to manage image in face-to-face interaction. In the face-to-face world, we can hear how we come across and we can receive feedback from our listener about how we sound and seem. Such feedback is less forthcoming from the silent page. The writer is challenged to know how she "sounds" or "seems" in a medium that does not talk back. The value of reading our composed words out loud is to hear the person we think we are projecting.

Historically, one of the common ways in which writers practiced self-portraiture was through letter writing. Personal letters required writers to express their feelings, thoughts, and personality on paper in conjunction with what was happening in their lives. However, the telephone, the mass-produced greeting card, and the rapid turnaround of e-mail have all contributed to the death of the thoughtful and leisurely composed personal letter as a routine practice of the literate. Written portraiture is now best known culturally as a high literary art, associated with the personal essay, memoir, or autobiography.

Although elevated to art in markets for the reader at leisure, portraiture has been demoted in much professional and workplace writing. The conventional wisdom associates self-representation within a text with taking unnecessary risks that can offend the network of readers who form the writer's superiors, clients, and customers. However risky, though, the fact remains that no writer can avoid self-representation and no reader can avoid attributing a persona to the writer. Readers typically look for the writer's personality whether the writer thinks to display one or not. Although readers can be turned off by a personality they do not like, they can be even more put off by a writer's voice that sounds flat, shallow, or manufactured.

A writer creating portraiture tries to create the felt presence of a three-dimensional human being on paper. Three-dimensional written portraiture can be undertaken from different points of view. A biographical sketch, or profile, portrays the subject from the third person or observer perspective. The portrait writer in this instance captures the portrait subject from the outside in, the writer and the subject being different people. We investigate portraiture of this kind in the next chapter. In contrast to this form of observer portraiture is first-person or *self-portraiture*. Autobiographical texts, diaries, and journals feature portraits from the subject's first person or self-perspective. The portrait writer, in this case, stands in as his or her own subject, starting from the interior of thought, looking out.

The focus of this chapter is the self-portrait.

What representational elements are at the heart of written self-portraiture? What kind of writing assignment can assure that the representational elements fundamental to it can be given focal practice? Like all the prototypical writing assignments featured in this book, this assignment challenges students to align independent representational elements. In the particular case of self-portraiture, the alignment is between elements of disclosure and enactment. *Disclosure* is the voiced inner thought that makes the writer's mind visible. *Enactment* is the action, scenically or narratively depicted, that displays behavior. If there is only disclosure, we get a monophonic or disembodied voice, something like the mad ravings of a crazed person out of a Dorothy Parker or Dostoevsky novel. If there is only enactment, we get the cinematic character whose actions are seen, but whose inner thought remains inaccessible. Three-dimensional self-portraiture requires the alignment, if not strict harmony or convergence, of both disclosure and enactment, affording readers an intersecting portrait of the author both from the inside-out and the outside-in. Readers need to see the writer's inner mind and motivation influencing and being influenced by his or her actions. The result is to give the reader a feel for the writer as a *stereo*, or three dimensional, *presence* (a person with a mind and body). The skillful alignment of inner thought and action is the key behind producing this stereo effect.

While this alignment is basic to a mature self-portrait, the self-portrait varies in relationship to two additional factors, the depth of self-characterization and the intended effects on the reader.

The *depth of self-characterization* refers to whether the writer puts herself at centerstage or in an ensemble of other agents. The levels of this factor range from deep to shallow self-characterization. Characterization is *deep* when the writer remains alone at centerstage and *shallow* when the writer represents herself mainly through an ensemble. In shallow self-characterization, the author becomes recognizable to the reader by becoming a member of a familiar ensemble.

The *intended effects on the reader* refers to whether the reader is meant primarily to register similarity or empathy with the writer (the reader is made to think— "the writer is like me and I can identify") or difference (the reader is made to think— "the writer is unlike me and I cannot identify"). This factor varies across three levels: *similarity, difference*, and *mixed similarity and difference*. Similarity is the effect of the self-portrait writer striving for reader empathy. Difference is the effect of the self-portrait writer striving to make herself a person with whom the reader will not relate. Difference is often negative and can lead to fascinating but still unlikable characters, as Dostoevsky and other great novelists have made us aware. At its best it betokens creativity and originality. At its worst, the eccentric, strange, and pathological.

Mixed similarity and difference involves building on both similarity and difference to create a self-portrait that could not be produced by either element alone. Mixed similarity and difference, for example, is needed to cause the reader to feel admiration for the writer, causing the reader to think, "the writer is similar enough to me to care about and yet different in ways I value."

Mixed similarity and difference is also at the heart of the approach and avoidance readers feel with first person writers who portray themselves in the throes of suspense. Everyone has unique pasts and futures, unique personal histories and unique prospects. Everyone, up to the moment of death, remains uncertain about what will come next. This autobiographical uncertainty causes uncertainty to every person's future-looking present (e.g, *am* I doing what I should to face what comes next?) and future-looking past (e.g., *have* I been doing what I should to face what comes next?). Within first-person suspenseful stories, readers can feel the difference of knowing that the writer's specific fate, in detail if not final outcome, belongs only to the writer. At the same time, readers can relate to the writer's vulnerability toward the unknown future, as the reader shares this vulnerability.

Relying on all the levels of these factors, we have identified five recurrent and relatively stable patterns of elements and effects that account for most of the successful self-portraits we have received when we have exhorted students to "make yourselves persons" on the page and to let readers "come to know you." We now turn to these patterns.

Variable Patterns of Self-Portraiture

The patterns discussed fall into the following categories of effect on the reader: (a) the feel of similarity with the writer through deep characterization; (b) the feel of difference from the writer, through deep characterization; (c) the feel of admiration for the writer, from mixed similarity and difference; (d) the feel of difference from the writer, though shallow characterization, and (e) the feel of suspense-driven empathy with the writer, caused by an unknown future binding writer and reader.

Similarity Through Deep Characterization

Writers creating the feel of similarity in the reader are challenged to convey signature thoughts and feelings rooted in personal actions. At the same time, they must link the reader's context with their own so that even anonymous readers can feel a connection, an empathy, for their point of view.

The artful writer after self-portraiture must indicate to readers that "This is my highly personalized thinking" and must culminate by getting the reader to think that "This is thinking to which you too can relate, once you understand my context." Most of us believe that we have reasons for doing the things we do and that these reasons can be shared with and supported by others. This is particularly true when we take the time to share the context of our thoughts as well as the thoughts themselves. If you see a person running down the street yelling, you will wonder why. If the person turns out to be a parent hunting down a lost child, the context makes the behavior understandable. The same reasoning applies when writers present situations in texts. Should a writer write about running down the street yelling and harboring dark thoughts, she may leave readers wondering why. If she then discloses she is a parent looking for a lost child, she will help her readers make the connection with her thinking. Building context into the writing provides a foundation for the writer to make visible the basis of one's thinking and a bridge with the reader. Employing external context to ground internal thought marks a powerful way to make the reader connect and care.

This principle turns out to be easier to state than to apply. Writing makes it relatively easy to plant on the page thoughts that are near and dear. However, we cannot communicate the near and dear to others without taking a reflective distance on it ourselves. Our closely held thinking must become strange to us if we are to learn to approach it as a reader must, from the outside. Yet, that is the rub: We find it hard to take a distance on the very things we care about most. When student writers try to get more intimate in their writing, their natural reflex is to become only more clichéd, stereotypical, or obscure. We are always close to our thinking as a response to events, but we seldom take the time to work backward to the precise contexts (both internal, in our heads, and external, in the environment) that might have led to our response. To establish similarity with readers, writers must piece together the connection between their distinctive thinking and the various contexts readers rely on to anchor it. The self-portrait writer must create an alignment between how her readers view her in thought and how they view her in contextualized action.

Writers of serious literature and writers in the professional world both rely on the alignment of disclosure and enactment for self-portraiture. In both cases, the writer lets the reader compare the self that the writer portrays in thought with the self that the writer enacts in and across scenes. In serious literature, fictional narrators invariably describe a self that is, in the conflict-defining phases of plot, out of balance with the self enacted, or enact a self that is out of balance with the self the narrator discloses. The imbalance between the self in thought and the self in scenes creates an instability that drives the narrative forward and sets the character's fate. Contrastively, in professional writing, authors do their best to use the self they enact to confirm the self they describe in words. Genres like the job application letter and résumé are designed to allow writers to portray a verbal image of a self to a prospective employer and then to justify the image by enumerating the accomplishments that have been enacted over time.

In our studio, we sometimes raise the bar of empathy through deep characterization by asking writers who choose this path to tie their deeply personalized thoughts and feelings to mundane contexts that their readers can witness and share. As an illustration of the labor of meeting this challenge, let us turn to the self-portrait project of Beth. Beth described her recovery from a breakup with a boyfriend and her efforts to hide her pain from her mother. Beth's first self-portrait started as follows:

> January 1, 1995. Background: The days seemed to be bad one day, good the next. The only predictable thing was my rollercoaster days. I recall a February entry in my diary, "Today I feel pretty damned good"

followed with "Yesterday was horribly painful." That pattern continued for months. Sometimes I wonder how I made it through. My poor mother. I could tell by our telephone conversations how unsettled and helpless she felt. Only it wasn't because of my relationship this time, but how its end had affected me. She could never understand my relationships—not my high school crushes, not my college romances, and not the latest—a three-year live-in relationship. But that was then. Now, here she was, 600 miles away, her relentless love more apparent than ever. So vivid are the days when I remember holding the mouthpiece of the telephone away from my mouth when she spoke so she wouldn't be able to hear me trying to gulp down the tears in my throat.

This last paragraph places us in the midst of Beth's depression over her breakup and her troubled relationship with her mother. Beth now recalls a day that seemed more hopeful:

I do recall one beautifully warm and sunny day. The reason I remember this day in particular is because it was the first day in an absurd number of months that I was conscious of anything around me seeming beautiful. Nothing had been beautiful to me. Nothing at all. For months. And then one day, things were different. I don't know how or why things had changed for me, but I remember how beautifully warm and sunny the morning seemed. Everything around me seemed beautiful once more. That particular morning was the first in an absurd number of months that I was conscious of anything beautiful. For months, I hadn't enjoyed my morning walks to work or my waits for the bus. For months, I hadn't admired the architecture along the way—not even the Hillman House, which had always been one of my favorites. I hadn't breathed the air created by the flowers that lived in those carefully manicured gardens with flowers. I hadn't even noticed the little kids I used to look forward to watching on their way to school, sometimes holding hands, sometimes racing one another, sometimes even punching one another out the way siblings often do. Each one of these things had been absent from my life.

Beth lets readers take a perspective on her depression by reviewing the kind of healthy thoughts she too seldom had. She now puts readers back in her depressed state of mind as they accompany her on the bus.

But that morning, there I stood, amidst several others, mostly regulars, who also waited for the 8:00 bus, and for some reason, I was feeling anxious. Those days, I had grown accustomed to crying in public. Suddenly, I was paralyzed at the realization that I was at the center of someone's gaze. The gaze was that of a little girl, seated across from me, who had obviously been watching me. Such an innocent face, not more than four, maybe five years old. Yet her forehead was crinkled. Not typical for such a young age. She was obviously troubled and concerned that I had been crying. She tugged at her mother's sleeve, not knowing to keep her voice down, begging, "Mommy? Why is that lady crying?" Her mother's response was quick and an embarrassed one. "Be quiet and behave yourself," she hushed her daughter, as she stole a glance at me before hanging her head down to stare at the feet of the women on either side of me. I smiled a genuine smile at the small girl, in an attempt to reassure her that I was all right. That moment I decided my life would have to change.

Beth lets her readers see a little girl's response to her show of despair. Beth's response in this first draft generates interest, but also includes commonplaces that make it pat. Can we possibly believe that the mere stare of a small girl can turn one's life around? The scene seems too Hollywood. How can someone so profoundly change based on such a slight and fleeting experience? On the scant information in her first draft, the reader might infer that Beth changes to avoid the embarrassment of blank stares when she cries in public. Yet, Beth had also mentioned that she "had grown accustomed to crying in public." She had, presumably, long overcome the embarrassment of the public display of her emotions. Consequently, Beth's first draft contains an unresolved contradiction. The interpretation that Beth changed because of public embarrassment apparently cannot be right. Without further information, Beth's reasoning, and hence her character, remains inaccessible. Readers did not yet have a portrait of Beth that shows her as a person.

Readers of Beth's first draft indeed reported that the scene did not ring true. Assuming that the scene with the little girl happened as Beth reported, Beth's thought seemed to these readers too compressed and, as a result, enigmatic. They advised Beth to bring in connections that could ground her thought, that could put them on track with her thinking. They told her she needed to go deeper into how the experience with the little girl had played into her larger thinking about the world and herself.

In a second draft, Beth more precisely describes the effect of her interacting with the little girl that day.

Suddenly, I was paralyzed at the realization that I was at the center of someone's gaze. The gaze was that of a little girl, seated across from me, who had obviously been watching me. Such an innocent face, not more than four, maybe five years old. Yet her forehead was crinkled. Not typical for such a young age. She was obviously troubled and concerned that I had been crying. She tugged at her mother's sleeve, and not knowing to better to keep her voice down, asks loudly, begging, "Mommy? Mommy!? Why is that lady crying?" Her mother's response was a quick and an embarrassed one. "Be quiet and behave yourself," she hushed her daughter, as she stole a glance at me before hanging her head down to stare at the feet of the woman sitting next to me. I smiled a genuine smile at the small girl, in an attempt to reassure her that I was all right.

And within seconds, she was looking at somebody else. Her concern had almost instantaneously disappeared and she was on to other things. It was that moment in which I decided things in my life would have to change. Before stepping off that bus, I promised myself that day would be day one of a new chapter in my life. I will never forget that little girl, nor her expressions. If only I could direct my thoughts and feelings as instantaneously as that little girl was able to. I never could have imagined that my life would be so different; improved; a mere eight months later.

In this new draft, Beth shows that she really was not so concerned with what the little girl thought. Rather, it was the image of herself, reflected in the little girl's eyes, that she had noticed. Seeing a child's fleeting attention prompted Beth to think about her problems in a different way.

I scrutinize the stare of this four, maybe five year old face, crinkled with concern. These young eyes and folded brow are obviously troubled by the sight of what to them probably appear to be a grown woman crying. How silly for an adult to cry, she must think. I think about that a moment. It is silly. The small girl tugs at her mother. The gaze was that of a little girl, seated across from me, who had obviously been watching me.

In that instant on the bus, Beth saw her problems as the little girl must have seen them—random, fleeting, and silly. Beth's new draft brings to the surface this new interpretation. Yet, after thinking through her second draft further, Beth realized that not even this description of her state of mind quite worked. If the attention of the little girl was so fleeting, Beth reasoned, why would she dwell on it and weight that child's stare as such a significant moment? In the weeks and months after her breakup, Beth knew she had grown accustomed to the momentary stare from strangers when she cried in public. Why would she find so much significance in the stare of this particular little girl? Could the girl's tender age have something to do with it?

Returning to the drawing board for a third draft, Beth recognized that what strangers thought about her was not the problem. What her mother thought was. Beth never cared that strangers saw her in pain. Yet, she had done her best to hide her pain from her mother. Until the bus incident, Beth believed she had been succeeding in shielding her mother from her hurt. The little girl's stare made Beth realize that if she could not fool a little girl, how could she possibly fool her mother? The little girl's stare made her realize what a trooper her mother had been not to let on what Beth only just realized her mother must have known for a long time.

> I sneak a smile at the little girl, who, in spite of her mother's orders, still watches me. I hoped my smile would provide her some relief. Shyly, she sneaks a smile back at me, her forehead relaxing a bit before someone else grabs her attention for a while. My brief experience with that little girl had a profound effect on me, even if only temporarily. I guess I had gotten so good at faking things, including smiles, that it seemed strange that this little girl would evoke a genuine smile from me. How strange it must be for a child that age to see someone my age crying alone on the bus. I feel almost silly, realizing how absurd I must have looked. My thoughts turn to how absurd and naive I've been to think I could disguise my tears from my mother during our regular telephone conversations, simply by holding the mouthpiece away from my face. Surely she must have seen through the façade.

From the first to the third draft, Beth's portrayal of herself moved from that of a cipher, reacting to a situation for no clear reason, to a human being, with thoughts and feelings rooted in her memories of past experience. Had Beth remained an enigma to us, we would have remained outside observers, left only to guess who Beth was. She would not have let us see her as a person whose reasoning we could share. Knowing she had to make her thinking visible within a believable context guided her to a successful final draft.

Beth typifies the discipline of many character-based, short-story writers seeking empathy through self-portraiture. The narrator's self-image is usually displayed retrospectively, in flashes of disclosures juxtaposed with actions derived from narrative or retrieved memories. The reader is allowed to witness the resulting convergence or divergence of the disclosed and enacted self and how the narrator ultimately responds to it. To craft this empathy effectively, the fiction writer must create the taut logic between self-image and self-enactment that Beth was able, over multiple drafts, to reproduce.

Difference Through Deep Characterization

A second pattern of self-portraiture focuses on taking a perspective that readers find different, and, one hopes, interestingly so. In contrast to empathy, juxtaposing mind and enactment in ways that readers find similar, difference creates interest through juxtapositions that readers do not recognize and want to learn more about.

Consider Eric's self-portrait, which recalls the various images and experiences of January 18ths in his life. Although histories and almanacs organize dates and years according to major events of importance, we generally assign personal importance only to anniversaries, birthdays or other life milestones. We typically do not invest personal meaning in arbitrary days of the calendar. However, in his self-portrait, Eric does. He organizes his thinking around a routine date, January 18th, the day he composed his self-portraiture. His unusual perspective brings an element of unfamiliarity, marking for some readers a feeling of dissimilarity they further associated with creativity.

> On this January eighteenth, I sat on the porch. The wind teased my hair, toyed with my open shirt collar, the pages of my book. Though yellow clouds contested its power, the sun radiated an April warmth. The ground trickled with snowmelt. Squirrels danced to early robins' miscued spring songs. A neighbor's inverted lawn chair took a warm gust like a sail and trolled over the brick street. Wind chimes clinked a broken-glass cacophony—the world sounded like Tinkerbell. I shut my book and tilted my head toward the sun. As the sun painted swaths of red and orange across the black canvas of my closed eyes, I imagined other January eighteenths.

Eric begins by describing the January 18th most recent to his composing, an unusually warm one. To make sense of the text, readers must be willing to see the world through Eric's eyes. They must notice and assign significance to the events and places that Eric remembers from other January 18ths.

> On other January eighteenths, I'm sure, I awakened to a bed of fresh, wet snow—the perfectly packable snowball kind—outside my window. Storm Center on the radio cycled through the alphabet—D schools, E schools, As—oh, please, let mine be canceled, too! "Gateway…" the pause between my school's name and the superintendent's verdict seemed eternal—or long enough for me to think, We must at least have a delay, otherwise they wouldn't have even mentioned it—"closed for the day." I whooped and tossed away the covers. Bounding into my parents' room, I imparted the joyful news. Then I burst into my younger brother's room and bounced on his bed. "School's closed, Josh. It's a snow day!" He rolled awake and looked smiling up to me.

Eric recalls other January 18ths, where the scenes change:

> On other January eighteenths, the sky over the Parkway dumped sleet in relentless pellets. The radio news said there were two separate inbound accidents. We had all left work early that day, but it didn't matter. Two lanes of red brake lights stretched ahead three miles to the tunnel—and who knows how far behind me. The wipers dragged icy wet streaks across my view, blurring the traffic. The washer fluid was empty. I stole a glance to the backseat floor, but saw no towels or rags. So, leaning out the window, I cleared a small zone with my glove. Daredevils drove along the shoulder. I'd always wanted to do that—but not today. I popped in Bruce Springsteen to let his words take me to far-worse-off worlds than mine: to depressed steel towns, to teenage runaways, to unfulfilled dreams. But his scratchy lyrics only reminded me of my own mess: "Baby, I'd drive all night…."
>
> On other January eighteenths, I'm sure, it was the wind, blasting out of the north and trying to peel off my skin. Though I had dressed in layers—T-shirt, matching thermal tops and bottoms, turtle neck, sweatshirt, wool socks; though I had covered my extremities in my forty-below boots, insulated gloves, scarf, headwarmer; though the outside temperature according to DeNardo was 18 degrees (not too cold, I thought); though the walk from my Oakland apartment to the Cathedral was only five minutes, I was unprepared for that invisible assailant to jump out at

me and knife right through to the bone. Forty, fifty miles per hour, at least bitter wind.

It was not snowing. In white swirls, but the arctic menace whisked the day's earlier snowfall from the bushes, from the sidewalks and hurled little ice daggers into my eyes and face. I turned my head, but caught a stinging faceful from the side. I may as well have been wearing my open-toed sandals—despite their holding up my legs. With each step, my raw, bitten feet showed me no signs of life disappeared in the snow. Hunkering in a Fifth Avenue doorway with a bum, I wondered if this is how the IceMan felt in the moments just before his preservation. Though my fingers didn't know it, I clasped them together, stepped through a whirlwind of snow and dead leaves, and hoped for an early spring.

By stepping through the various scenes that fell on the calendar day, January 18th, Eric provides readers with glimpses of himself and his view of the world. At the conclusion of his self-portrait, he returns to the scene with himself on the porch. He reminds us one last time that his subjective experience of the date, not the date itself, lends significance to what we have seen.

Ah, early spring is one thing; but a warm January day is a freak, a tease, ephemeral. I opened my eyes and felt my face and its warm, winterbleached skin. Tinkerbell still tinkled. Squirrels still danced. Robins still chirped their preview. The neighbor's chair sailed along. I closed my eyes again. In a while the yellow clouds swallowed the sun and the wind exhaled a chilly breath. Gradually this January eighteenth would relent to normalcy, to the cold front. It would not be 67 degrees tomorrow. In fact, they said, it would snow. Where will the robins go?

As Eric takes readers on his tour of January 18ths, he keeps himself and his thinking at centerstage. He adds a third dimension to his words by creating a felt difference between his disclosure of thought and the conventions for remembering ordinary calendar dates. The readers' engagement with Beth's thinking depends on their following her trail of thinking. Readers connect with Eric, like many unconventional voices of fiction and nonfiction, because his habits of seeing and thinking about the world differ from what we know. Beth's reader finds a human writer through shared reasoning ("Oh, I understand"). Eric's reader finds the human writer by coming to appreciate his off-center perspective ("Oh, I see").

Admiration Through Deep Characterization

Empathy and difference cast opposite effects on readers. The first ties writers to readers; the second unties them. The effects may seem to nullify one another, but they do not as long as the difference is perceived to be positive, a difference that can build on empathy rather than undermine it. Positive difference, we have seen, can take the form of creative difference, modest elements of which are evident in Eric's understanding of January 18ths. It can also take the form of a difference that throws sympathy on the subject. When empathy and positive difference are combined, the effect is *admiration*. The reader can be motivated to look up to the writer based on differences she establishes with readers.

In his self-portrait, Steve provides an example of the consequences of first failing, and then succeeding to achieve the reader's admiration. Steve's self-portraiture recounts his bicycle ride home and his encounter with a Miata driver.

> It's a Friday night after dusk, and I'm on my bicycle, flying down the side of Mt. Washington, passing pokey drivers inclined to obey the speed limit, keeping pace with the speeders. By the time I hit the bottom of the hill, my eyes are blurring with wind-spawned tears, and I bullet past the Liberty tubes, crossing the bridge that takes me over into the South Side. Approaching a red light with a number of cars stacked up in front of it, I blithely pass the autos on the left-hand side to wait for a green at the head of the intersection. There's a Miata across the way. I hate those wretched little cars. They're barely a half-step up from those toy convertibles that Shriners drive at parades. I'm hovering at the red, and I decide that the Miata looks like it's going to make a right, which means that I can follow it left down onto Carson Street.
>
> The light goes green and I'm off, cutting into the intersection. But something goes awry. Instead of going right, the Miata comes straight on, and fast. There is a single, long heartbeat, as I feel disaster ebbing in from the side. But the Miata screeches to a halt at the last second. It's nearly a bad accident and, of course, it's completely my fault. I jerk my left turn sharper and escape the intersection unscathed, but I hear the Miata wheeling around behind me.
>
> Oh criminy, I think, this guy wants to yell at me. I hop the bike up onto the sidewalk—cardinal rule when arguing with car drivers: get out of the road—and turn to see a beefy guy quite at odds with his petite lit-

tle sports car leaning toward his descending passenger-side window. He's wearing a baseball cap, and he looks pissed. What the hell are you doing? he bellows, neck veins bulging, across the diminutive form of his female passenger. From within the car, I hear the faint strains of Bruce Springsteen. His date stares determinedly at the dashboard. Usually, I've found that dignified restraint works best in these situations. I put on my best diplomatic face and gesticulate apologetically. "I'm sorry," I say earnestly, "I thought you were making a right. I didn't mean to cut you off."

Apparently unsatisfied with this response, Mr. Miata suddenly jerks out of his seat. In a swift motion, he's looming over the side of the car, his finger pointing. The situation is immediately much more dangerous. This guy could squash me like a cockroach. "What the hell are you doing?" he roars a second time.

One of my feet goes to the pedal strap, and I'm ready to bolt at the slightest move on his part. However, still in diplomatic mode, I try the truth again. "I said, 'I'm sorry, I thought you were making a right.' It was a mistake, and I'm sorry." My voice is noticeably more nervous, but at the same time, I can't believe that I'm actually apologizing to a guy that drives a Miata.

And clearly, Mr. Miata isn't going to let this go. "They should take all you bikers off the roads," he snarls, and takes a half step around the car toward me. And before I can stop it, my mouth says, "Tell you what, retard: Why don't you and your sporty little Miata try and catch me?" So much for the diplomatic approach.

And I'm in the straps, peddling down the hill, Carson Street four blocks away. Off the curb, into the street, downshifting, I'm picking up speed. I hear the Miata door slam shut, the sound receding behind me. But now, I hear the engine come to life, and it's coming. Bike vs. sports car. Ordinarily not much of a contest. But Carson Street is getting closer. Three blocks, two blocks. My tires are humming on the pavement, no engine to block out the sound, but the Miata is close, a bumblebee in my ear, maybe not more than ten feet away. The road is a line of racing stars, reflected in the halogen light, and Miata is almost on top of me, and I wonder for a millisecond if this guy will actually run me down, as I lean hard into my turn onto Carson Street—and straight into, and through, the traffic.

> I hear the Miata shriek to a halt behind me as I fly up the centerline of Carson, dodging side-view mirrors and wandering pedestrians. The Southside is choked with cars and people, just as I expected. With great satisfaction, I leave Mr. Miata fuming blocks away. Well, actually, that's all a lie. As I said, dignified restraint is really the way to go, even if that last bit is a nice little fantasy (one I cursed myself for not pursuing once I saw how congested Carson Street was). After Mr. Miata's last comment, the one about getting bikers off the road, I simply held my tongue and stared at him doe-eyed. As usual, this brand of thug isn't used to dealing with diplomatic restraint, so he simply grunted, climbed back into his little Shriner-mobile, and drove away, his girlfriend still cringing. Not as exciting an ending, I will grant you. But at least I ruined his Friday night. On the other hand, I pedaled home in a great mood.

Conceivably, readers can empathize with Steve if they can see the challenges of urban bicycling. However, Steve's first draft portrays him as a rather unsympathetic character. In spite of his underdog status on the roads, he seems like a creep. He may set himself apart from readers, but he does not make the empathic connections that help us value his difference with us. Steve wanted to win the admiration of his readers. He wanted to paint himself as a rogue artist practicing a little known urban art, not a creep on a bicycle trying to make life on the road miserable for drivers. A rogue artist sees urban cycling as a form of creative self-expression. Irritable city drivers pose only a minor occupational hazard of the artistic practice. The rogue artist puts more emphasis on the art he has mastered than on gloating over the victims of his actions.

Steve attempted a second draft, focusing on making his character more empathic. Underlines are added to his insertions and strike-outs to his deletions.

> It's a Friday night after dusk, and I'm on my bicycle, flying down the side of Mt. Washington, passing pokey drivers inclined to obey the speed limit, keeping pace with the speeders. By the time I hit the bottom of the hill, my eyes are blurring with wind-spawned tears. I bullet past the Liberty tubes, crossing the bridge that takes me into the South Side. Despite my aggressive nature, I rarely run red lights; <u>too dangerous, too stupid.</u>

In this new draft, Steve adds words of caution about his role (too dangerous, too stupid) to signal to readers that his behavior, despite its risks, is high-minded and principled.

There is a <u>red</u> Miata across the way. I ~~hate~~ have always found those ~~wretched little~~ cars somewhat amusing. They seem hardly removed from those toy convertibles that Shriners drive at parades. While I am hovering at the head of the intersection, waiting for the green, I decide that the Miata looks like it is going to make a right, which means that I can follow it left down onto towards Carson Street. Thus, I'll get moving quickly, and besides <u>and this is how my reasoning usually runs</u> The light goes green and I'm off, ~~cutting into the intersection~~, <u>the sooner I can get out of the way of these cars the better.</u> <u>The light goes green and I'm off, cutting left.</u>

Steve includes the Miata's color (*red*), to indicate, perhaps, the coolness with which he can construct a detailed assessment of the scene around him; perhaps also to hint at the fiery and flashy personality of the Miata owner. He deletes much of his hostile attitude toward Miatas (*hate, wretched little cars*) as well as descriptive verbs (*cutting into the intersection*) that would make his actions seem dangerously reckless. Steve is still in motion (*I'm off*), and his motion is still sharp and abrupt (*cutting*), but he now makes clear that his motion is beholden to a conventional purpose, namely getting safely through the intersection. Steve relies on a disclosure (*the sooner I can get out of the way of these cars the better*) to make absolutely clear that his actions, though swift and unbridled, remain within the prospects of a driver who is finally responsible.

The next passage is a mostly new insert into the second draft:

But something goes awry. Instead of going right, the Miata comes straight on, and fast. There is a single, long heartbeat, as I feel disaster ebbing in from the side. The Miata screeches to a halt at the last second, almost kissing my back tire. It is nearly a bad accident and, of course, it's completely my fault. I jerk my left turn sharper and escape the intersection unscathed, but I hear the Miata wheeling around behind me. Oh criminy, I think, this guy wants to yell at me. Well, that was my fault, so I decide I had better stop and talk to him. Hopping the bike up onto the sidewalk—cardinal rule when arguing with car drivers: get out of the road—and turn to see a beefy guy quite at odds with his petite little sports car leaning toward his descending passenger-side window. He is wearing a baseball cap, and he looks pissed. *"What the hell are you doing?"* he bellows, neck veins bulging, across the diminutive cringing form of his female passenger.

Steve still confesses that the fault is his. Yet, now he adds another, internal, admission of fault and a willingness to stop and talk to the Miata driver about what he had done. These revisions block the perception that Steve feigns a spoken apology, as if he were only pretending to be contrite when he is not. Steve, rather, now conveys an apologetic tone, one that sounds authentic. The driver, in this draft, no longer plays the innocent victim, but devolves into a character of ungracious anger in light of Steve's contrition. The driver's female passenger is now cringing at what she hears her companion saying. Steve has turned her into a character witness for himself.

> From within the car, I hear the faint strains of Bruce Springsteen. His date stares determinedly at the dashboard. Usually, I have found that dignified restraint works best in these situations. No one really wants a fight. I put on my best diplomatic face and gesticulate apologetically. "I'm sorry," I say earnestly, "I thought you were making a right. I didn't mean to cut you off." Apparently unsatisfied with this response—which is, I might add, the truth—Mr. Miata suddenly jerks out of his seat. In a swift motion, he is looming over the side of his car, broad shoulders filling out his Penguins jacket, forefinger pointing accusatorily. The situation is suddenly much more dangerous. This guy could squash me like a cockroach.

In this new draft, Steve adds that he does not want a fight. He tries honesty. No more smart aleck enjoying a dangerous encounter, Steve plays a concerned rider confronted by a potentially dangerous hothead.

> "What the hell are you doing?" he roars a second time. One of my feet goes to the pedal strap, and I am ready to bolt. However, still in diplomatic mode, I try the truth again. "I said, 'I'm sorry, I thought you were making a right.' It was a mistake, and I'm sorry." My voice is noticeably more nervous. I manage to keep the tremble out of my voice, but at the same time, I cannot believe that I am actually apologizing to a guy that drives a Miata. And clearly, Mr. Miata isn't going to let this go. "They should take all you bikers of the roads," he snarls at me, his fists clenching.

Managing to *keep the tremble out of my voice*, Steve signals his discomfort, perhaps fear, with the confrontation, but also his capacity to keep cool under pressure, an attitude that a reader can respect.

In a flash, I get angry. Is this jerk trying to impress his date? Is he a playground bully? Did he miss a Ritalin dose? I mean, clearly I was in the wrong, but this creep is itching for a fight, one where he would have an obvious physical advantage. So before I can stop it, my mouth says, "Tell you what, retard: Why don't you and your sporty little Miata try and catch me?" So much for the diplomatic approach. And I'm in the straps, peddling down the hill, Carson Street four blocks away. Off the curb, into the street, downshifting, I'm picking up speed. There's barely a pause as I hear the Miata door slam shut, the sound receding behind me. Now, I hear the engine blaze to life, and it is coming.

In the redraft, Steve's rogue character surfaces in response to the Miata driver's crudeness and obnoxiousness. Even though some readers felt that Steve's reaction bordered on the extreme, they acknowledged that they could admire Steve's coolness and sense of competitive sportsmanship under pressure.

Bike vs. sports car. Ordinarily not much of a contest. But Carson Street is getting closer. Three blocks, two blocks. My tires are humming on the pavement, no engine to block out the sound, but the Miata is close, a bumblebee in my ear, maybe not more than ten feet away. The road is a line of racing stars, reflected in the halogen light, and the Miata is almost on top of me. I wonder for a millisecond if this guy will actually run me down, as I lean hard into my turn.onto Carson Street—and straight into, and through, the Friday night traffic. I hear the Miata shriek to a halt behind me. The Miata slams on its brakes as I fly up the centerline of Carson, dodging side-view mirrors and wandering pedestrians. The Southside is choked with cars and people, just as I expected. With great satisfaction, I leave Mr. Miata fuming blocks away.

By the time we reach this passage, Steve has likely won us to his side and we can more easily take delight when he eludes the Miata driver.

Well, actually, that is all a lie. As I said, dignified restraint is really the way to go, even if that last bit is a nice little fantasy (one I cursed myself for not pursuing once I saw how congested Carson Street was). After Mr. Miata's last comment, the one about getting bikers off the road, I simply held my tongue and shrugged. As usual, this brand of thug is not used to dealing with diplomatic restraint so he simply grunted, climbed back into his little Shriner-mobile, and squealed away, his girlfriend still cringing.

Not as exciting a denouement, I'll grant you. At least I ruined his Friday night. Myself, I pedaled home in a great mood.

In the later draft, Steve portrays himself as a skilled craftsman of his own actions, actions that manage to be daring and risky without being malicious. By redrafting this way, Steve was able to make his actions on the road seem more admirable than reprehensible.

Difference Through Shallow Characterization

Thus far our examples have all involved deep characterization, where the foreground of the writing is dominated by a single mind, disclosed and scenically enacted. Deep characterization can involve multiple characters, but usually only one *main* character—the writer. In the space of some short stories and novels, however, a writer can probe the interior thought and action of multiple characters. Deep characterization and ensemble writing in this context are compatible.

In the case of self-portraiture through shallow characterization, the goal of the writer is to show the habitat in which she resides. The writer connects with the reader by having the reader connect with the ensemble of characters that surround the writer. This form of empathy is rooted in the idea that you cannot learn about a person without first watching her scenically, interacting with other characters. The writer's thought may be on stage for only spare moments, with little or no introspection. Still, the world of the writer can be sufficiently characterized to make the world familiar to the reader through similarity and difference. Once the world of the writing becomes familiar, then acquaintance with the writer involves coming to know the writer's place in that world. Granted, the allure of the writer is largely inherited from the allure of the world. But it is a character allure that need be no less compelling than that provided through deep characterization.

Still, as a short form and even a longer one, building character identity through world identity is a challenging undertaking. As any short story writer and novelist can attest, it requires a keen patience for noticing the various ways individual identity is refracted through those with whom the characters interact.

The following self-portrait by Matt illustrates the creation of difference through shallow characterization. Matt describes a trip to an unusual computer store, Elmo's, in the small town of Brownsville, Pennsylvania. His self-portrait is interesting because he was trying to paint an image of himself as a willing member of a dark and seedy world with which the reader would probably feel difference.

It was 8:35 PM on a Friday in January, and it was time to go to Brownsville. Brownsville is a small town that lies approximately an hour and a half southeast of Pittsburgh. Brownsville isn't good for much anymore, except for late night runs to buy software for Amiga computers; it's the location of the last true Amiga dealer in western Pennsylvania. This night, I could not go to Brownsville alone. I breezed by Ted's house. He was finishing his after-work meal: another pizza from the joint across the street.

"Get in the car, we're going to Brownsville," I said as I made myself visible beneath the cold, wet light of his Beeler Street porch. He spoke hesitantly. "What the hell is Brownsville?"

Matt shows a superior attitude toward Brownsville and bullies Ted to go with him. As a writer, he makes no effort to win his readers over. Nevertheless, he is betting that the situation holds enough potential interest—in a context of difference—to keep his readers along for the ride.

Standing in the same position, I returned, "It's a city. I have some business to do there this evening. We're going to a place called 'Elmo's'" I showed no sign of discomfort in the raw winter evening; I didn't want to be asked to come inside. Ted disappeared for a moment and then reappeared, wearing a sweatshirt, cap, and heavy winter coat. I took this act as acceptance, and so we started for the car.

Matt shows no effects of the cold just to manipulate Ted. Although he could have been more visual about how he suppressed shivering muscles, he is effective enough to imply his interest in controlling his friend.

Brownsville isn't the only place that I go when I just need to get away. Jim's Truck Stop in Somerset isn't a bad place. They have life-size Elvis lamps there for a mere $49.95. As we pulled away, I laughed at what I had said exactly one week earlier . . . "Will that be all?" screeched the unattractive lady at the truck-stop checkout counter. And then I said, "Two Tastykakes, a bottle of Yoo-Hoo and an Elvis lamp, what else do I need?" That was probably the best reply I could have given in that situation.

Matt credits himself with superior observations (e.g., screeched, unattractive) and banter at the expense of the cashier without testing his self-assessment. Through a tone of self-congratulation that seems closed to feedback, the self-portrait writer can convey a feeling of smug self-containment. Some of Matt's readers reported that they wanted to keep reading just to find out whether cold water is ever thrown on Matt's self-satisfied persona. However, Matt's sense of contempt for this small town culture does not waver and is never challenged.

> The man darted for the entrance, not acknowledging my offer. I already knew what was going to happen. As soon as that man disappeared behind that door, something would be stolen, or someone would be shot and that would be the end of it. I can't even explain why I remained seated for this, but after about three minutes of silence, what appeared to be the man's wife stood in front of me. A sort of evil truck-stop check-out-counter lady. "What flavor Skoal you want?" she asked, as if she were right behind that counter. She rested her heavily tattooed forearm on my door. Experiencing this woman suddenly made me realize why my older brother got steamed when he found out that I chewed tobacco—it wasn't because he was a dentist; I should have been out of there by then—but I said "Wintergreen" instead. Another long silence passed and finally the man came out, holding a cardboard box and a bag. He threw me the bag and climbed back in his truck. We pulled away.

Depicting the scenes in more visual terms could have made Matt's context more vivid. In addition, readers could have learned more about this adventure had he—in a part of his text not illustrated here—deepened the backstory about the suburban upbringing that he mentioned he was trying to escape. Still, Matt's draft does illustrate how even an unattractive subject, characterized from difference, can be interesting to follow if the world of the character holds interest.

Empathy and Difference Through Suspense

Self-portrait writers can produce both distance and empathy by sharing with readers the uncertainty of the future and the suspense of not knowing what will happen next. They can maintain a distance from readers on the assumption that the reader's fate is not their own. Yet they can produce empathy by virtue of the reader's sharing their general feeling of vulnerability to an uncertain future. This effect is not unique to self-portraiture. Authors of mystery stories build this combined distance and empathy between their main characters and readers through suspense. A suspenseful story keeps the reader on the edge of her seat, engaging the world of the text to see what will happen next.

Suspense relies on a feeling of immediacy. We feel we are reading not just what the writer thinks but what the writer thinks *now*. We can sense an intimacy with the writer's thought simply by knowing we feel we are sharing the feeling of uncertainty about the future at the same time.

Aaron's self-portrait provides an example of creating empathy and distance through the suspense he had to endure as a pet owner. He recounts the story of his nighttime encounter with Kashka, one of his cats.

> Kashka, one of our cats, woke me up this morning. She left bloody foot-prints on the sheets when she jumped off the bed. Half asleep, I noted the footprints and the wet matted hair on her face. It didn't register until she yowled.
>
> I once read that cats make about 25 different sounds. I know the normal ones: feed me, pet me, and leave me alone. This one was new. Kind of a low, growling, angry whimper.
>
> What was wrong? I looked at Alison, my wife, who was sleeping peacefully. I looked back at Kashka. She was sitting in the doorway, facing me. In the glow from the street light, her eyes were big yellow lid-less globes. Even though it was pretty dark, her pupils were thin vertical slits. Her striped face was covered with black blood. She didn't look like our cat.

At this juncture, Aaron and his reader are both unsure about the situation. Typically, pets do not show up in a bedroom covered with blood. Soon, Aaron finds that the blood on Kashka presents a situation worse than the one he first feared.

> She growled at me again. It raised the hair on the back of my neck, matching the hair on hers. What had happened to her? I couldn't see a cut on her face, and since the blood was on all of her feet, it wasn't a cut on a foot. So it wasn't her blood, right?·Then whose was it? Where was Desmo?

The suspense mounts when we find that the blood does not belong to Kashka and that the second cat, Desmo, cannot be located. We also begin to get some glimpses of Aaron from the inside out, learning how he perceived the situation.

I got up, naked, trying to casually toss the sheets off. I got tangled and thumped to the floor, half hoping it would wake Alison up. She didn't move. Kashka disappeared through the door, hackles still raised, tail lashing angrily. Leaving Alison asleep, I followed Kashka out of the bedroom to the bottom of the stairs.

I didn't turn the lights on, but carefully peered into the living room anyway, shivering a little. It was cold and dark. It hadn't been this dark in bed. Kashka curled up the circular staircase, leaving me at the bottom.

I didn't want to follow her. On the other hand, Kashka didn't hesitate going up the stairs, so there wasn't something waiting. So what was bleeding? And where was Desmo?

Kashka's actions create a foreboding about finding a lifeless object. Desmo has yet to be spotted and Aaron's thoughts, laced with fond remembrance, turn to dread.

Desmo was our second cat. I got him because I figured two cats would provide more excitement than one. Alison was away, so I figured I'd surprise her and went to one of the local animal shelters. I found a small black kitten that rubbed up against the cage when I got near and purred and gently bit my fingers when I petted him. When I went to look at the other cats, he yowled until I came back. Twenty minutes later I took him home.

This is Desmo, the note I wrote to Alison says. He's very affectionate. He likes to stand on my chest and rub against my face. Unfortunately, he smells funny and has bad breath. But he's nice!

He stopped smelling, stayed affectionate, got fat, and became a part of our family. He raced and chased with Kashka during the day and slept between Alison and me at night. Not tonight, though.

Aaron lets us come to know him better even as he builds the expectation that we will find a dead Desmo. This strategy increases the likelihood that we will identify with Aaron, if only because he has taught us to share not only his uncertainty of the situation, but also the depth of his emotional investment.

I called Desmo! quietly, not really wanting to wake Alison up, not wanting to hear myself, wanting to hear Desmo scramble across the floor

upstairs and see his big round orange eyes staring down from the landing over my head. I wanted my chest to stop hurting.

No eyes, no reassuring purr. Kashka growled upstairs, but I was
afraid to go up and find Desmo sprawled on the floor, dead of a sudden
heart attack. Or caught under something, bleeding to death. I already
felt guilty for stacking the old television on the pile of boxes. What if one
of the antennas had speared him?

I shivered again and turned on the upstairs light. Full of evil premoni-
tions, thinking I was being silly, I went up the stairs.

I stopped before I'd make it to the landing. Desmo was laying on his
side with his back to me in the middle of the floor. There was blood
soaking into the carpet all around him. Kashka stalked over to him, back
arched, tail whipping. She sniffed at him, then slowly, deliberately, and
gently, clawed at him. I gagged. I didn't want to watch.

Finally, we learn the truth at the same time Aaron does.

Suddenly both cats leaped up, hissing and spitting and biting at a furry
thing that flipped into the air. They dove at it, then sprang for cover when
I jumped into the room, yelling to clear them out, heart in my throat. I
almost slipped and fell, but saw what they were playing with. They had
killed a rat. A big one. Full of blood.

Kashka and Desmo circled me, hunched low. I hissed to keep them
away. They glared back resentfully, Kashka growling. "Get out of here," I
growled back, a naked man crouched over their kill. I went downstairs
for paper towels and a garbage bag, leaving my own bloody footprints,
angry, goosebumps fading, my face hot. When I went back up, Desmo
was clenching the rat, kicking at it with his back legs. I threw the garbage
bag at him, making him scramble, then started mopping up blood.

When I went back to bed, Alison asked me if anything was wrong.

"No," I said. "Go back to sleep."

As Aaron builds the narrative suspense, he keeps us with him every step
of the way. Through a skilled combination of disclosures laced through
the narrative, we follow not just the story of the cats, but the story of
Aaron as well. Weaving together immediacy and uncertainty, we come
to know and care for Aaron in a story that originally did not seem to be
about him at all.

Summarizing the Written Models
in Relation to Self-Portraiture

Let us summarize how the writing models of this chapter pertain to principles of self-portraiture in writing. All self-portraiture builds on the alignment of self-disclosure and enactment in the world. This juxtaposition is the fundamental principle by which writers make themselves objects of acquaintance in texts. Variations on this principle involve the depth of characterization, either centered on the single author (deep characterization) or capturing the author as part of an ensemble (shallow characterization). Variation also involves the specific effect—empathy or difference or both —produced when a self-portrait is rendered. In addition, an effect combining empathy and difference can be brought home to readers through suspense.

Five patterns across these variations have proved robust models in the practice of our studio writers. These involve empathy through deep characterization, difference through deep characterization, admiration through deep characterization, difference through shallow characterization, and the achievement of empathy and difference through suspense.

Beth exemplifies empathy through deep characterization, wanting readers to connect with her thinking about her response to a little girl. She needed multiple drafts to build the logical ties between her disclosures and actions that made her thinking both visible and the object of reader empathy.

Eric exemplifies the seeds of creative difference through a deep and unconventional characterization of otherwise ordinary events.

Steve illustrates admiration through deep characterization, showing how one can combine empathy and positive difference to create an admirable, even if roguish, self-portrait.

Matt reveals difference from shallow or ensemble characterization. He includes scenic details and an interesting, even if unsavory, cast of characters to make himself a player in a colorful world.

Aaron works a self-portrait based on empathy and difference through suspense. The uncertainty of the future both binds and individuates us. Aaron's story relies upon linguistic immediacy so that we learn about his fate as a pet owner at the same time he does. The story he reports can remind readers that the fragility of his particular situation is no different than the fragility of their own.

Self-Portraiture in Professional and Public Writing

In professional contexts, admiration and light characterization in relationship to an ensemble are the central effects sought in the cover letter for a job application. When a person applies for a job, she needs to create an admirable portrait of herself. Showing oneself as part of an ensemble is also important. Employers want to know that they are hiring a team player, one who will respond well and contribute to a healthy work environment. The job letter, responsive to these expectations, requires the writer to point out both how she has taken creative initiative and how she has made teams successful.

Job letters for managerial positions also require producing empathy for oneself as one looks into the uncertainty of the future. Writers must show how they manage others under situations of stress and uncertainty. Just as Aaron tried to keep readers with him when he was searching for Desmo, the manager's job letter must try to keep readers with her as she outlines her managerial style —which is how, under various "what-if" scenarios, she moves a group from the present into an uncertain future. A job applicant's answers to such questions help define a managerial style.

In public contexts, self-portraiture is fundamental to civic-minded writers who must clarify the context of their thinking when they espouse positions that seem questionable or controversial. On November 24, 1998, the Pennsylvania State House of Representatives rejected a funding bill that would have given Pittsburgh and Philadelphia new sports stadiums. Many citizens of Pittsburgh had been counting on the governor's promises to have the bill passed into law in order to save their baseball team. When the bill was rejected, Pittsburgh residents were angry with the governor for a promise broken. They were also angry with various legislators from the Philadelphia area who voted in a bloc against the bill. Two weeks later, one legislator from the Philadelphia area who was part of the "no" bloc published a column on the op-ed page of the *Pittsburgh Post-Gazette*. His column was designed to win back the empathy of angry readers. Deploying empathy, exactly as Beth, the Philadelphia legislator reconstructed for his readers the hidden context of his vote so that they could see the rational link between his context and his vote. Using empathy from a future perspective, the governor also published a piece on the same page of the same newspaper on the same day. He called for the anger to subside because the cause was not yet lost. He urged that readers had to stay with him—even if it meant prolonging the suspense—if the story was to have a happy ending.

Finally, it is worth noting that in his psychological investigation of leadership, Gardener (1995) observed that a prominent feature of all successful leaders is their ability to align their stories about themselves with their policies and actions in the world:

> [L]eaders exercise their influence in two principal, though contrasting, ways: through the stories or messages that they communicate, and through the traits that they embody. Sometimes, the single leader alternates in emphases. . . . Churchill first developed a story about the need to maintain the glory of Great Britain, and he then embodied a courageous stand through his activities during the Battle of Britain. A tension may develop between stories and embodiments. Indeed many political leaders have gotten into trouble when the facts of their lives seemed to contradict the stories they were conveying. But in the happier event, stories and embodiments reinforce one another (p. 37).

We expect leaders to make their actions match their talk and we expect them to continue to do so over time. In this way, we become acquainted with them not only as persons but as consistent persons. We should not forget that not all juxtapositions of mind and behavior are positive alignments. We can just as well become acquainted with people through their inconsistency as well as through their consistency. Most characters of literature are interesting precisely because of the glaring inconsistencies between how they see themselves and how others see them. Nonetheless, few such characters could win modern elections or would compete in the professional world under the persona of leaders! Conversely, self-portraiture that consistently aligns disclosure and enactment reproduces, in compressed form, the over-time stability of words and deeds we expect from leaders. Little wonder, then, that self-portraiture as a principle of writing that compresses this alignment figures so prominently in texts, like job resumes, letters of inquiry, and essays of introduction, where we wish to demonstrate to readers our attractiveness as potential employees, colleagues, and leaders.

All human beings lead interesting lives, whether they think so or not. However, only writers skilled in self-portraiture know how to make the interest in their lives visible on the page for readers.

2

Observer Portraiture

Observer portraiture covers the principles required to bring third parties to the attention and acquaintance of readers. Much as a painting portrays a subject on a canvas, observer portraiture focuses on the portrayal of another person—neither writer nor reader but a third party—through a text. Observer portraiture is a useful palette option any time a writer needs to acquaint a reader with third parties. This option becomes a dominant choice when the writer's purpose is focused on profiling an individual. Yet, the option is also useful across a variety of writing contexts when the writer's purposes are mixed and include acquaintance with a third party only as part of a more complex design.

Observer portraiture supports the same coming-to-acquaintance experience for readers as self-portraiture. Like the writer of the self-portrait, the writer of the observer portrait relies on empathy and difference to develop the reader's acquaintance with the subject. The writer is challenged to maintain enough empathy with the subject to keep readers involved, even when the subject of the portrait would seem to defy empathy. Hitler's most recent and celebrated biographer, Ian Kershaw (1998, pp. xxi), framed the challenge of empathy in the negative portrait well when he observed that, "A feasible inbuilt danger in any biographical approach is that it demands a level of empathy with the subject which can easily slide over into sympathy, perhaps even hidden or partial admiration."

Despite their common interest in developing an acquaintance experience for the reader, the observer portraitist cannot rely on the same tools as the writer of self-portraits. The self-portrait writer is an active participant in the acquaintance relationship. The writer of the observer portrait is no longer the target of acquaintance but the matchmaker trying to help an acquaintance form between the reader and a third party.

Although it may not seem obvious at first, this presents a huge difference in the work involved in developing acquaintance experiences for the reader. We saw in the last chapter that self-portrait writers acquaint themselves with readers through internal disclosures and scenic or narrative enactments. What we did not mention is that the self-portrait writer can rely on powerful independent processes to initiate acquaintance with the reader, even when acquaintance with the reader is not a conscious goal of representation. Every writer relies on the reader's sensing the writer's language and presence on the page as an integral part of the reading experience. The self-portrait writer, merely as a language user, is already putting her language and mind on display for the reader.

The writer of observer portraits cannot rely on these implicit aids to satisfy her goals of acquaintance. The language and mind of the portrait subject are not naturally emergent in the words of the text. The reader cannot sense the presence of the subject merely as a passive side-effect of the reading experience. Rather than the elements of first person acquaintance, the observer portraitist must rely on three elements to capture third person acquaintance that we have yet to introduce.

First, the writer must provide readers with the experience of sensing the presence of the subject in physical space. By describing the subject in a scene, a space that the reader can envision in her mind's eye, the writer can furnish the details that readers are accustomed to using in their face-to-face interactions to infer the thought, attitude, and physical presence of other persons. The details to recreate this experience involve much of what a forensics expert might call a suspect's physical description. However, it also carries with it physical evidence about persons that only novelists usually take the pains to describe, such as bearing, carriage, physique, body contour, facial shape, features, fashion, hair and skin texture, odor, and, generally, the overall presence one feels when one shares physical space with that person. Through this textual detail, readers can come to see the subject's face and body up close, come to learn about smiles, frowns, furrowed brows, crinkly eyes, hand gestures, fashion, and walk.

Second, the writer must allow readers to eavesdrop on the subject's own words. We feel acquainted with a person when we hear what they have to say, even as eavesdroppers on conversations in which we are not participants. Acquaintance involves hearing the dialect and regionalisms of the subject's expressions. It involves hearing the tone, attitude, and intonation behind the words in various contexts. It involves hearing the words of a subject in long monologues, when the subject is holding forth and others are listening. And it involves tracking the subject's words in dialogue, when the subject is sharing the floor with others. The combination of the subject's physical bearing and words recreates for the reader an internal image of sharing proximate space with the subject.

Third, the writer must let the reader experience the subject's actions over biographical time. When we think of ourselves as knowing a person by acquaintance, we typically have the ability to say we have been keeping up with that person or (more intimately) going back with her, long enough to see trends and patterns that bespeak character. Acquaintance with a third party suggests having some access to their life experiences over time. Few readers ever physically meet the persons they become acquainted with through a text. Nonetheless, writers can give readers the feel of a cumulative and shared past with a subject by focusing on the subject's past in the particular detail that only a biographer or close acquaintance could know. By telling readers some of the stories of the subject's past, a writer can provide readers with an understanding of how a subject acts, or has acted, in different decisive situations throughout her life.

Observer portraiture in writing, in sum, involves elements of representation that simulate for the reader the experience of third person acquaintance over physical space, quoted language, and biographical time. Space, time, and the subject's own language provide separate and potentially convergent experiential channels for making the acquaintance of a third party through a text.

In the last chapter, we observed that all hard representational effects in writing stem from the alignment of independent representational elements. Observer portraiture is no different, as it requires developing for the reader a unified portrait across the three representational elements we have just described. The difficulty of achieving a convergence across these elements should not be underestimated. A person's physical presence in a particular scene need not reflect or reinforce his specific language or his past. These elements, chosen randomly, don't have to add up to a converging picture and often do not add up. Still the writer of the observer portrait is given these elements as resources with which to make them add up, at least add up enough to stimulate the reader's feeling of acquaintance.

The writer of the observer portrait is challenged to combine these diverse elements from varying roles: portrait photographer, interviewer, and biographer. As interviewer, the writer makes readers experience the presence of the subject as an interactive partner in real time. As portrait photographer, the writer must seed the text with revealing images of the subject's face and body in physical space. As biographer, the writer tells the subject's story, recalling defining events from the subject's past. In the face-to-face world, a sense of shared space, biographical time, and the subject's interactive language are cues we use and combine to come to know persons. The writer of the observer portrait must compress, in a few hundred or thousand words, the varying cues of acquaintance that the face-to-face world makes available over weeks, months, and years.

The observer portraitist takes the reader through these disparate experiences of the subject while trying to make the reader see convergences. There must be enough convergence across experiential views to create a person with whom the reader can feel acquainted. There can never be enough convergence to build a subject of completely consistent and uniform identity. That is simply not realistic. People are neither perfectly consistent nor perfectly coherent in their outlook. Unlike the puzzles cut by a jigsaw, the puzzle pieces of life never perfectly fit together. Human beings are complex and harbor mysteries that even they cannot figure out, much less observers. Learning more about people in the face-to-face world often does not remove our questions about them, only sharpens, and hones them. Getting to know a person requires mastering the loose ends as well as the tight threads. Well-crafted observer portraiture can do no better than we do in the face-to-face world. And it need do no worse.

The Subject Stereotype:
A Foundation for the Observer Portrait

As writers of an observer portrait embark on developing a memorable subject, they do not start with a mental picture of a human being already filled in. That is where they would like their research eventually to take them, but it is not where they start. Where they start rather is with a subject stereotype, a familiar frame on which to try to hang the details that make the subject an individual. The subject stereotype provides a wireframe image of the subject, with familiar default characteristics that the writer's subsequent research fills in, elaborates, and modifies.

Stereotyping involves categorizing people. Stereotypes may be unfair, but they need not be. To manage in the social world, we often must make quick and imprecise inferences about people whom we do not know. If we did not or could not make these inferences, we would find it difficult to make decisions about dates, friends, landlords, baby-sitters, dentists, plumbers, and roommates. Stereotypes also function to help us remember people for their uniqueness. Because we can stereotype people, we do not have to remember every small detail that they share with others of the same type. For example, we do not have to remember that Max has a crewcut if we also know he is going through basic training. We can rely on our stereotype of new recruits to retrieve that information on demand, without having to tag it uniquely to Max. This allows us to focus our energy on remembering a person's truly distinctive traits and not bothering with storing what the person inherits from a category. We function in our public and personal lives as well as we do because, through stereotypes, we can make rapid and reasonably reliable assumptions about the strangers we meet and interact with.

Stereotypes are thus not all bad. Neither are they all good. In truth, they are as much a mixed blessing for writers as they are for nonwriters. Just as they help nonwriters with categorizing and recalling information about individuals, they help writers get characters defined on the page with amazing speed and efficiency. Just write the words *fat and jolly, depressed and withdrawn, proud and defiant, prim spinster*, or *powerful tycoon*, and the writer can get the reader busy sorting through an internal card catalog of people and types. Novelists and situation comedy writers could not make a living without good working stereotypes to start from. On the other side of the ledger, if writers couldn't get their subjects beyond stereotypes, they could never recreate truly interesting acquaintance experiences for readers. Writers cannot limit themselves to stereotyped subjects precisely because stereotypes are types rather than fleshed out individuals.

Screenplay writers call a baseline stereotype a *premise* for a character. The importance of the premise can be seen in work that a novelist whom we studied did to develop a particular female character. The novelist had submitted her work to a publisher who accepted it for publication on the condition that she revise the female character in question, a character whom the publisher judged to be weakly developed. In about a month of work, the novelist revised the character and the revision was eventually accepted for publication. Curious to know how the novelist had reworked the weak character, we researched the initial draft and the revision over the course of some 300 edits made. We found that the problematic female character in the first draft lacked a clear premise—the character simply could not be stereotyped. The novelist had given the character hundreds of internal disclosures in order to show the character's unique inner complexity and turbulence. Yet the novelist had forgotten to give the character the blueprint that would allow the reader to recognize the type against which the character's uniqueness could stand out.

Writers need to establish a baseline premise for a character so that readers can say, "Oh, I know the type." The acquaintance process relies on maintaining hypotheses about type that are continually tested and refined with new evidence. We keep coming to know people better when we keep finding, to our surprise, that they are more than the type we had pegged them for.

In the face-to-face world, we rely on type information about a person in order to get closer to the unique person. A text adheres to this face-to-face principle of acquaintance, albeit in a highly compressed form. Like humans in the social world, readers engaged in texts need initial wireframe images of an observed subject—the subject stereotype—to make sense of the further, unexpected, detail that is to come. The subject stereotype is the place where acquaintance with a person begins, but not where it ends. Stereotypes are necessary for getting a recognizable character on the page quickly. Yet, if writers do not add additional individuating texture to the stereotype, readers will never move past the type to an individual. They will never experience an individual with whom to form an acquaintance.

Moving Beyond the Stereotype versus Shifting Stereotypes

Moving beyond the subject stereotype is easier said than done. The writers we studied tend to fall prey to a common confusion, thinking that texturing (and, by implication, breaking) a stereotype can be achieved merely by shifting from one subject stereotype to another. Rather than developing an individual, the writer replaces one undeveloped stereotype for another. Andrew's observer portrait of William Ricci illustrates this common problem.

> Sergeant William Ricci, of the Rockport University Police, would like to get you into shape. Physical, mental, and spiritual shape that is. Ricci changes from his police uniform into a martial arts uniform, and walks down a hallway to a small gym with high ceilings.

Andrew tells us Ricci's name, profession, and place of employment. Beyond those generic tags, Andrew leaves it to us to infer what we can about Ricci from his actions in the gym:

The walls of the gym are lined with the young men and women dressed in a manner similar to Ricci, except for their white belts. Ricci raises his fists, and greets the students with a salutation of "Tang Soo" (pronounced Tung Soo). Ricci walks to the front of the gym, and the students quickly line up, four abreast facing him. Ricci sits at the front of the class, and folds his legs inwards, Indian-style. At a signal from an assistant, the students also sit, and begin to clear their minds, preparing for class.

Andrew then moves out of the scene to establish what's going on within it.

Ricci teaches the Tang Soo Do course for the Physical Education program, listed as Karate in the coursebooks. He seeks to make a good impression on his students, and help improve their mental health through martial arts.

Andrew next provides an interview element where Ricci's words disclose what he has been doing in the gym:

"Martial arts should be enjoyable," said Ricci. "Many people have a bad exposure to something, and they don't want to do it anymore. I try to make the class the first exposure, which many times it is, and make it a good experience." According to Ricci, martial arts should improve the confidence of the student. To do this, the teacher must earn the respect of the students.

"I've seen instructors whose students respect them, out of fear. It's a forced respect," said Ricci. Ricci observed several schools that are harsh on their students, because their instructors begin full contact sparring in the first few weeks of training. "They are glorified streetfighters," said Ricci of the instructors.

Andrew moves us back to the gym so we can match Ricci's actions to his words. He uses the historical present tense to lend immediacy to his writing. His observations about Ricci and his writing seem to unfold at the same time so we feel as eyewitnesses on the scene as we learn that Ricci is a tall, supple man.

After meditation, the class rises, and is led through stretching exercises by Ricci. One of the most surprising moments of his class comes during stretching, when Ricci, who is six foot four, drops into a split and touches his chest to the floor. After stretching, Ricci announces that practice will

begin with "hadan makai," Korean for low block. It is the first move that
the students learn, and the first move that begins subsequent lessons.
Turning his back to the students, Ricci begins the lesson by with a gruff
shout combined with execution of a low block.

Moving between the action in the gym and Ricci's commentary on that
action, Andrew gives us enough to form a stereotype of Ricci as "the
strong but peaceful martial arts instructor." We have seen this stereotype before in Hollywood. Ricci plays the martial arts expert who
preaches nonviolence and the maintenance of the mind and body.
Although different readers may infer slight variations, most of Andrew's
readers took this Hollywood stereotype as his character premise. In his
early drafts, however, Andrew did not stabilize on this premise. Instead,
he offered a bothersome detail about Ricci that seemed to flip premises:
"The students follow, shouting in unison. Ricci continues to call out a
count in his deep smoker's voice."

This smoker's voice violates the stereotype of the martial arts
instructor out to set an example of fitness and vitality. Andrew's readers
were forced to reconsider the characterization of Ricci they thought
Andrew had first thrown them. What could make a health-conscious
person smoke? As readers, we can turn to Ricci's other role as a police
officer. Police officers support different subject stereotypes. They support the image of the action hero practicing karate and preaching a philosophy of nonviolence and organic health. They also support the image
of the beefy civil servant addicted to donuts. We would not be jarred to
see a police officer molded in this last image with a cigarette dangling
from his mouth. Andrew's readers could start Ricci from one known
stereotype or another. They complained, however, that they wanted
Andrew to decide on his baseline for Ricci before beginning to complicate it.

Andrew realized that on his first draft he had tried to complicate
Ricci before settling on the wireframe to give to the reader. The result,
as his readers reported, was not to liberate their image of Ricci from stereotypes but to move their vague understanding laterally, from types to
other types. Consequently, in Andrew's early drafts, his readers
reported feeling at arm's length from Ricci, knowing him only as a
changing lists of categories.

Andrew realized he could make progress by staying with Ricci's
interest in health as his basic character premise for another few paragraphs and offering Ricci's cigarette-smoking as a piece of anomalous
detail that could pose a problem for the narrative and drive it forward.

If we think about people we know beyond stereotypes, we recognize that they are always more complicated than any type we can peg them for. No character is perfectly consistent. Some are contradictory at base. Yet our very ability to piece together character inferences in a productive chain depends upon our willingness to lay down some baseline assumptions from which to start and take a direction. Andrew had all the right insights to develop Ricci, but in his early drafts he had not firmly settled on his starting point for initiating the acquaintance relationship with readers.

Both in the face-to-face world and in texts, the acquaintance experience is an ongoing detective story, never fully closed, that seeks to reconcile the gaps between an individual's appearance and reality. Such appearance-reality gaps describe any individual. Writers are not the only human beings to participate in this detective work. They are, however, the only human beings to use words to recreate, on paper, the experiential cues we employ in the face-to-face world to develop acquaintances.

In certain cases, the writer can focus the entirety of his detective story on the subject's appearance alone. Randall, for example, focused his observer portrait on his grandmother and decided that her smile, if highlighted, could move readers from types to a unique person.

> My grandmother always likes to tell stories. She has an awful lot of them to tell, too, and I always listen to them all with an attentive ear. Her bright green eyes sparkle when she tells me stories about when she was the younger. She has pictures, too. A whole shoebox full of them, all in black and white.
>
> Even in black and white her face is regal. Engulfed by a mink stole and hat, my grandmother looked like a movie star from the early 1940s. The few lines by her eyes are the only clues to her hard life during the Depression when she sold flowers on a street corner in uptown Manhattan to pay for a piece of bread. The picture was taken in 1946 and she looks to be about 25 years old although she was born in 1906. If you look back and forth from the picture to my grandmother's wrinkled face and silvery white hair you would find it hard to believe that it is the same person, but the smile is unmistakable: proud, happy, filled with life. Her teeth are dentures now, but that makes no difference. She always keeps that picture on her night stand to remind her of the days when she lived on Park Avenue in a 17th floor suite overlooking downtown Manhattan.

> She likes to tell stories and shows pictures while waiting for the soup to
> boil. Right in the middle of a story, she gets up and hurries into the
> kitchen and you can hear her bustling around, banging pots and dishes
> together, washing utensils (you need a full set of utensils for her soup)
> and glasses. Then she bustles her way back into the living room, places
> a heaping bowl of soup in front of you, and continues with her story.

Randall uses biographical and on-scene elements to characterize his
grandmother at different stages of her life. In her youth, she "looked
like a movie star from the early 1940s." She was the flower girl who
"sold flowers on a street corner to pay for a piece of bread." Now, she
is the grandmother who "bustles" and "places a bowl of [homemade]
soup in front of you."

Taken on their own, these characterizations are difficult to imagine
as references to the same person. Each paints images and moods, moreover, that take potentially contradictory directions. Her grandmother's
lost beauty could be linked with cynicism and despair, or taken as a sign
of fond memories still cherished. Her hard life selling flowers during the
depression could mean bitterness and resentment. Yet it could also
mean a deeper appreciation for her days on Park Avenue. Her bustling
through the kitchen as an old lady could mean she has no escape from
domestic duty. Yet, it could mean pride in being able to give so much to
her grandson.

These elements leave us with many riddles about Randall's grandmother and many possible answers. Randall did not want to pursue
them all, nor could he. However, he realized he could address one small
riddle about his grandmother's life by looking into the physical evidence
of her face. He found that her smile could be used to unify the reader's
on-scene (old lady) and biographical (the young lady photograph) experience of her. He saw that her smile provided continuity and convergence across these representations. By focusing on visual detail, such as
a smile, to unify different elements, a writer can make different representations converge into a single one. The result is a stereo effect, reinforcing a single observer portrait from different viewing angles.

Sometimes, as in Randall's case, the face and body hold small
answers to a person. Randall's case, though, is the exception more than
the rule. The curiosities and mysteries of a person's life are seldom
developed or resolved through such a convenient piece of visual evidence. Typically, the writer will want to draw on additional interview

and biographical elements to sharpen the lines of the subject, even as loose ends remain.

Linking the Visual Detail to the Person of the Subject

Visual detail, we have seen, is important in helping us see aspects of a person that we would not have inferred from a stereotype. Visual detail can include features from the larger environment, not just the subject's face and body type. What a subject wears and carries are also part of the scene that can reveal character puzzles. So too are where the subject lives, the car he drives, the brand of toothpaste and deodorant he uses, and the furnishings of home and workplace. The writer can get close to subjects and reveal unexpected features of their character by describing their property, belongings, and surrounding—in a word the *stuff* that makes the external environment their own.

Many writers whom we have studied understand this principle. However, they do not always appreciate that the details they select about the subject's environment must refer back to the character of the person. In an observer portrait, the subject's environment cannot be the dominant element. It surfaces only to reveal more about the subject's character. When the details about the subject's environment become dominant, the writing becomes scenic rather than the framing of an observer portrait. The portrait inadvertently widens into a description of a landscape that just happens to include a person.

Kenneth's portrait committed this inadvertent widening when he set out to profile his friend, Ayanna. In the opening, he succeeds in giving us an image of Ayanna as we meet her.

> I was met at the door with a warm smile from my friend Ayanna. She was dressed as always, in the most comfortable T-shirt and jeans that she could find. Her hair was pulled back in to a small ponytail and held together with a scrunchie. As she greeted me in the doorway, I noticed that she was barefoot. Not normally an exceptional thing but it was significant on this day because I had been so used to seeing her in black hiking boots—and she never had them off. Her nails were unpainted and she never wore even a hint of makeup so I was able to make out the features that fit her half-black/half-Indian heritage.

At this juncture, Kenneth turns his attention to his impressions of Ayanna's apartment.

Earlier this year I helped her move into her new place and it had been about two weeks since I'd seen it last. That's why I was knocking at her door then. She called me up and ranted and raved about how cool her new apartment was and how she could not wait to show it off. I can't say I really knew what to expect.

When I thought about it, I remembered that I had only known her for about a year and the last place she lived in didn't leave her much room to express herself. Sure, I had spent a lot of time with her but, you never really get to know someone until you see him or her there at home in their own environment. I will admit that I was rather surprised at how eager she was to present her new place. I proceeded to her apartment as soon as I could.

I walked through the door. She all but ran in before me anxious to get the impressions of her first guest. The first thing I noticed was the light gust of warm air. It seemed to hang there in the doorway as if to signify that I had just entered Ayanna's domain.

There was a slight dimness contrasting the light from the hallway. Before me was a strange curtain made of some kind of white colored twine. It reminded me of visiting the homes of my mom's friend when I very young.

My grubby little hands would not touch a thing. If they did, I could expect a most unpleasant and violent response. In any case, I proceeded to make my way into the main room as the door closed behind me. The dimness disappeared and as my eyes adjusted to the light and as the cleverly placed curtain was sliding down behind me it appeared as though I had walked into a movie scene. I took a slow look around; the light bounced off the soft plush carpet and set a warm gold like glow about the room.

Along each wall was hung a movie poster depicting violence, horror, death, and destruction. There were pictures of Mel Gibson (her favorite actor) and various friends in random clusters on the walls. At the center of attention across from her bed and the constant glow of her Power Mac stood her big screen TV. All around it an intense video library of cult films, classics, action, and horror, complete with Japanimation. To the right of the television, sits perfectly balanced a samurai sword. Its blade was sharp as a hair and it was polished to a high shine. I admit I was impressed. "Well, what do you think," she asked me. "I like it, how could

I not!" I saw her face full of glee at the simple sounds of awe in my voice. She happily explains the meaning of the new displays and then the significance of its location.

We often sit and swap stories and ideas about philosophy, cinematography, and the joys of violent and dramatic forms. For that, I will always be grateful. I'll never forget the first time I met my friend Ayanna.

Kenneth's writing hints at character connections to be made without making them. He uses the spatial detail to fill in striking objects in Ayanna's apartment ("The first thing I noticed . . . ," "Before me . . . ," "It reminded me . . .") that fan out across decor (e.g., strange curtain) and cultural icons (e.g., Mel Gibson, Japanimation), but that do not converge on a strong portrait.

By way of contrast, Eric's observer portrait illustrates spatial detail that more effectively converges on the owner of the space, his subject, Paul Dixon, a workaholic, novelist and social activist.

He sits at the monitor, face glowing blue. His fingers tap the keyboard, clicking like castanets. Rat-a-tat-tat. Rat-a-tat. Littering his desk are a coffee mug with swill, a drained paper clip dispenser, an origami frog, a pen-filled cup with the words "Stolen from Jonathan's Bar Mitzvah," bescribbled Post-its, a 1994 letter from a friend, a pair of his grandfather's cufflinks, and a box of James' saltwater taffy. Undisturbed by such clutter, he slides his glasses up to the bridge of his nose, then continues the castanets. If you were a fly on the wall, you'd be dancing. Then you'd also be poised in a prime place to watch Paul Dixon at work on his first novel.

Pushing aside some of his clutter, Dixon stares into the monitor's blue aura. "All this stuff helps me think," he says. "I don't think I could write in a sterile environment. All these things are little slices of my life. They're part of me, and that helps me to write about my own feelings." He unwraps molasses mint taffy and pops it into his mouth. The castanets begin. Rat-a-tat. Paul Dixon's writing a book. Doing some good.

Eric shows us glimpses of Dixon through his stuff. He shows us, more specifically, how Dixon's stuff helps support and mobilize his characteristic actions, his incessant writing. From the never ending typing on the computer, the coffee mug, the Post-its, and the paper clip dispenser, we know Dixon works long hours. From the cufflinks and letter he does not discard, we know Dixon maintains attachments to family and friends. From the novelty cup, the taffy, and the origami frog, we have some evidence of an eclectic taste and a sense of humor. Providing this detail gives readers the cues that they need to see inside Paul, his attitudes, perspectives, and thoughts. And by returning to Dixon's words, actions, and prospects at the end, Eric makes us feel the writing as an experience of coming to know the occupant rather than a real estate tour.

Integrating On-Scene and Biographical Elements

On-scene and biographical elements play different but complementary roles in revealing character. On-scene elements create a visual vividness and an impression of immediacy. Biographical elements focus on broader traits about the subject across different situations and periods of life. They tend to be sketchier and less vivid than on-scene elements. Nonetheless, they provide important vistas associated with personal identity: a religious, regional, and ethnic affiliation, a family heritage, an individual life span, and a contemporary generation of peers. Capturing the subject's actions in time thus provides a useful complement to capturing her in space.

As Randall's observer portrait illustrates, the writer creates a powerful observer portrait when the reader can capture the subject at the intersection of both views. Although Randall captures this intersection through a physical smile, Mary's observer portrait of her aunt offers a more sustained examination of a subject occupying visual space and time. Mary's aunt was a teacher with a learning disability that caused her to work ploddingly and methodically. The aunt could have considered herself disabled and avoided a challenging job. Yet, her entire life, Mary's aunt had this dogged determination to be a teacher.

We see this doggedness in the first scene of the writing, where Mary lets us glimpse her aunt grading papers late into the night.

> It's 11:00, an hour past her bedtime. She sits at the kitchen table, a squat, plump woman, with an array of papers fanned out before her. The papers are five- to seven-sentence assignments from her second grade class. She picks up each paper and reads it thoughtfully, twice. She corrects mistakes with a bright red felt-tip pen. She reads each a third and final time, and then holds it in her left hand while she leafs through a second pile of papers for the spelling assignment done by the same student. She studies that paper, already graded, and sets it to the side. She searches yet another pile, and pulls out an arithmetic assignment from the same student. She compares the three, then marks a grade on

the first one. She returns all three sheets to their respective piles, checking to make sure that she's putting the right assignment in the right pile. More often than not, another student's paper catches her eye and she pauses to look for a while before she picks up the next ungraded sheet. The next paper, and each paper to come, follows this same slow, meticulous process.

Her face gives away her opinion about each student, unconsciously, as she reads his or her paperwork. When she picks up the ungraded sheet, she stares at the name in the upper right-hand corner. If the child is a good student, her face is expressionless as she reads, and her minor corrections with her red pen seem effortless. If the student is one who doesn't pay attention in class, scores badly on tests, or has handwriting problems, she frowns, and usually shuffles to find other examples of his or her work before she even begins reading. She will study the marks the student received on other papers before returning to the unmarked one, and will press down on her red pen hard to mark mistakes—as though she were cutting through a thick, heavy cake with the utmost concentration.

Mary turns briefly to first person to explain why her aunt must work so hard: She refuses to let her disability rob her of a challenging career.

I have gotten to know her classes this way, watching her grade sheaves of inch-high writing on blue-lined sheets, late into the night, every evening of the week. The year that I started college, my aunt began teaching elementary school again, began to make the desk my cousin had worked at in high school into her own workspace, and told my uncle that he was now in charge of dinner. Because now, after such a long stretch of inactivity, the learning disability which had once caused her to read slowly was even rustier with disuse. The years that she spent at home raising my older brother and me was a 25-year marathon of cooking, washing, cleaning, and errands. The slim, petite schoolteacher who had taught carefully and methodically in the late 1960s was now a mass of heavy machinery, slow and ponderous cogs and wheels. If my aunt worked at a faster pace, I have no doubt that she would have been a doctor. Like most parents, she was an overprotective expert on the common cold, and recognized its symptoms a mile away (and was no less agile in her predictions 600 miles away, over the telephone).

Nevertheless, she seemed to have a knack beyond just maternal instinct. "That's a fracture," she stated flatly at my brother's soccer game, when his teammate was kicked in the wrist.

Moreover, it was. "That's impetigo" was her greeting on one visit, referring to some faint red marks studding my cheek. "It's just zits," I argued, but yet again, she was right. "That's not poison ivy," I remember her saying, when I returned from the woods muddy and scratched and itchy. Sure enough, it was poison oak, slightly bubblier and twice as contagious.

She was always abreast of the latest antibiotics and the rumors that surrounded them. My pediatricians became used to her accurate diagnoses and commands. "Penicillin," she demanded, marching me into the doctor's office. "She has strep throat." If we waited for the culture to come back positive before we filled the prescription that the doctor dutifully wrote, it was a mere formality. "Does Seldane D cause your heart to race?" she called to ask me one day. "Never mix it with other antibiotics. I read that it causes heart palpitations."

However, what doctor has the time to pull out each of her medical texts, and compare and contrast all the information they contain, while the patient sits in stocking feet in the examining room? No. My aunt would have trouble finishing medical school within her lifetime, and then, she admits that she'd probably never finish with her first patient.

Mary's on-scene shot of her aunt now segues into a biographical sequence, opening a wider window on her life.

So, for the last five years, she's stuck to teaching. After the first year, my family expected it to get easier. But as time wore on, we began to see that my aunt was the proverbial old dog who wouldn't learn new tricks. She refused, at my father's urging, to type her class plans into the computer; instead, she wrote sheet after sheet of her impeccable, voluptuous script. "It would be a lot easier for her if she knew how to save time," my uncle confided to me one day. But she has to do everything the long way."

I knew what he was trying to say. My aunt was from the old school, a generation of women trained to be wives and allowed entry only into some professions, including teaching. Not only that, her natural slowness made her shy away from the embarrassment of anything new. In 20 years out of the work force, she had missed great leaps in technology and now her eight-year-old students had to explain how to operate a CD player. Stubborn and unyielding, she neither had the emotional nor intellectual weapons to battle the changes that had taken place while she had been at home.

Given the modern, feminist perspective of my generation, where women feel the pressure to bite off more than they can chew, just to show that they can "do it all," it was hard for me to learn how to appreciate my aunt. Nevertheless, I have inherited her stubborn thoroughness, her intensity, and her old-fashioned interest in people rather than numbers. I have learned about dedication in a way that only a role model can display. I have watched her up close, grading sheaves of inch-high writing on blue-lined sheets, late into the night, every evening of the week.

Mary's opening on-scene element of her aunt prepares us so that when we later learn about her aunt's past, we are not surprised. Knowing the aunt's past and sense of determination, in turn, reinforces the striking image of the character we had first met at that table, hunched so determinedly over all those papers.

Splicing in Interview Elements

Interview elements allow the reader to create observer portraits that include the subject's perspective as reflected in his own words. These elements should not be confused with the informal talking and interviewing the writer might do with the subject while preparing to write. Talking and interviewing will fill hours of audiotapes. Interview elements are the quotes the writer includes to lend support to the acquaintance experience he has planned for readers. They help the reader experience the subject's own words as an enhancement of the acquaintance relationship.

Aaron nicely illustrates this function of interview elements in his observer portrait of Jane Brooks. Brooks works in the admissions office at Carson College. Her job is a grind. Her long hours are etched on her face. She is overworked, but she is also not one to back out of commitments. Aaron finds that readers do not have to rely solely on descriptions or actions to convey this aspect of Jane when Jane's words can also convey it.

> "I have to go out with my sister tonight," Jane Brooks says wearily. "When I agreed to, I didn't realize what I'd be doing at work." She waves her hand helplessly. She's working 15-hour days, sleeping badly, and has dark rings around her eyes.

Interview elements are also useful when the writer worries that readers won't take his word without support from the subject. Aaron learned about Jane's deep passion for boxing and discovered that one could not know her without knowing her long time love affair with the sport. Aaron was nonetheless surprised by this information and concerned that his readers wouldn't believe him were he left on his own to tell them. So he uses Jane's words to back the credibility of his reporting.

> To keep herself happy, Jane watches boxing. ("She likes boxing?" one of her coworkers asked me. "I'd never have guessed. She's so calm.") She's a dedicated Tuesday Night Fights fan, and wants to get HBO so she can see more big name matches. A month later, she's still talking about a woman's match, which preceded the latest Mike Tyson fight. "The Bruno-Tyson fight sucked, but the women's fight was great. Slugging like heavyweights with stamina and speed like featherweights. The winner almost broke the other's nose, a great shot—POW!" Her enthusiasm is tangible, her smile wide, both are contagious.

Aaron shows Jane as a person who would never back down from and quit on a challenge. He presents the visual evidence in her office. He presents it in her face. He discovered he could also confirm it in Jane's own words. So he made sure to bring her words in as well.

> "When I was in second grade at Winchester-Thurston," she says, "there was this girl who used to push me around. One day I fought back. I ran at her, but she knew karate or something—probably just this one move—and flipped me onto my back. It really hurt, but I got up and charged her again. She flipped me again. So I got up and charged and she flipped me repeatedly until finally she waved me off. She shook her head and said she was sorry. She never bothered me again."
>
> "Why do you stay?" I asked her. "You were happier before, you liked what you were doing more, and you worked less. Why stay?" "Because I'm not done," she answers. Translation? She won't leave feeling like she could have done more. She doesn't want to leave until she's won.

When an interview subject is verbal and reflective, her own words can do much to expedite the reader's acquaintance with her. Bear in mind, though, that without a character baseline and on-scene and biographical elements to fill in the subject, the subject's words can't alone enhance the acquaintance experience of the reader further. They will remain isolated quotes, self-reports, leaving the reader too little to acquaint with.

Threading Converging Traits
Through Independent Representational Elements

A common flaw in the observer portrait is to include the three design elements (on-scene, biographical, interview), but to overlook that the different elements are there to converge toward a stereo effect. Just as self-portraiture relies on the three-dimensional effect of revealing oneself both in thought and action, observer portraiture relies on the stereo effect of seeing a subject's *converging* traits reinforced across on-scene, biographical, and quoted experiences. The stereo effect is diluted when different elements point to entirely different and unaligned traits.

Joy, for example, portraying a friend named Forest, starts the reader in an on-scene element where Forest is deathly ill.

> Forest sits on the corner of the couch, legs crossed, arms resting on either side of his slender frame. He is tall (six foot four to be exact) but his posture suggests a man much smaller. Like a branch heavy with snow, his body is curved and bent, void of physical strength. A plastic bag containing over forty vitamins rests next to his 12 ounce glass of distilled water. Focusing hard on the glass, Forest releases just enough energy to take a drink. He extends his right hand, picks up the glass, moves it to his lips, takes a drink, puts the glass back and returns his hand to his side. He repeats this activity until the glass is empty. Each drink drains his energy. The nurse keeps an eye on his progress and when he gets close to finishing the glass, without missing a beat, she fills it again giving Forest a comforting smile. "Just five more glasses to go," she said. Trying hard to return the gesture, Forest forces the corners of his mouth up. It's hardly a smile, but the message gets across. Dropping the weight of his cheeks like a pair of dumb bells he says, "I never thought I'd end up like this."

The man we first see in this scene and hear in quotes is sick and shaken by what has happened to him. In the biographical elements, by contrast, Joy shows us a confident workaholic who was ambitious from an early age:

> Dreams of wealth and power set in early for Forest. He started a lawn mowing business at the age of twelve, mowing over thirty lawns a week. "I made three to four thousand dollars a summer. My parents couldn't afford to buy me a car for my sixteenth birthday so they encouraged me to start saving money at an early age." By the time his sixteenth birthday rolled around Forest had enough money to buy a Mazda Z28. "I loved that car. It was the opposite of everything I had known. That car was flashy, expensive and made a social statement."

Forest goes on to achieve fame and fortune running a design firm. In her first draft, Joy mentions, only in passing, that Forest worked so hard that he did not pay attention to his health. We do not see this aspect of him over time or on-scene. Rather, we get one Forest (energetic and successful) over time and a second Forest (sick and resigned) on-scene. The result is to use different elements to reveal different phases of Forest's life without centering a portrait of him. Unlike a less character-based biography, related to narrative history, where the writer tells the story of a person's life in phases and over time, an observer portrait tries to capture enduring traits about a person, with each trait revealing itself on-scene, over time, and in the subject's own language. In an observer portrait, writers are free to reveal multiple traits about a subject, as space allows. However, no trait offered, taken by itself, will add to deepened portraiture if it is not threaded through multiple and independent represented elements. Without understanding the stereo effects that are built into mature observer portraiture, novice writers tend to use words not to reveal a subject, but to bury him under a heap of adjectives and descriptive phrases.

In her second draft, Joy knew she wanted to capture traits about Forest that spanned his workaholic past and his current life of poor health. Thinking back to the hospital scene, she recalled that Forest's workaholism as a designer had once starkly revealed itself even in the hospital room.

> Forest sits on the corner of the couch, legs crossed, arms resting on either side of his slender frame. He sits back seemingly unconnected to his environment. He is tall, six foot four to be exact, and like a branch

heavy with snow, his body is curved, bent over from carrying life's burdens. Silently, he absorbs every detail in the room. He lowers his eyes, appreciating the sterile white floor. He sees the blanket on his hospital bed changing color in the light. Breaking his silence, he briefly opens up his world to the people around him. "Look at the texture of that blanket. Do you notice how it's almost three dimensional under natural light? The material is not as dynamic with florescent. It's a really beautiful blue in the right light." The doctors don't know how to respond to his observations.

By showing us a mind that could not stop working and that would shamelessly push a body beyond its limits, Joy had put her finger on a trait that she could more consistently thread across healthy and sickly stages of Forest's life. She could then use this trait to build a more integrated, over-time portrait of Forest.

Familiarity and Objectivity

Readers need to see the observer portraitist as being fair to the subject and fairness requires a balance of objectivity and familiarity. *Objectivity* means that the reader is able to distinguish the writer's perspective from the subject's. The reader perceives the writer as trying to tell the truth about the subject, not simply reinforcing what the truth as the subject sees it. The observer portraitist uses the subject as a source, but must reserve the right to come to her own conclusions about the subject. Insisting on the profiler's need for objectivity, Remnick (1996), who earned much of his literary reputation on the celebrity profile, remarked, as evidence of his objectivity, that his subjects do not always recognize themselves in the way he depicts them.

Familiarity means the writer is perceived as having both access and open-mindedness to the subject's point of view in the course of building a complete portrait. The observer portrait can not be a hit-and-run assault, or a smear, carried out from the distance of a negative stereotype. The fair writer must be perceived as trying to understand the subject's story in the subject's terms before drawing any final, independent, conclusions.

The writer's viewing distance must not be too far from the subject to lose familiarity nor too close to lose objectivity. When the portrait writer manages this delicate balance, she has achieved the perception of fairness.

Kerry's observer portrait relates to these matters, as she manages to keep an objective viewing distance while profiling her three-year-old daughter, Rebecca. She begins with on-scene and biographical elements that are strikingly accurate and all too typical of three-year-olds:

Today she insists! She must wear the blue lam dress-up gown. She has played in it so much that threads dangle from its ankle length skirt. A neon pink winter parka and white plastic winter boots with pink accents completes her ensemble. Beneath her dress-up gown is her favorite pink T-shirt from the St. Louis Zoo. As she opens the door of Magic Years pre-school, all eyes in the room glance in her direction. A small voice shouts "Becca's here!" and a burst of running feet cross the room as several kids rush up to greet her. She raises her arms in protest but there is a smile on her face. She says, "No Kissing! No Kissing!" while a teacher peels a few of her admirers away.

One child hangs up her coat while another takes her backpack and puts it in the cloakroom. She goes in and retrieves the Barbie she brought to play with for the day and heads over to the sand table to join her classmates. I say, "Bye Becca, have a nice day." She mumbles "Bye Mom" under her breath but doesn't look up.

Kerry then proceeds to develop Rebecca from the type, *typical three-year-old preschooler*, to a unique little girl.

I wonder if I should explain to the teachers why she is wearing a blue lamé dress-up gown to school, but instead mention only that there are different clothes in her backpack, if she wants to change. Then I leave. Her teachers know she has a will of her own and a very acute sense of personal fashion. One day she insisted on going to school in her paja-mas. When I forcibly changed her clothes, in spite of her crying and anger, she just waited five minutes, went back to her room, and changed into the clothes she wanted to wear. After a couple of these horrifying episodes, I learned to let her wear what she wanted to wear. Usually she just insists on wearing a dress, tights, jewelry and pretty shoes. Her favor-ite color has always been pink.

Becca will be four years old in three months time. She is independent and charismatic. Dimples appear and deep blue eyes flash when she shows off her elfish but stunning smile. She has dark straight brown hair cut short and very fair skin. Her features are small and rounded like any child. A 'Y' shaped scar imbedded in her right eyebrow is the only imperfection in her beautiful face. She acquired it at the age of 13 months when she fell onto the corner of grandpa's coffee table. The shape of her eyes bears reminders of some Asian genes in her past. She is rather tall and thin for a three-year-old. She walks with grace and a bit of a swagger. It's hard to believe she weighs only thirty pounds, her presence is so much larger. Yet, I can still pick her up and whirl her around like I used to do when she was a toddler.

She likes to take small things like beads, rocks, and toys, and deposits them into her secret places. The cabinet under the bathroom sink is one of her special spots. Her sense of order manifests itself in another way too; a radar-like inventory system. She knows where every small thing is in our house. If I can't find my keys, I will ask Becca. She knows they are important to me, so she won't take them and hide them away. She will probably know where they are.

Becca has always been so willful, that no punishment would work. She did just what she wanted to do, regardless of what we said or did. If we told her to sit on the naughty chair, she would flatly refuse. She wouldn't go near that chair. Even if we picked her up and sat her on it, she would jump up like that chair was covered in molten lava. We don't like to hit our children but at one point we decided to try it because nothing else worked. When we hit her, she would stand up and look at us defiantly and say "It didn't hurt!" We stopped trying to hit her. We just decided to hold our breath and try and keep her from killing herself until she reaches an age when we can reason with her.

To increase familiarity, her closeness to Becca's perspective, Kerry plays a visible character in some of these scenes. In one present-tense, on-scene element ("I wonder if I should explain to the teachers . . ."), she reveals her thoughts in first person. She also makes herself a visible character in other biographical elements that refer to unique past events ("When I forcibly changed her") and to recurring ones ("If I can't find my keys, I will ask Becca"). Yet, to maintain objectivity, her distance from Becca, Kerry avoids writing from the intimacy of a mother's point of view. She lays out facts about Becca that an on-scene observer, not solely a mother, could confirm.

Mixed Portraiture:
Blending Self-Portraiture and Observer Portraiture

In fiction, main characters are the characters who are textured beyond an opening premise. Minor characters tend to remain stereotypes who do not learn, grow, or change significantly during the course of events. Often, there are multiple main characters. In nonfiction portrait writing, there can also be multiple subjects portrayed. In our studio work, students have sometimes found it useful to develop themselves as characters even as they portray a subject with whom they have a longstanding relationship. This melding of self and observer foci results in *mixed portraiture*, a combination of self-portraiture and observer portraiture.

Susan's observer portrait is an example of how self- and observer portraits can be combined. Nana, Susan's deceased grandmother, had remained a living presence for her long after her death. By going through family artifacts, Susan learned more about Nana's perspective, could better interpret what Nana's facial expressions had meant in the many scenes they shared together. Most relevant to mixed portraiture, Susan found that by looking into Nana's life, she could see more clearly into her own.

Susan begins by presenting a sense of her home, family photographs, and describing her memory of one person in the photograph, her grandmother.

> As you walk up the stairs to the second story of my home, you'll see a family history of photographs. It's a common convention, which I saw for the first time when I was newly out of college, visiting the home of my best friend and roommate. Her father had framed and grouped old photos of earlier generations that suggested the thread of their unity, understanding, and love. My family gallery has similar pictures of great grandmothers and unknown ancestors along with more contemporary scenes. We hug and laugh and look at the camera hoping it will capture only moments that will please us. However, one picture of my Nana and me shows a different view of our family. It doesn't please me, but it reminds me in an instant of the story of our lives together.

Susan tells us that Nana was not happy about the prospect of becoming a grandmother. Her reluctance makes Nana an interesting puzzle to pursue.

Upon being given the news that she was about to become a grand-mother, a word never used in her presence later, Nana did not hide her considerable unhappiness. Luckily my mother's first child was a boy. I was told much later that his birth came first as a relief and then as a joy to her. A new boy was somehow not a problem. She wouldn't be so lucky the second time around.

This snapshot of my Nana with her only granddaughter is a beautiful picture, I think, in its accidental composition, but I see the eyes that I remember so well—disapproving and unhappy—and me trying as usual to get away. Nana often wondered why I couldn't be more like my brother, a good, happy boy who never fussed or gave her a minute's confusion. While I tried my best to please her, doing those things she so admired in him, the picture reminds me of the outcome of those attempts.

Susan fills in the details of this lingering image with a particular episode, one that relives how Nana caused her to feel inadequate.

One day stands apart from all the others. My mother had gone to get her hair done, Nana was left to watch me, a 5 year old sitting carefully on a dining room chair that had been placed against the wall. My fingers held the edge of the stool, slow motion movement until I became aware that she was watching me. I looked up and heard, "Look, your brother was doing this when he was only four." I saw a drawing of quite a nice tiger, worthy of any refrigerator display. I asked for the crayons and drew the same animal, only one-year late.

Susan now skips ahead in time to Nana's death. As she sorts through Nana's things and finds photographs of Nana as a younger person, she connects with Nana in ways she had not before.

And though I kissed her at every family gathering as was required, and held her hand as she lay dying, and wished with all my heart that she would open those eyes again, we never were any closer than the frozen moment captured by that family snapshot. After she died and my grand-father joined her, we had to clean out their home. Sadly, I thought of it as a buried treasure moment. In dividing the furniture and throwing away the junk, we came upon more family photos.

Reflecting on the aging process, Susan hints that Nana's strained relationship with her must have come from Nana's anxieties about aging. Susan wonders whether she will inherit the same anxieties and with the same consequences for her children and grandchildren.

> The stills I lingered over were old, the ones destined for my hallway gallery. They included photos of Nana when she was much younger, even then having a look that made me think that she must have always been unhappy with something. I looked at those pictures for a long time admiring their age and patina and feeling sorry for her sad expressions, until finally I saw something else in the old image. Always, I'd thought of the two of us as dissimilar creatures thrown together by an accident of fate, but now, in her young eyes with the skin pulled tight and smooth, I saw my own.
>
> I've since come to see her unhappiness with me as the unsuccessful struggle of a victim of time, with no tools to deal with the reminders of passing generations and her own youth. But in that moment it frightened me to wonder if someday there would be another grandchild whose existence I also couldn't bear to face, who would pull away as I did, unable to understand why I held her so sternly in my gaze.

After a first draft, Susan came to think she had created a link between Nana in the photographs, Nana's anxieties, and her own anxieties about inheriting them. Nonetheless, she felt the link was still not as well developed as it needed to be. She also felt that her analysis of Nana was plausible, but also stereotypic. Aging is a common fear, hardly unique to Nana. Susan felt she had to make Nana more distinctive to the reader if she was to expect the reader to understand how Nana had *distinctively* influenced her own thinking.

In her next draft, Susan focused the writing, using scenic detail more judiciously. She edited out the incidental detail of how the wall photos came to be mounted and got right to the point about why she noticed them.

> Because I control time here, my mother never has to be old on this wall. It's my gift to her. Besides, it's my history and I tell it as I please. I've always thought that those old photos, stained with yellow and holding the forever young, are like the welcome of a nice warm kitchen after being out on a blustery day. They shelter me and tell me I belong here.

Susan has created a context, happy and optimistic, about what family photos have come to mean for her. She then disrupts the mood by describing a picture of herself with her grandmother.

> My family gallery has similar pictures. We hug and laugh and look at the camera hoping it will capture only moments that will please us. However, you will find one snapshot of my grandmother Nana and me that captures a different view of our family. It doesn't please me, but it reminds me in an instant of the story of our lives together.

In the first draft, Susan told of Nana's discomfort with a granddaughter. Now, to give the reader a closer look at Nana, she lets us overhear snippets of her parents and Nana interacting, with the words and attitudes mostly lost to faint signals but the context and its mood left intact.

> Picture this: My mother and father glow as they tell my grandmother that they're going to have a child. Her reaction surprised them. How could they do this? They'd made a mistake. They tried to talk to her. "Mary, the you'll love this—a baby—my god." She cried. They tried to understand, but finally they left.

In this second draft, Susan does not leave her grandmother, or herself, a stereotype. She uses the death of her grandmother and the opening of her estate, as an occasion for developing the mystery of Nana's life.

> I went back to her home with my family one last time after my grandfather died. Their house had to be sold and we had to clean it. As I threw away the junk in the attic, I felt I was really on a dig for artifacts. I didn't have to search for long when under the wrapping in an old gift box I found a picture of Nana when she was much the younger. I couldn't stop looking at it. I thought I liked its age. That wasn't it.

Susan uses the photograph of Nana as an essential clue to the mystery. Like all good mysteries, the clue allows Susan to notice information that was available to her all along but whose importance and relevance she had overlooked. In an earlier draft, Nana's eyes in the photograph revealed Nana to be "a victim of time." Aging makes a person a victim of time just because the time in a lifetime can never be recovered. Susan now came to see in Nana's eyes a vulnerability she had not before recognized. Nana's life was one of missed opportunities that had made her cynical. It was not just that time was passing. The time that had been available to her had been a disappointment. Susan, a young girl with a world of opportunity in front of her, reminded Nana of the time she had lost.

> Nana and I always acted like the repelling poles of two magnets held together by force. How could we connect? Now, in her the young eyes with the skin pulled tight and smooth, I saw my own. I guess I should have looked into those eyes long before that day. Nana always thought that fate should treat a good, pretty girl like her very gently. Life was diffi-cult. Her father drank and beat his wife. So she ran from that to a hus-band she didn't love. He was supposed to be rich . . . but he wasn't. How could she accept a baby girl who reminded her that her opportuni-ties were over while mine were just beginning. With all that youth had denied her, a new girl in the family must have been difficult to bear.

Susan's glimpse into Nana now helps her understand her own perspec-tive better, the fear that what happened to Nana could happen to her.

> It has occurred to me often since then that only the like poles of magnets repel. That frightens me. I wonder if someday there will be another grandchild whose existence I also can't bear to face. I wonder if some-day I will have a grandchild who will pull away as I did, unable to under-stand why I hold a stern gaze on her.

Using mixed portraiture, Susan was able to blend a portrayal of Nana with a self-portrait. As Kerry's example showed us, the writer must be cautious not to let her own perspective distort the view she gives of the subject. However, as Susan's example also shows, the mix-ture of self and observer portraiture, when done well, can allow the writer to capture information about an ongoing relationship that nei-ther type of portraiture captures as well on its own.

Summarizing the Writing Models in Relation to Observer Portraiture

Observer portraiture develops an image of an observed subject through the convergence of three independent representational elements: on-scene, biographical, and quotes.

Andrew's early draft illustrates perhaps the most ubiquitous misstep that novices take when they try their hand at portraying a subject on the page: mistaking developing a subject with shifting the subject from one subject stereotype to another. The result is to shift a character across types without adding the individuating elaborations that make types into persons.

Writers must provide the small details about people that override the defaults implied by any character type. The detail comes in the scenic experience with the subject, the quotes she supplies, and the biographical record.

Confirming the same traits across visual space, biographical time, and subject quotes supports readers in feeling that they are learning the same things about a person through different channels of experience.

Randall offers an example of how different views about a person can be confirmed and combined through the use of physical details that endure over time. In Randall's case, the detail was his grandmother's smile, connecting the aged woman of today with a young woman in a photograph taken decades earlier.

Visual detail about character is not limited to the face and body of the subject. It extends to the environment that the subject inhabits. Kenneth's early draft illustrates that if the writer wants to portray a subject through her stuff, he needs to make sure the stuff converges on a person rather than fans out across details that never converge back on character. Eric, making sure to focus on stuff that supports or enables a character's defining actions, illustrates the positive application of this principle in the case of Paul Dixon.

Mary's writing shows the integration of visual detail and biographical time. Her portrait of her aunt shows how defining character features, like her aunt's determination, are strengthened when the writer can show these features textured across both visual scenes and biographical time.

Aaron illustrates how interview elements lets the writer recruit the subject's voice to confirm or comment on the way the writer intends to portray the subject as an object of acquaintance.

Joy's first draft shows the pitfall of including different representational elements that fail to converge into a single portrait. Merely generalizing about a person does not capture the stereo effects of observer portraiture unless the writer takes care to thread converging traits through different representations. Absent the sense of convergence across diverse representations, readers will not experience a single object of acquaintance.

The observer portrait has a high potential for losing objectivity when the writer and subject are intimate. Kerry maintains her objectvity in a portrait of her daughter by staying with descriptions that remain at arm's length from her motherly perspective.

Susan, writing about her Nana, shows how observer portraits do not have to leave the writer out of the picture. Portraying a subject's life can involve saying something meaningful about the writer's own. A mixed portrait allows a portrait writer to pursue mysteries in her own character even as she pursues them in another's.

Observer Portraiture in Professional and Public Writing

The principles of observer portraiture apply to professional and public examples of writing as well as to the everyday examples produced by our students. Journalists create observer portraits to acquaint their readers with celebrities and newsmakers. Sometimes the portraits are flattering. Sometimes, as happens in underground and tabloid profiles, unflattering and unfair.

Observer portraiture is a central representational element in the genre known as the reference letter, where the writer must characterize a job candidate to a prospective employer. Consider the following opening paragraph, taken from an actual letter of reference for a candidate to a senior professorship in a research university. The writer starts by showing how the candidate stands out from his peers creatively.

> I am taking the liberty of offering a letter of recommendation in support of an applicant for your position. You will perhaps recognize my name from John Doe's list of references. I want to express my strongest enthusiasm for John Doe, both as a scholar and as an individual. A glance at his resume says plenty about his professional standing, but its reader would not necessarily know much about the impact of Doe's work on his area of study. His first book quite simply revolutionized the field, pushing it as hard as Tom Smith [the name of a prominent established writer] had begun pushing it. No one in his area of study, I think, writes with the combination of lucidity, force, and sophistication that graces Doe's work. Doe's books have won rave reviews. The books are as readable as they are revolutionary.

Creativity is necessary, but not sufficient grounds for hiring a person if the person is a scoundrel and a low-life. To make the person admirable for the job, creativity must be combined with the human qualities that make the person a role model and team player. The writer concludes with these qualities.

No doubt some of your other applicants will have scholarly credentials that approximate Doe's. But John Doe is an unrelentingly decent, caring, honest, pleasant, and humane person. Were you to hire Doe, you would be hiring a colleague of the highest quality, a model for your younger faculty members as well as a willing and expert participant in the departmental and college chores for which only senior professors are eligible.

Although the reference letter can contain on-scene, biographical, and interview elements, the biographical elements will tend to dominate. The on-scene and interview elements will make visible the candidate's specific actions and work habits, but not his or her physical appearance. There are laws against taking into consideration a person's race, age, and ethnicity for hiring. The reference letter, for this reason, tends to suppress the visual close-ups from the observer portrait.

The various wrinkles and potential missteps underlying observer portraiture should not conceal the relative uniformity and elegance of the principles on which such portraiture depends.

That said, no matter how tight an observer portrait, loose ends will always remain. That is not a limitation on observer portraiture, but a tribute to the richness of human life. A writer's stories about a life can at most be what Remnick (1996) called a "glimpse."

All humans are interesting. Only writers, however, skilled in observer portraiture, know how to bring readers unforgettable glimpses of perfect strangers with nothing but words.

II. Landscapes

3

The Feel of Extended Space

Landscaping evokes imagery of objects occupying physical space across wider horizons of viewing than are typically available in portraiture. Faced with the problem of describing the layout and activity of a panoramic scene, we have come to instinctively rely on communication with pictures and illustrations more than with words. Floor plans, diagrams, landscape paintings, photographs, and video recordings are just a few of the tools that we use to communicate different features of physical spaces. Words, conveying meaning in discrete semantic bits, are poorly equipped to reference areas across a contiguous space.

Writing and physical space seem strange bedfellows, a strangeness that becomes dramatically apparent when we consider our earliest exposures to written information. When we first learn writing in school, we are shown how words carve up the physical world into discrete categories that tend toward the generic and the abstract. Consider the common sentences, "The cat is on the mat" and "John sees Mary run." The ideas these words conjure have no anchorage in physical space. The common nouns (cat, mat) and proper nouns (John, Mary) referenced could reside anywhere in physical space. The sentence tells us nothing about the size, shape, or color of the cat, of the mat, or where on the mat the cat lies. We are not told which cat or mat or (for that matter) which John or Mary is being referenced. The sentences contain category types rather than individual tokens. Sentences we consider transparently simple, even as beginning readers, omit much visual and location information. Yet we barely notice its absence. From the outset of our careers as readers, we classify these sentences as trivial to understand even though we understand them only sparsely in terms of the visual and locational information they code.

In this chapter, we examine scenic writing as a prototype to better understand the representational principles available to the writer when she wants to evoke physical space with words. Unblended, scenic writing is most likely to appear in fiction and screenplay writing. The writer may compose the physical world within which the characters interact; or may compose physical scenes into the memories of characters while they act or interact in dialog. Since the 1930s, science fiction has portrayed empires held together across worlds light years apart. Oliver Morton (1999, pp. 84-87), comparing Isaac Asimov's *Foundation* stories to George Lucas' *Star Wars* films, conjectured that "the printed word is much better at conveying [spatial] immensity than film is." He observed that, onscreen, galaxies look like "beachballs." Written science fiction is better at capturing vast size over speed, he proposed, because our concept of infinite space is shaped from the imagination even more than from the perceptual system.

In unblended form, scenic writing that focuses on bounded space constitutes what Spirn (1998) called a *language of landscape*, a language with its own rules of expression. Scenic writing is indispensable if a writer is to create, for readers, a sense of spatial ambience. This chapter describes a scenic writing assignment we devised, one that asked students to give readers the experience of "an environment" with words.

To describe the challenge underlying our scenic writing assignment, we need to introduce the element of displacement, an element that captures an important default of written information. Chafe (1994) defined *displacement* as the assumption that the world of the text is removed in time and space from the world of the writer and reader. Under the assumption of displacement, the reference context is removed from the communication context. When addressing a listener, speakers create displaced utterances by referring to situations outside the here and now. For speech, displacement is an option but not a requirement of communication. When A and B are talking, they may choose to talk about the couch they are both sitting on or the TV show they are both watching. However, they may also choose to talk about the bad loan that cousin Fay took out two years back or the retirement of Uncle Charlie two years hence. The reference of the talk may or may not live outside the immediate production context of the talkers. In writing, however, where the writer and reader are spatially and temporally distant, displacement is a communicative default if not a requirement. Only in specialized forms of writing, such as passing notes or instructions, will the text reference the here and now of the reader.

Requiring the displacement of the reference context from the communication context has its advantages. It can stabilize and make portable the world of the text, allowing the reader to plunge into the same world whether in a library or on the beach (Kaufer & Carley, 1993). Displacement in writing further explains why writers and readers can each work in parallel, asynchronously, and in spurts. It explains why texts do not have to be composed or read in real time, as part of a single live transaction. Texts can be composed over many sittings that take place over varying time intervals. It also explains why writers can produce texts that are, on average, longer, more planned, and more internally complex and consistent than the utterances speakers, on average, produce (Kaufer & Butler, 1996). None of this would be possible were not the world in the text displacable from the immediate world of the writer or reader.

Displacement is a basic assumption of asynchronous communication. Chafe contrasts displacement with another assumption, *immediacy*. Displacement means that the world of the communication resides outside the here and now of reader's immediate world. *Immediacy* is the complementary assumption, namely that the world of the text does inhere in the reader's here and now. The reference context overlaps with the immediate context of the reader. Under the assumption of immediacy, what is said references the immediate environment of the person saying it and the people listening.

Displacement is the communicative default of composed text. Immediacy is the communicative default of unplanned or spontaneous speech.

Beyond defaults of communication media, displacement and immediacy do double duty as representational elements in their own right. In the next chapter, we shall investigate the representational use of displacement in a narrative history assignment. In this chapter, we investigate immediacy as a representational requirement of scenic writing.

Scenic writing works its representational magic by activating immediacy, not only to override the natural displacement of writing, making the words seem to *reside* in the reader's here and now, but also to set the representation, making the words seem to *configure* the reader's immediate reality. By highlighting immediacy as a representational principle and by attenuating the reader's sense of displacement, the writer makes the reader feel the illusion of not reading at all. The reader rather feels the words with the weight of immediate spatial reality.

Done well, scenic writing causes the reader to feel present in the world of the text. The forests, trees, and mountain trails in the text, do not, of course, literally sprout in the reader's face. However, the writing can seem sufficiently striking in visual immediacy to cause the reader to interpret the reading experience as a perceptual experience.

The scenic writer coaxes the reader to feel as if the words are functioning as her own eyes and ears. If the reader turns the words into mental imagery, the illusion can make the words no longer feel displaced. This is not necessarily because the writing feels like speech, but because the experience of the world in the text takes on the proximate and unfolding immediacy characteristic of speech. The reader may recognize the words as the expression of an offstage guide who is simply reinforcing what the reader's mental senses can independently see and hear. The words may come to seem eerily redundant and unnecessary, especially if the reader's imagery is now driving the representation.

Pictures striving for photographic realism derive their representational power from their capacity to represent, point-for-point, concrete particulars occupying precise time/space coordinates. The photographer cannot photograph a generic cat, but only one of Felix or Tabby occupying a specific location at a specific time. The uncaptioned photograph may not identify the cat's unique time and place, but it will always reveal it, and so will always make its identification in time and place a project for further research.

The scenic writer overrides the defaults of generic elements of representation, capturing objects in their specific time and place. The elements responsible for scenic effects form components of many well-documented genres. They participate in the on-scene elements of an observer portrait; the task-focused space referenced in an instruction manual; and the descriptive detail of a travelogue. These various genres recruit scenic elements to create in the reader an impression of contiguous space.

Words versus Cameras

Photographs can surprise and disappoint, as well as please, because they invariably provide more detail than the photographer intended to frame. Photographs can show us the new baby that was born in a family. However, in the process, they can also show us that the proud parents who are holding it look haggard and bleary-eyed. The photograph may not have been taken to record these changes in the parents, but it nonetheless makes that contextual information available to any viewer. Photographs capture details that the photographer could not have fully absorbed when framing the shot.

Texts are poorer at saturating the visual information available within a region of space. Write the word *dog* and you will likely build a skeletal image, a wireframe of a dog that is no dog in particular (Kosslyn, 1994). If we then ask you, what color is the dog and what kind of dog resides in your mind's eye, you may not know. Unlike a photographic detail preserved as soon as the shot is taken, such as the exhaustion of the parents, the details of a mental image need not be resolved fully as a condition of their being built. Suppose you have an image of a 100-pound yellow collie in your mind's eye and someone asks you, "How long the collie, nose to tail?" Given what you know about collies, you may be able to respond by making some length calculation on your mental image. Yet, the research of Kosslyn (1994) suggests that your image of the collie is not likely to have included a serious length dimension until you are faced with the question about its length. Readers can develop the particular detail of mental images as they need to. Mental images are more dynamically manipulable than true-to-scale photorealistic pictures.

Because word-induced images lack the detail and fixity of photographs, one might think that the experience of realism conveyed in texts is itself weaker than the experience of realism conveyed in photographs. Curiously, this is less the case than we might first expect. Readers are able to experience literary persons and scenes as real without insisting on the dense texturing of photographic realism. We can fall in love with literary characters and scenes without ever noticing that, within the standards of visual realism, our images of these characters and scenes remain dream-like and spotty. Everyone knows Huckleberry Finn, but how many know the texture of his hair or the motion of his hips as he walks? This is visual-spatial knowledge, knowledge that we acquire when we share physical space with a person or when a writer is skilled enough in observer portraiture to give readers the experience of this knowledge. Nonetheless, readers can, from a text, form an image of Huckleberry Finn as a real person even without pinning down these low-level visual-spatial properties.

Readers thus don't require photorealistic detail and accuracy to experience texts as bearing on the real. They not only don't require it; they also don't welcome it. Only novice writers try to imitate true-to-life cameras in their descriptive practices. Such dogged imitation leads to reams of unreadable prose. Imagine trying to write every descriptive fact about the room in which you are reading this. You could fill volumes for the effort and no one would care. Writers simply cannot do what cameras can do or in the way cameras do it. Nor would they hold the attention of readers if they could.

Where the camera can be comprehensive in the information it frames, the writer must be selective. For the camera, the focus is determined from the selection of the shot to frame. Once the shot is framed, selection is complete. For the writer, the focus is determined by the information selected within a frame. Once the writer trains her eye on what to write, the process of selection begins.

A writer tells stories about a space by shifting viewing frames and angles. In this sense, a text is like a film, another powerful medium for visual story-telling. In film, the labor divides into separate activities. Filmmakers shift frames, but the frames shifted need to be carefully edited under the guidance of a story editor relying on a written screenplay. Writers, by contrast, compose, shoot and edit frames within the same medium. Visual framing, editing, and story writing collapse into one role and medium. Shifting and editing frames of space, writers can organize texts to form spatial stories.

The spatial details selected in scenic writing are selected precisely because of the role they play in a scenic story, relying on contrasts and conflicts to resolve. Outside a spatial story to tell, spatial detail becomes incidental. Taken as an isolated visual fact, an office building's glass and marble facade is a throwaway detail wasting page space and the reader's time. Yet if we notice a striking visual contrast between the glass and marble on one side of the street and the broken brick and decaying wood on the other, and if we learn that the different sides of the street reflect a stratified economy, the selected detail "glass and marble" now, almost single-handedly, carry a good story.

Making the most of these trade-offs between words, pictures, and word-induced images, the skilled scenic writer captures a space by finding the fewest high contrast words (e.g., "glass and marble") that induce the tension needed to carry a story about a space. Miminalism and efficiency in word selection are important for psychological as well as stylistic reasons. The reader needs to be able to build the image quickly, as many surrounding words in the textual stream can't be assigned a final interpretation until the image has been resolved. For example, how we understand the word "drill" in a sentence varies dramatically depending upon the spatial imagery (e.g., a school, a dentist's office, an oil rig) we have built in our mind's eye prior to encountering it. Should the reader work too hard for the right image of "drill" with too little unifying context, the words will leave the image stillborn.

When Words Fail as Mental Pictures:
Patterns Harmful to Visual Writing

We can be more systematic about the minimalism and efficiency at issue in building word pictures. When a writer's efforts to coax a reader toward a mental image fail, she has likely fallen victim to one of various image inhibitors. We consider five specific patterns of writing that inhibit the capacity of words to activate mental pictures for readers.

1. Visual Redundancy

Visual redundancy arises when a writer throws more words at an image than is necessary or desirable. Consider a first draft and revision of one of Mary's passages:

> "Old women emerge from the grocery store lean on each other ~~and trudge down the sidewalk~~ with plastic bags of food sagging at their sides."

The phrases "old women" and "lean on each other" already prompt images of slow movement, that is, trudging. Readers of the original sentence, feeling this redundancy, complained that when they parsed the word *trudge,* they felt their image of plodding movement, already clear in their mind's eye, becoming cluttered. Readers literally expressed their complaint as "too many words," but their legitimate complaint was not the number of words but the stagnant effect of adding words that are redundant with an image readers already hold. In a second draft, Mary removed the "trudge" phrase and her readers judged that the sentence was improved.

2. Selecting Words Low in Visual Vividness

Words are not equal when it comes to guiding a reader's construction of imagery. Some words are more visually vivid than others. They guide the reader's construction of imagery more precisely and efficiently than less visual words. As the linguist Manfred Bierwisch (1996) pointed out, words can vary in the mental instructions they give readers about the features of a space. Many words of English, perhaps the majority, offer no guidance whatever to readers about how an image of physical space is to be developed. Words like *for* and *because* function as glue for sentences, but provide no help when constructing spatial images.

They are what Bierwisch called *aspatial terms*, words that offer no mental instructions about how to texture a space.

Other words, like *colored*, *wet*, and *solid*, are what Bierwisch calls *implicitly spatial*. They specify a visual attribute without specifying a specific visual value. The word *colored*, for example, tells a reader to fill in a space with a hue, but it does not say which hue. The same is true for *wet* and *solid*, which give us a general attribute without specific detail (what kind of wet? what kind of solid?). *Oil* and *water* are both wet, but their wetness must be represented differently in accurate imagery. Styrofoam and concrete are both solids but require representations that differ in the texture of solidity.

Still other words, like *striped* and *squeeze*, are what Bierwisch called *intrinsically spatial*. These words are more successful at guiding readers to fill in spatial images with specific features. Our image of a *striped tiger* starkly contrasts with that of an *albino tiger*. Our visual image of a *squeeze* visually contrasts with a *pinch* or a *punch*. Although Bierwisch does not mention this, the spatial characteristics of words seems contextually variable. Words like *clever* and *silly* seem aspatial when describing a person, pulling out personality rather than visual contrasts. Yet they become intrinsically spatial when describing a smile, as a clever smile and a silly smile suggest different curvatures of the mouth.

Writers skilled at scenic writing know to search for intrinsically spatial words. By contrast, the writer who stays content with implicitly spatial and aspatial words will fall prey to the lawyer error of judging a scene before describing it. When we report to someone that we have just witnessed a *hit and run* or a *theft*, we reveal what our mind has concluded while keeping our listener in the dark about what our eyes have actually witnessed.

Bierwisch also pointed out a class of words that he called *strictly spatial*. These are words like *slanting* and *near*, which have no meaning other than to define the spatial orientation of single objects and the spatial relations between objects. Writers good at getting readers to texture space must have a working knowledge of these words as well.

When experienced writers aim for scenic effects, much of their revision results in changing aspatial and implicitly spatial words into intrinsically and strictly spatial ones. In the following passage, written by one of our students, notice the revision from the implicitly spatial *aligning* to the intrinsically spatial *turning*. Also note the revision from the aspatial *with* to the strictly spatial *toward*.

"It's an unseasonably warm March afternoon. The people out on the patio aren't reading their books; they're ~~aligning~~ turning their chairs ~~with~~ toward the sun and squinting through their sunglasses."

Aligning depicts a spatial goal and result (alignment), but not the specifics of the motion taken to achieve it. *Turning* adds specification to the motion, making it easier to construct an image of what the people are doing with the chairs. *With* presents an interesting case because it has both an intrinsically spatial and aspatial meaning. As an intrinsically spatial word, *with* can mean *near-to* or *next-to*, denoting spatial proximity. This, however, cannot be the meaning of *with* in the passage above because the chairs and the sun are not physically near one another. The aspatial meaning must be in effect, referring to any relation, abstract or concrete, specified or unspecified (e.g., I'm studying cooking, along *with* algebra). By revising the aspatial *with* to the strictly spatial *toward* (meaning, *facing in the direction of*), the writer gave specific guidance to the readers' image of the moving chairs.

Another source of visual vividness, known since Aristotle, is *metaphor*. Metaphors are good at tapping into our visual memories to capture movement and shapes that would be otherwise hard, if not impossible, to convey to a reader. Consider Christina's expressive challenge. Reporting on the movement of her cat, she watches as her pet jumps for a string, misses, and lands on its back, in a supple arch that flattens gracefully against the couch. Christina knew she had no geometrical language to describe the shapes and motion she was seeing. She also knew that she would not be able to connect with her readers even if she had. She did know that what she could not name through geometry, she could name through a resemblance with the familiar. The cat's movement was so fluid, Christina realized, that were the cat a liquid rather than a solid, the motion it made would resemble a substance *melting* into the couch.

> The rear of the body tenses and wiggles, preparing to leap. The string dances above him and in a flash he stretches his hind legs, poised to jump. The attempt is in vain and the fluid body melts, back first, into the floor.

Ann was trying to describe the hard-to-describe movements of a swimmer with an unpolished crawl stroke. Tapping into her visual memory, she realized that the movements of this unpolished swimmer bore a strong visual resemblance to a Spanish dance whose movements her readers would have in memory: "Beginning with the crawl stroke, she windmills her arms and thrashes her feet in a passionate flamenco with the water."

The consequence of selecting words high in visual vividness is to facilitate the reader's mental imagery. Failing to select such words, in turn, makes the reader work harder by asking her to infer, piece-by-piece, what can be recalled in a single vivid memory.

3. Visual Implausibility

Textual descriptions need not be physically accurate to be effective for stimulating reader imagery. Metaphors are a case in point of words that are effective for imagery and inaccurate. Nonetheless, even metaphorical constructions are governed by constraints of visual plausibility or suggestiveness. Visual plausibility means that the image has a coherent content, apart from accuracy. Words that fail to stir a reader's sense of visually plausibility inhibit imagery.

One writer wrote the following in a first draft scenic writing assignment:

> "The couples, both young and old, rotate their ears toward the music of a lone French horn, floating out of an open window of the Music Building."

The language here is not visually plausible, much less accurate. Even if music metaphorically floats, French horns do not, nor do ears rotate, even metaphorically. The writer had meant to pull from the scene that the music was pleasing. Yet, she soon realized that, lacking visual plausibility, the passage did not even metaphorically suggest the intended image. To revise, she searched her memory of the scene for a more plausible rendering, and this led to the following, more imagistically effective sentence:

> "The couples, both young and old, smile in the direction of a lone French horn, visible through an open window of the Music Building."

Visual plausibility creates for the reader a sense of realism. This sense is enhanced when the words in question are familiar to the eye but not to what we consciously categorize or verbalize. Describing actions within a sports bar, Tammy makes the following familiar yet under-verbalized observations about a table of women:

> The women, on the opposite side of the bar, share an order of chicken
> wings. They eat without moving their eyes from the television. The
> woman on the left sucks the juice off her thumb while her two friends
> wring their hands in hot sauce-stained napkins.

Tammy's image resonates with our own visual memories of such spaces. However, when we make these observations in similar spaces, we generally avert our gaze and focus elsewhere without stabilizing in words what we have seen. By keeping her eye riveted on the action and taking the time to formulate it verbally, Tammy gives her readers a chance to retrieve their own visual memories of such spaces, stored previously only in a visual library without a verbal index. Small visual detail whose weight we have felt, but never named, raises the stock of the writer as a reliable eyewitness.

4. Unsmoothed Clause Boundaries

The goal of visual writing is to make the reader experience reading as seeing. Let us consider how this works within the normal Subject-Verb-Object structure of English. Take the sentence, "the yellow cat pounces on the blue mat." With each clause, the writer shows a preference for concrete nouns (cat, mat), visual properties (yellow, blue) and visual motion verbs (pounce). The selection of these words contributes to the overall visual effect of the writing. However, if we take the same words and chop them up into marked clause boundaries, such as "The cat, *which* was yellow, pounced on the mat, *which* was blue," the sentence loses much of its energy as a visual stimulus. We can hear the writer's serial judgments about the cat and mat, but we do not so easily burn an image in our mind's eye of an animal in motion.

Smoothing the bumps between clauses is essential for visual writing. Such bumps are signaled by function words, especially *that, which, who, for,* and *because.* You can often eliminate these words to smooth the reader's ride between clauses. Compare:

> He believed that he was going to have a good time. (bumpy)
> He believed he was going to have a good time. (smoother)
> He believed he'd have a good time. (smoother still)
>
> He believed her statement, which was a positive sign. (bumpy)
> He believed her statement, a positive sign. (smoother)

He saw the boy whom he hadn't seen for years. (bumpy)
He saw the boy he hadn't seen for years. (smoother)

He was starving, for he hadn't eaten all day. (bumpy)
He was starving, having not eaten all day. (smoother)

To minimize the chances that syntax will get in the way of the reader's projection of imagery, the visual writer, during revision, looks for opportunities to do clause smoothing. Some of the diction errors stylists call *wordiness* derive from clausal transitions so unsmoothed that readers have a hard time building effective imagery from them. Consider a sentence from Christina's first draft writing, which described the motion of her cat in the following terms:

Motor running, the dark orange fur ball leaps up to the couch in order to receive his reward of strokes and scratches.

The reader gets a lovely start on an image of a cat, airborne, happy and expectant of the prize to come at landing. Before building the image in its entirety, however, Christina inserts the generalization (his reward) she wants the reader to take from it. The words *strokes and scratches* come in anti-climatically. No longer part of the image, they chain to the semantic abstraction, *reward*, which the cat anticipates.

In a second draft, Christina revised to:

Motor running, the dark orange fur ball leaps up to the couch for strokes and scratches.

Grammarians within structural composition would say that Christina had made the sentence less wordy. Indeed, she has. Yet, from the standpoint of representational composition, the payoff is much greater than a word shaved here or there. She has taken advantage of the fact that the major Subject-Verb-Object relations of the sentence consist of visual nouns (orange fur ball, strokes, scratches) and visual motion (the verb phrase *leaps up to the couch*). In their relations, the nouns and verb simulate the framing of a single seamless gaze. The short English connector *for* is enough to code the purpose of the motion without interrupting the visual shot. Christina's clause smoothing allows *strokes and scratches* to remain visual details within the shot rather than verbal generalizations looking into the action from the outside.

5. The Writer's Mind Getting in the Way

A further barrier to visual writing is placing the writer's mind in the way of the reader's line of sight into the text. When writers bring the world to the reader through a direct and unmediated presentation, what the writer thinks—so visible in self-portraiture—only gets in the way. The writer's mind obscures the world the reader wants to access through her own senses. Alyce focused her scenic writing on a group of blind ice skaters she observed at a skating rink. She was struck by how different from her stereotype of handicapped people the blind skaters looked. During her drafting, Alyce worked on the following sentence formulations of this observation.

(a) The blind persons are not at all inhibited by their handicap.

(b) The blind persons are totally uninhibited by their handicap.

(c) The blind persons walked with a look of confidence.

Although Alyce wanted to convey what she saw to readers, sentence (a) conveyed only the interior of her mind looking out. The *not* furnishes a denial, a difference between what she saw and what she expected to see. As readers, we learn that Alyce was surprised by what she saw, but we are still left not knowing what she saw. In sentence (b), Alyce has eliminated the denial and revised the phrase *at all* into the single word *totally*. Both phrase and word are intensifiers. They report the intensity of Alyce's thinking and feeling as she makes her observation. They do not, any more than sentence (a), resolve for the reader what she saw. In sentence (c), however, Alyce manages a sentence that gets her mind out of the reader's way.

Through different sentence formulations, Alyce was able to revise her subjective impression into a shared observation. With sentence (c), we can see what she saw to cause her intense surprise. Drawing upon the element of empathy, she now gives us the basis to share that surprise along with her.

The sole difference between Alyce's strategy and Beth's self-portrait (see Chap. 1) is that Beth, aiming for empathic self-portraiture, needed to give readers her context to follow her thought. Alyce, aiming for scenic writing, wants to share the world she sees while keeping her own thoughts implied and offstage. Compared to self-portraiture, the empathy gained from good scenic writing is muted and understated. The empathy is there for the scenic writer to produce nonetheless.

Structural grammarians and mavens of style often call words like *not*, *at all*, *totally* and other words expressing the writer's thinking "metadiscourse." Here's how Joseph Williams (1994) defines metadiscourse:

> Metadiscourse is writing about writing and reading. This includes connecting devices such as *therefore, however, for example, in the first place*; and expressions of the author's attitude and intention: *I believe, in my opinion*; comment about what the writer is about to assert: *most people believe, it is widely assumed, allegedly*; remarks addressed directly to the audience: *as you can see, consider now the problem of.* (p. 234)

Within structural grammar, it is well-known that metadiscourse can be useful to the writer's intentions. It is also well known that metadiscourse can be harmful to the writer's intentions. Within the categories of structural composition, one is hard pressed to explain the boundary between good and bad usages. A theory of writing as representational composition is better equipped to explain it. When a writer's focus is on her internal perspective, metadiscourse will be necessary. When it is on making the world of the text directly visible to the reader, metadiscourse, standing between the world and the reader, will be neither necessary nor nice. It will be detrimental.

To summarize, when writers fail to stimulate visual imagery, the reasons generally have to do with one of the five patterns we have reviewed: selecting words that are visually redundant; low in visual vividness; low in visual plausibility; or selecting words that create interference either because they are too complex to support effortless image making or too inner-directed to give the reader an unobstructed line of sight into the world of the text.

The Language of Landscapes

> "Landscape, as a literature of lived life, must be experienced in place to be fully felt and known. And skill in the language of landscape amplifies the experience."

These are the words of the landscape architect Anne Whiston Spirn (Spirn 1988, p. 81). Spirn has helped us see that the stories we find to tell about natural things depends upon the implicit cultural frames we have learned to impose. There is a systematic culture-boundedness in the way we pull stories from landscapes. For example, news reporting imposes its own frame of reference for telling stories about spaces.

What sells are stories that grips an audience for months and years. Spirn chronicled how the reporting of a California fire from October 1993 to May 1996 evolves from a language of burning to blowing, raining, slipping, growing, and (finally) rebuilding.

> October 93: Burning: Wildfires burn out of control. . . . Spicey, smoky smells . . . fill the air. Flames flash and flicker. . . . Residents stand numbed.
>
> February 94: Raining: The earth is still bare and brown. . . . Burned shrubs stand out. The size of branches tell how hot the fire burned. Twigs were vaporized. . . . Prickly pears [are] masses of blackened flesh. The mulch has formed a crust. Winter rains cut deep in soil stripped of plant cover. Sandbags line the street.
>
> February 94: Slipping: Thick brown mud, flowing, slides down slopes. Slides [are] to come on burned slopes.
>
> May 94: Growing: Flaming orange poppies . . . bloom brightly. . . . Long green grasses cover burned over slopes. A few houses are under construction.
>
> May 96: Rebuilding: The air is full of buzzing insects, birdsong, hammers. A huge prickly pear, once blackened, is overgrown by luxuriant new growth of other shrubs. (pp. 86-87)

In each window of time, the focus is on present-tense process verbs and states. Each verb and state recounts something about the fire or something that stands out in contrast against what happened before.

The organization of spaces can be periodic as well as historic, with the periods defined by the local inhabitants of the space. As Spirn observed, "Most landscapes are designed to be sensed through movement, at a particular tempo, for a specific duration, in a rhythm" (p. 90). Historians are often given the authority to define spatial periods. For example, the distribution of rich and poor neighborhoods in Pittsburgh are often explained through a historical look at the steel industry and the effect of elevation on wind patterns. In historically-enriched scenic writing, the writer brings volumes of learning to add a fourth dimension to the acuity of what one sees. Even when the historical forces that shape a space have disappeared, the residue of these forces often remain visible and the space cannot be understood without interpreting one's immediate visual environment from the lens of the distant past.

Whether equipped with an extended historical and geographical perspective or not, the scenic writer must bring her own senses to understand periods within a space:

> Gravel crunches underfoot, grass swishes, a wooden bridge thumps hollow. To a blind person, snow may give a sense of walking through an endless, undifferentiated nothing, for it muffles sound. In some time and places, sense of sound seems heightened, discrete sounds amplified: when air carries sound farther at night, and in early morning; where ambient noise is low, in a quiet cloister, where sounds bounce off walls (partial quote of John Hull; cited in Spirn, 1998 p. 97).

The spaces of interest to the writer are formed from active and recurring human processes. A bar may be a place for courting but not serious courtship. Although it is a place to see and be seen, a public laundry affords a space where people can be seen without their necessarily having a strong reciprocal interest to see. What we call a territory, a clearing, a gateway, a home, a meeting place, a family room, an asylum, a hiding place, a workplace, or sanctuary, are all human habitats that been formed for human purposes (Spirn 1998, p. 121). Habitats that show similarities in space and shape, further, can still harbor vast differences in cultural significance. A walking path used for exercise in wilderness or developed land is commonly a trail. A walking path used for meeting and exchange is more promenade than trail. A walking path used for ritual is more processional than either trail or promenade. A walking path used for invasion is typically described by the military column that fills it, a descriptive practice that allows battle scenes to be told from the perspective of strategy as well as geography. In all these cases, the writer must understand the cultural significance of spaces in order to make possible the noticing of interesting spatial stories.

All stories must have protagonists, agents from whose perspective we see the story being told. In the self-portraiture of the journal, the protagonist is none other than the writer. In observer portraiture, the story is about an onstage subject, yet the story belongs to the writer and it is through the writer's eyes, often viewing implicitly from offstage, that we come to see the subject. Were this not so, fairness and objectivity in observer portraiture would not be the issues that they are.

What, or who, are the protagonists for spatial stories? In much travel writing that describes vast geographical terrains, the writer uses prominent objects in the space to construct, as protagonist, the character or outlook of a people who inhabit it. Travelogues often describe the isolation of the Chinese in terms of the mountains that have protected them from invaders over the millennia. The American colonists were defined in part by the forests they needed to clear for settlements. Westward expansion required seeking passage through the Rockies. The settlement of American cities depended on the psychological as well as the economic relations formed between people and rivers. However, landscape writing is not restricted to uninhabited spaces. People make among the more interesting protagonists from which to tell the story about a space. The writer herself, embodied in the space, can be the protagonist from which the story is told.

In our studio explorations of scenic writing, we have asked writers to enter a space, study it for stories that emerge, and then select zooms, pans, and scans (discussed later) to "shoot" the story. Our writers are given the choice either to make others the protagonists of a spatial story, or themselves an offstage presence from which to tell a story about occupying a space.

Sustaining Complex Scenes: Zooms, Pans, and Scans

Every landscape feature, such as a mountain, embodies at least one complete expression—its own formation. Describing the elements is like looking at a landscape—scanning the scene, then successively zooming in and out on significant details, letting the context blur but keeping it always in view (Spirn 1998, p. 85).

Spirn seems to be making metaphorical reference to the camera when she described the written description of landscape. However, shifting viewing angles and distances on a physical space is not a recent import into writing. Rather, the assortment of viewing options opened by the camera were artistic replications of at least some of the options already available and practiced in the writer's craft. Of the orders of scaled distance one can travel from atomic structures to distant galaxies, Spirn noted, "only about a dozen of the scales—from the moon to the surface of the skin—have been directly experienced by humans" without the aid of technology (p. 172). Not coincidentally, these are the same levels of scaled distance that writers have, for centuries, captured for the page.

Like the camera operator, the writer has always supported zooms, pans, and scans over a space. Spirn invites us to think of a square meter as the baseline of human interaction and experience, the range of close companionship, the surface of a desk to engage work, and the width of a sidewalk or a gate to pass through. If we take this imaginary scale as our baseline, she observes, we can understand zooms as regions of space on a landscape that make significant reductions on this baseline (p. 172).

Zooms shift our attention from entities to the detail of their properties. Rather than the presence of a companion, we sense a hand. Rather than a gate, its latch. Rather than a tree, its bark.

Zooms are the landscape writer's way of focusing the reader's imagery on details that would not normally get close visual attention. Zooms reduce the viewing distance, making objects seem closer than we normally experience them. The effect can be heightened intimacy, realism, or both. Zooms can heighten subjectivity or objectivity, placing objects close to the heart or under the microscope. Zooms provide the intimacy of focus and angle we associate both with the deepest subjective passion and the most objectified intellectual curiosity.

Revealing that the handle of the hammer his grandfather gave him is "hand-carved hickory" is a zoom a writer might use to add realism to the reader's image of the family heirlooms. Zooms keep the reader's attention on the small details that matter to a spatial story, detail that a less discerning story teller would have missed.

Beth offers a good example of the realism the writer can achieve with zooms when she describes a sudden downpour at a South American beach:

> Just minutes before, the rain had poured down and several oiled bodies ran for shelter under the nearby hotdog and American pizza stand. Most of the beachdwellers had thrown their sandals on and grabbed their towels, bags, and beach umbrellas while running across the street to the stairs of the underground train station.

By zooming in on the people at a narrower and closer-than-conventional viewing distance and angle (*oiled bodies* and *hotdog and American pizza stand*), Beth effects a realism by furnishing detail that gets under the radar of our stereotypical memories of beach scenes. The zooms invite our eye into the experience of the scene, creating the feel of "being on-scene."

Pans are the opposite of zooms. They increase the viewing distance, making objects more distant and blurring them in wider panoramas. As Spirn observes, increase the one-meter baseline of human interaction tenfold and one feels the presence of a room or a tree without necessarily feeling the companionship of any particular entity alongside. The ears and nose remain effective at this scale, but the eyes lose detail and touch has no effect. Increase the meter area a hundred fold and one feels the presence of a city block, a stadium, a museum, or a large yard. The eye can see out to the horizons of this space but may not be able to make out the objects that lie at the horizon. Further panouts in the spatial area cannot be apprehended from within the space. The viewer needs to hop an airplane and, ultimately, a spaceship to experience the space (Spirn, 1998, p. 172).

Pans draw back from a scene, emphasizing the placement of objects in relation to one another. Pans are useful for expressing the ambience of a space, abstracted from the objects that fill it. Pans support zooms by making visible the larger perspectives that make the small detail so meaningful. The indicate the narrative connection that can be made by showing the hammer in close-up followed by the father teaching his son to use it.

Watch how Maria creates an effective visual experience of a billiards game by zooming in on the cue and then panning outward to wider views of the scene. The shot is described in zoom to give it weight and the pans move the reader beyond that detail to the larger context of the table, the player, and the game room.

> A pool cue is poised gracefully over the green flannel surface and a white arm draws back briefly—then stabs out quickly—striking its prey. A "crack" sends its victim down the table. A wiry young man wearing jeans and a navy blue T-shirt smiles triumphantly, and then backs slowly and quietly out of the light.

Scans shift the reader's imagery from one region of a scene to another. They do not change the reader's viewing distance, but they do change where in the scene the reader's attention is fixed. Scenic writers require scans because the spaces they want to write about are typically too multifaceted, too extended and complex, for a reader to take in in one fixed image. Scans help the reader continually readjust her mental imagery to keep pace with the words.

By combining pans, zooms, and scans, the writer can help the reader build a spatial story through a few well-selected, edited, and shifting details.

Susan intersperses pans, zoom, and scans to capture the ambience of a coffeehouse. Through sequencing narrowing zooms with widening pans, for example, she sought to capture the crowding, bustle, and noise of the space. All the while, she pans from table to table so we can eavesdrop on different visual happenings. She begins by describing the streams of sights, sounds, and rhythms evident from a panning shot:

> It's a steady stream of windbreakers and backwards baseball caps mixed with trimmed beards and crisp cotton shirts made sloppy by the rain. As the crowd grows from 9 to over 20, they turn up the volume of the buzz and mix in more change clinking, coffee machine grinding and cappachino maker steaming. It changes the makeup of the orchestra, adding new instruments for color as well as volume. Tom Waits finishes up his set, replaced by a second act on the accordion.

Susan now directs our attention from table to table, catching out-of-context snippets of conversation that, in the overall experience, resembles a child's parlor game.

> A few words drift in and out here and there. "So, you want to do this?"" . . . it's eight o'clock. . . ." "I put on my little tie . . ." " . . . and call my mom and I was telling her . . ." "but otherwise I have no doubts . . ." " . . . because, quite frankly, you're no longer in her dreams." It sounds like the children's story game where each child adds a new word to the tale.

Viewed from the distances and angles through which the patrons experience the coffeehouse across tables, the patrons are strangers only accidentally sharing the space. Panning out, however, from the perspective of a sound technician on a crane, reveals that the space conducts an overall vocal energy that peeks and dips in unison.

> As time passes, the stories come and go in waves, moving up and down in volume from internal cues. While the drinkers sip from their cups and pick up a caffeine edge, the crowd shifts from a slow steady andante to a light-hearted allegro.

To show us that the ambience of the space is multi-layered, Susan moves us from the universe of the room to the self-contained universe of single tables. At any one table, the patrons are friends, lovers, and acquaintances. A novel could be written about any of the relationships. Susan dwells on single tables with a novelist's eye for detail.

> "The young romantics are doing the mirror thing. Sitting across the table from each other, both have their hands in prayer folds and look right into the other's college romance eyes."

Susan's description of the couples' hands and eyes are precise descriptions of the bodily orientations of two people absorbed in one another. Susan could have told us that the couple looked in love, which would have thrown away the detail and left us wondering what the look was. By describing the scene as she does, Susan gives us visual evidence of their feeling and puts us on the scene as eyewitnesses so we can see the look for ourselves without having to take her word.

Mixing zooms and pans skillfully can leave readers feeling that the writer has caught the panorama of sights and sounds that define our experience of a space. When we translate what we see into words, our brain tends to throw away the details in favor of summary abstraction. Unlike Susan's visual description of the coffeehouse, our words might have been: "The coffeehouse combines music, noise, and talk to make a vibrant atmosphere." This sentence generalizes from the space, suppresses the detail, and discourages us from peeking in. Susan's mix of zooms, pans, and scans do much better to keep our mind's eye in the space.

Finding Spaces to Find Stories

The surest way to keep a reader riveted to a text is to tell a story that makes the reader care what will happen next. To locate stories about a space, writers must dwell in various spaces for a while and then, after some exploration, look for the spatial stories that emerge.

Although designed rather than innocently discovered, spatial stories must always give the reader the feel of an eyewitness watching the stories emerge out of the space as a natural perception. Out of visual detail comes visual contrast. Out of visual contrast comes conflict, opening the way for one anticipated resolution or another. Such stories often require nonroutine looking and noticing, watching the space for narrative rhythms and patterns at non-conventional viewing distances and angles. This is precisely why knowing the techniques of zooming, panning, and scanning prove so important in orchestrating a spatial story. Once the writer has a basic story to tell informed by visual detail and contrast, the writer can begin to break it down into different shots (zooms, pans, and scans) that she thinks are best for pulling the story out.

In our studies of writers searching for spatial stories to tell, we found that writers often make the mistake of focusing too narrowly on the mechanics of visual writing before composing an interesting visual story. Aaron's first draft writing of an airplane taking off is a good example of why visual writing needs a compelling visual story to guide it.

The Boeing 757 is huge, over two hundred feet long, but the passengers in coach are packed in like proverbial sardines. There are over one hundred of them, jostling for space, squirming uncomfortably, playing with the seat backs and the folding trays. The airplane lights make them look pale and sickly, almost ghostly. The air is heavy with deodorizers, making the plane smell worse. The passengers all look unhappy, loading luggage into overhead racks, slumping into their seats, defeated. The plane hasn't even left the terminal yet.

The copilot comes on the intercom. Everyone instinctively looks for him, then looks around for the speakers. The copilot sounds like an AM radio announcer, deep voiced, pleasant, reassuring: "We'll be leaving the lovely Greater Pittsburgh International Airport shortly, so please buckle your seatbelts. We've been cleared to runway A4, so we'll be taxiing for a few minutes, but we'll have great views of downtown for those of you on the starboard side of our aircraft." The 757 pauses on the takeoff runway, and the engines speed up. The 757 suddenly roars down the runway. The wheels leave the ground. The runway bumping is gone and everyone looks relieved. When the plane turns, it retracts its landing gear, making the plane dip suddenly. The 757 roars up through 17,000 feet, the flight attendant call button dinging quietly but urgently the whole way.

Like a wide-angle photograph of a mundane space, Aaron's text is visual writing without a visual story interest.

Holly's first draft writing has a problem similar to Aaron's draft. She describes a ballet studio known as the Drill Deck. By focusing on visual detail, she overlooks the importance of a visual story. Furthermore, she tries to mimic a real camcorder. She provides fast and fleeting pans of relatively disconnected zooms around the room.

The Drill Deck has three concrete walls that are painted royal blue on the bottom three feet of the wall. The rest of each wall is painted white, excepting the nicks, leftover masking tape, and black rubber marks. One wall displays panels of full-length dance mirrors. Chairs line its opposing wall, which supports a metal bar used for ballet.

Two guys stand in the middle of the room in the midst of several folding chairs. At the far corner of the room, two people move around as they casually talk to each other. In the other far corner, a small orchestra of no more than 20 musicians plays Russian folk melodies.

A young man with olive skin and dark brown hair with dark circles under his eyes sways to the music. He looks up, closes his eyes, and gestures with his hands while moving his lips. He turns, alone, responding only to the music. It stops, and the man rests against the ballet bar.

The orange-tanked woman continues discussing dance moves with her partner, "You can't really get a good bounce if your feet are spread apart." The curly-haired woman is joined by her partner, and they both sit on the table. The third couple waltzes over on the far end of the room. The curly-haired woman asks, "When will people stop realizing that it's a myth that if you go to Paris, the waiter will just out of the blue ask you to dance or something?" "Ok, somebody's been dreaming," replies the young man in khaki pants.

The couple on the table observes the couple dancing in the far corner of the Drill Deck. "What are you doing over there? You're not supposed to push her around the floor!" The man looks back at the observer and smiles. The woman in the orange tank top adds, "It's better than picking her up off the floor."

The woman in brown skin-tight leggings stood in front her partner, her weight shifted to one leg. He put his hand on her hip and lunged to one side, arm extended upward. The music began. The woman slinked forward, running her hand down the side of her body. Her thin arms adorned her walk. The partner breezed up to her, and lunged to one side. The woman turned her nose up and pushed him out of the way. He came back and pulled her close, she raised her knee up to his waist. He dipped her, resting his forehead below her chest.

Holly's description of the dance studio illustrates two common problems in attempts at visual writing. First, as we saw with Aaron, a visual story must precede and guide the visual writing. Without the spatial story, scenic writer will recreate the experience of amateur video, with its disconnected shots of vaguely related images. Second, the writer needs a visual story to know how to set up the establishing shots for the visual detail. Had Holly started with a good visual story, she would have known it cannot all be told in zooms.

Kerry offers an interesting visual detail with enough contrast to tell a story of a playground scene. She captures the rhythms of noise and quiet throughout the day, as if we are watching the story unfold from the playground's perspective.

Loud chaotic noises punctuate the air. Children are shouting, screaming, squealing, talking, and laughing. To the left, inside the school building, the school band is playing scales in "unison" (well almost). A four-and-a-half-foot boy screams as he bursts down the stairs, collapsing on the asphalt. He rolls over onto his back. His eyes are closed and he is still. Then one eye peeks open as his friends come bounding down the stairs brandishing their imaginary weapons. He suddenly jumps up, firing his forearm machine gun. He runs to the playground area, firing behind him all the way. He lands on his knees in the soft field of wood chips, while his playground enemies return the fire in hot pursuit.

The band inside the school competes for airtime with the children on the playground.

The band is beginning a song inside the school now. The introductory chords swell rapidly, then die to silence. They begin again after a few moments. The sound of screaming children ebbs and flows between the band's attempts to get it right.

Kerry chronicles the "death" of recess as the kids trickle off the playground, checked off by the monitor one by one, until the playground is quiet and empty.

The attention of the crowd of kids on the swings has suddenly been occupied by something behind the corner of the light brick school building. First children leave the swings, then the war game ends. Children move quickly and steadily to the left and disappear behind the building. As the crowd dissipates, a lunchtime monitor is revealed. In half a minute, the playground is empty except for a reluctant group of stragglers who lazily meander in the same direction the others have gone. Looking after the children, the monitor hugs her clipboard and walks confidently out of sight.

The end of recess brings peace for a time. However, as we soon find out, it is merely a lull before the next burst of activity.

The playground is quiet for a few seconds. Then the door on this side of the building squeaks open. Two first-grade boys run out, then two more. A flood of children follows. All at once the equipment is full again, and the noise is as loud and strong as before.

Two first grade girls are swinging side by side in unison. They are trying hard to keep the rhythm going and stay together. Soon, though, they
lose their perfect harmony and begin to find an individual pace. Many
more children wait beside the structure for their turn on the swings. A
couple of the boys in the crowd begin pushing the swingers, making
them go higher and higher! Then one of the boys begins grabbing at a
swinger's feet as she goes by. They are giggling as she tries to move her
feet away from the boy's advancing hands.

Kerry shows us how, in the midst of all the activity, certain subtle
regularities surface on the playground. First, in games of tag, the race
goes to the strong. Second, the swift, the smallest, and the slowest are
often picked to do the chasing. Third, being part of a family, whether
imagined or real, is hard work—and, sometimes, bad things happen.
We are shown that the playground is a place where children can work
out these life lessons in an active, social, and ultimately safe context.

A game of tag has just erupted in the waiting crowd. The smallest girl is
"IT." She chases joyously across the asphalt, by the gym door, through
the woodchips, around the swings, past the climbing equipment, around
the home tree, back to the asphalt. But the other children are so much
bigger and faster that she can not reach them. She gets discouraged and
stops running. With shoulders slumped, she walks to an unoccupied corner of the playground. There, three of the big tag players run up and hug
the home tree. The smallest one isn't paying attention to them anymore.

The smallest girl is sitting on a swing now. Four girls surround her.
They are arguing over who is going to be the big sister: "I'm Dada!
You're Mama!" "I'm the first big Sister!" "No, I'm the big Sister!" The
largest one (Dada) has picked up the smallest one and is trying to carry
her like a baby but her charge is clearly too heavy and tall. She puts her
down.

"See what happened to me?" a girl says as she shows her friend a
splintered finger. "Want to see what happened to me?" says the other.
"My sister bit me! I was reading a book, my sister was in a time-out, and
she walked up and bit me! FOR NO REASON!"

Three fifth grade girls have gathered by the edge of the swings. They
are whispering to each other while two fifth grade boys swing. A first
grader runs up to the chanters and yells "Hey you guys, Gramma's
dead!" They stop briefly to listen, then resume chanting while they follow

the messenger to the spot under the climbing equipment where Gramma is laying. They put the small one down and pull Gramma out from under the climber. They take Gramma by her arms and ankles and ceremonially carry her over to a different spot. Just at that moment two boys rush the group and all the girls (including Gramma) jump up screaming and scatter.

The group reassembles. The chanting and carrying resumes. This time the chanting catches the attention of the monitor, over all the other playground noise. She approaches the group and tells them this activity is against safety rules. They can't carry the small one any more.

Kerry uses scenic writing to open up for us how, no matter how loud and intense the play, recess inevitably comes to an end and the playground settles back into a state of quiet and repose.

A whistle blows through the commotion. A second whistle blows. The children begin to line up near the side of building by grade, class, and gender. A small group of boys is running around the cluster of queues. The monitor yells "I was just about ready to let you guys go first, then I saw you messing around. Now you will go last!" The lines are dismissed one by one according to good behavior. The playground monitor picks up her clipboard and starts to gather up the jackets left lying on the ground. A boy runs back to retrieve his jacket. A little girl comes next. The monitor gives them both a bunch of jackets saying "If you know who these belong to, you can give 'em to them," The kids rush back into the building. The rest of the jackets will go into the lost and found. The monitor and her clipboard go in. The playground is empty. The only sound is the wind and the song of a single happy bird, welcoming the first day of spring.

Through the realism of the writing, Kerry shows us more than just the space of the playground. She uses zooms and scans to show us how the playground is a place of positive activity and peaceful silences. We watch the mood of the space change as one segment of the day transitions into another.

The Implicitness of the Writer's Perspective

The writer cannot tell a story without a perspective. Yet, what happens to the writer's perspective when she wants to feature a world outside her own mind? If the writer's mind is permitted the visibility it has in self-portraiture, the writing will seem subjective as well as spatial. The writer seeking a purely scenic effect needs to suppress the reader's having the experience that a story *is being told* to him. The reader must rather experience herself pulling the story from the scene through natural perception and inference. To maximize the scenic effect, therefore, the agency of the writer as storyteller should be unobtrusive.

Making the narrator unobtrusive imposes a difficult challenge for a novice scenic writer. The writers we studied often yearn for a simple dichotomy. They either think (1) the instruction to be subjective negates visual writing; or that (2) the instruction to be visual negates the need for a strong subjective point of view consistently controlling the writing.

Randall's draft writing illustrates the first tendency. He wanted his spatial writing—of his fraternity house—to include his perspective. Yet, his reflex was to think that including his perspective meant making it visible, in the manner of self-portraiture. This led him, in a cascading chain of design decisions, to minimize the visual detail and focus on what he thought he saw, rather than what he saw. The result is less an achievement of scenic writing than Randall's personal journal entitled "My Fraternity."

> "Don't let the cats out!" is usually the first thing anyone hears upon entering the corner room on the third floor of the KDR Fraternity House. Nobody sees very much right away. Their visual perception is probably on sensory overload as it tries to process everything, such as the myriad colors of posters, hundreds of CDs and tapes scattered about. There are also decks of cards strewn across the dusty glass coffee table, and two little streaks of fur making their break through the visitor's ankles to pick a fight with the cat next door.

Conditional adverbs like *usually* and *probably* and quantifiers like *nobody* all focus us on Randall's thinking more than what he (and we) can see. These words define a perspective that generalizes over many persons, times, and places.

> When Jamie is home, the air in the room is filled with a deep, thick fog of cigarette smoke and the loud, rhythmic sounds of techno or ska booming out of four strategically placed speakers. When Randy is home, the air is filled with the same fog, but accompanied by the strident chords of Led Zeppelin or the mellow flows of Bob Marley and of the Grateful Dead. If both are there, the fog is thicker and the music just sort of alternates until one of them leaves.

Once again, this is not visual writing at its purest. We cannot see conditionals ("When Jamie is home . . ." or "When Randy is home . . .") or contingencies ("If both are there, the fog is thicker").

> The first thing most people do upon entering this room is light a cigarette and find a seat, though neither is required. Finding a seat can be easy or it can be a difficult chore. The once-white couch fills up quickly on a first come, first serve basis and, once filled, it becomes difficult to navigate the numerous ankles, beer cans, kitten toys, and books that make for a challenging obstacle course. The reward for completing the obstacle course is twofold: the blue, padded, rocking seat by the desks (if it hasn't been claimed yet), and a severe bump on the head. You see, the final leg of the obstacle course requires the participant to duck beneath a large, wooden loft while being careful not to trip on the laundry pile below. For the unskilled or unprepared, this can prove to be too much and usually results in a large, painful bump on the head.

This passage contains still more choices that compromise visual writing. Randall provides generic characters (*most people*) taking generic actions (*entering the room* and *finding a seat*) with probabilistic events (*usually results*). The text is a window into his thinking, not a stimulus for his reader's visual imagery.

By way of contrast, Andrew avoids the either-or choice between visual and subjective writing. He maintains his writer's perspective, though in a muted form that ties in with and actually complements the visual quality of the writing. He describes the scene in a campus newspaper office in which he is the managing editor. He displays an attitude toward that space that is as subjective as Randall's. Yet, Andrew tightly ties his attitude to the visual features of the scene, patiently letting the details of the space emerge to support his point of view.

> It is production day at the Tartan office, and at 9:00 in the morning, the News Editor is the only person in the office. She is tired, and struggles to keep her attention on the computer screen. Last night she did preliminary layout after attending a two and a half-hour long Easter mass, and didn't get enough sleep because of daylight's savings. The other editors have overslept.

That the news editor is the only other person in the office is a visual detail. That she is tired and struggling is an inference based on her face and body and further supported by the added, non-scenic information (which must have come from Andrew) that she attended a Mass and lost an hour of sleep. Granted, we are being exposed to Andrew's thinking, but his thinking is so closely allied with the visual setting that we do not feel his mind obstructing our view.

> By 12:30, the editors have arrived. The Photo Editor brings the color slides and black and white negatives from the darkroom. Tufts of bright red hair poke out from his baseball cap, hastily donned to obscure his unkempt hair. He cuts each roll of film into strips 6 frames long, and carefully (never touch the emulsion!) inserts them into file preservers.
>
> Examining negatives of an exhibit at Forbes Gallery, the Photo Editor and Diversions Editor discover that a sculpture of a penis and testes is prominently displayed in the exhibit, and they collapse laughing on the light table. The Photo Editor returns from the darkroom a few minutes later with a print that shows the penis pointing at a few gallery patrons, and tapes it to the photo wall.
>
> The photos on the wall are predominantly of staff members with goofy looks on their faces. The Systems Manager is depicted with a drawn mustache, bushy eyebrows, a pierced tongue, and a title card from the cartoon Life in Hell that declares "1001 Faces of Your Lover." Next to the Systems Manager is a picture of the Managing Editor's roommate, his face wrapped tightly with wires, which his hand is trying to peel away.

Again, Andrew keeps the writing focused on the visual details of the particular scene, letting us learn about the fun and clowning the goes into putting a paper together.

The one potential non-visual entry involves the Photo Editor's unkempt red hair beneath a baseball cap. Andrew can see the red hair. He can see that it is unkempt. He can see that it is mostly hidden under a baseball cap. These are all visual facts. However, Andrew includes an inference beyond these facts. He registers that the Photo Editor dons the baseball cap *in order to* hide unkempt hair. Andrew cannot see that intention.

Does this writing slip into Andrew's mind? Is Andrew disclosing himself? Yes. Still, this inferred motive only reinforces a general picture that we, as readers, have been able to visually confirm for ourselves: a frenzied pace of life that is dangerous to personal hygiene. Andrew's thoughts enhance the visual exploration he invites us to do. His use of subjective inference extends the visual implications of our own mental imagery.

Andrew keeps us moving in time as well as space. Rather than focusing on changes in Andrew's internal thought, the chronology of his text is driven by changes in the production room as the deadline nears.

> Nearby the photo wall, around 1:20, the Forum Editor begins to perform a one-man production of Antigone, albeit in a more colloquial form. He is dressed in a Boy Scout uniform he purchased at a thrift store, and uses two small plastic ducks as puppets for his vocalizations of the various parts. "I will bury Polyneices, he is our brother!" "You are mad, it is forbidden in Thebes!"
>
> Most of the editors give him a quizzical look, and then go back to work. Moments later though, the Assistant Diversions Editor has joined him in an impromptu rendition of Death of a Salesman.
>
> "Hi, I'm Willy Loman!" says a fluorescent pink plastic duck. In the background a song from the Casino soundtrack is playing, a classic Italian piece, complete with an accordion.
>
> The pizza arrives at 6:00, 12 large pies from Papa John's. The staff members sit in a line one side of the hall across from a matching line of pizzas. Some staff members eat hurriedly, cramming slices of pizza into their mouths, or take a few slices back to their desk so that they can eat while they work.

Time drags on in the newsroom and the scene continues to change.

> The night drags on, each editor struggles to be the first one to leave the office for the night, and the battle is won by the Forum Editor at 7:28. He leaves, grumbling about homework that he has to complete that evening. The Diversions Editor leaves around 10:00, to prepare for a test in the morning.
>
> At 2:00 A.M., the production staff sacrifices to the god of Varityper to speed up the printing. Bored of waiting for the printer, the Sports Editor builds the "Tiki God of the Varityper." It has the body of a plastic soda bottle, with legs and arms made from red pens that pierce the bottle and exit on the other side. The clothing is made from scrap paper, with arcane symbols scrawled on with a Sharpie. Once he has assembled the Tiki God, he walks around the office chanting hymns in gibberish.
>
> Even later, around 3:00 A.M., the News Editor, Features Editor, and Sports Editor are all sprawled on the couch, exhausted from the day. The Sports Editor stands up, and shuffles over to the print spooler to see how long the wait will be for his last page. He notices that the computer is

acting strange, the clock in the upper-left corner has started to malfunction. The seconds tick forward quickly three seconds, in about one second's time, and then suddenly tick back two seconds. It continues to flash forward and backwards at a fever pitch rate, slowly managing to progress forward in time. "Hey, look the print server's gone nuts!"

At 3:50, the paper is zipped into two portfolios by the Editor-in-Chief, and handed to the courier. The courier has a handlebar mustache, and an odor of cigars and liquor that follows him out of the office. The remaining editors put on their coats, heft their backpacks, and begin to leave. Each one mutters goodnight and they all walk back to their rooms. All of them will oversleep and miss their morning classes.

Andrew is careful to avoid the timeless perspective of personal reflection, an internal focus that interrupts a sustained scenic effect.

In his closing, Andrew again combines the visual (". . . put on their coats, heft their backpacks, and begin to leave") with the inferred ("All of them will oversleep . . ."). Andrew's writing shows how subjectivity need not be incompatible with visual realism. There need be no contradiction between scenic writing and point of view.

Eric illustrates the second early-draft tendency of novice visual writers, which is to think that choosing for visual writing is choosing against a coherent and controlling authorial perspective. Eric describes a cross-country trip on an Ohio highway. He had done a fine job using visual writing to let the space speak for itself. His choice of verbs is especially praiseworthy. Notice the image of the tires *slurping* puddles on a wet highway; the car *sucking*; road stripes *creeping* and then accelerating as they *shoot* under the bumper; bridges *clanking*; mile markers *descending* as they count down to a destination coming closer; and drivers, once passed, *shrinking* to halogen specks in the rear view of the passing driver.

Rolling over wet Ohio highway to Toledo, the tires slurp through puddles. The car sucks white midlane stripes which creep closer—then suddenly, shoot under the bumper. Metal bridge joints clank beneath the wheels; like a metronome, their rhythm hypnotizes. The green mile markers descend. Beyond the rain-streaked window, a red Chevy pickup draws near. The driver's head bobs to radio tunes, while his lips purse to whistle. He glances left to check out the couple in the red Shadow that he's passing at 75. Stroking his brown left sideburn, they shrink to halogen specks in his rear view mirror.

Eric had made his own perspective on the space a quiet one. Yet, notice the bump felt when, without warning, he shifts the scene to the interior of an oncoming minivan heading in the opposite direction.

> Crammed into a minivan, the family of seven approaches. While dad checks his map, little blondes bounce on top one another. Little Keds wave in the window. Mom turns in her seat and waves her hand, trying to calm the restless. It's still a long way to Wisconsin, and she knows they're tired of car songs. An older son draws out the magic answers of a Yes and No book. A curly brown-haired darling sucks his thumb while he sleeps, curls pressed against the glass. The indignant teenage daughter drowns them all out with her Discman. She doesn't really notice the Dodge hurtling by on the left, seventy-two miles from Toledo.

Eric shifts his perspective, and the reader's, into a different car. In the early part of the draft, Eric did a good job coaxing the reader down the highway with an implicit guiding hand. Yet, many readers of Eric's first draft reported feeling disoriented from the passage above. His text relies on disconnected zooms with no pans to integrate the perspectival shifts. Readers were left with a set of images that were difficult to connect into a single story.

The writer should not conclude from Eric's first draft that shifts in visual perspective are a mistake. Visual perspectives in scenic writing can and do shift. However, writers need to be careful to signal these shifts so that readers are prepared to shift with them to maintain consistency across the visual point of view. Although readers do not need the scenic writer to be explicit about point of view shifts, the writer needs to provide, at least implicitly, a guiding hand to readers when such shifts occur.

Steve's writing, about an airport departure gate, illustrates another intermingling of perspective and spatial description. His draft uses a focal character that he refers to in the third person, as *longhair*. Zooming in, he uses imagery to indicate the shaped objects (*croissants of carpeting*) and surrounding activity in and around the airport.

> It is 2:35 in the afternoon. A longhair shambles into the north end of concourse D at Atlanta International Airport. The colors of his courier bag trail behind him as he drifts through the waiting area, which is, gently put, a wreck. Bare spackling covers the sheet-rocked walls, makeshift signs uncertainly point the way to bathrooms, baggage claims, parking. Croissants of carpeting sit against the wall at odd intervals, rows

of vinyl chairs are collapsed helter-skelter onto the ground. Beyond this office-lounge turmoil, through 15-foot high noise-deadening windows, Valujet DC-9s and Delta widebodies migrate to their assigned nests under low clouds.

The longhair treks past one of the glass panes, ebbing to a stop at the end of a wavering line of travelers. While he squints into space through horn-rimmed glasses, the line lurches periodically toward a counter marked D-22.

"B-b-b-b-b-b," sighs the longhair through flapping lips as he jerks another meter closer to the counter. Bodies pack the north end of Concourse D, and the general mood is of resigned irritation.

Like Susan's description of the coffeehouse, Steve shows us the diversity of sounds and people that punctuates the activity of the airport. The line of travelers responds collectively when the young toddler breaks from it, letting us see how people, as individuals and as a group, respond.

The transient mob generates a mid-level murmur, an unceasing "yea-ggd-whererrys-abrshigaggg rrstlllayovvvlate" that mingles with cheery commentary emanating from ceiling-slung monitors and occasional out-bursts from the overhead: "Valujet announces the arrival of flight 407 from Chicago"

Presently, a toddler clad in this season's Gap Kids pastels bounces along the line containing the longhair. The round-headed infant makes happy sounds as it runs away from Daddy, and the heads stacked up in front of D-22 turn to track the thing's progress. Behind the longhair, a withered matron beams through her wrinkles as it goes jouncing on by.

In zoom, from longhair's perspective, the ticket agent is just a mustache behind formica. Using third person, Steve presents the incidental motions and appearance of nearby passengers.

Around 2:50, the longhair bumps up against the counter at D-22 and gazes at the mustache hovering behind the mottled Formica. "Your name, sir?" says the mouth underneath the mustache. "K-U-H-N," replies the longhair, handing his license over. Sitting off to the right of the longhair, a middle-aged woman with dyed blond hair and yellow V-neck claps shut her John Grisham novel. Putting down the paperback, she unfolds her legs, straightens her sweater, rubs her eyes, flicks her hair back, pulls out her shirt collars, runs her hands over her stomach twice, folds her hands together, crosses her legs, closes her eyes, and becomes perfectly still. "Here the writer are, Mr. Kaahn" says the mustache, handing the longhair a blue piece of laminate bearing a depiction of Valujet's happy mascot and the number "59." "Thanks," replies the longhair, but the mustache has already turned his attention to the beaming matron who is next in line.

The longhair pads four rows of chairs to the right of D-22 and flops into one of the black vinyl cups. He begins dividing his attention between the text in his hands and the tanned young woman sitting directly across and five seats over.

The book is untattered, clad in blue and gold, about eight inches by five inches, with widely set type on white pages. The cover reads The Odyssey of Homer. The tanned the young woman is vivacious, covered in leather trousers, a tight tummy shirt, and looks to be about 5'10". A bellyring gleams from her smooth midsection. The blue laminate lies chastely across her opaque thighs. The longhair ogles her, then returns to his book, his squint occasionally rising to take a fresh look at the bellyring.

In zoom, Steve captures the sounds and activities of boarding. He shows how, from longhair's perspective, the laminated ticket demands close—zoom-worthy—attention because of the role it plays in allowing people to board the plane.

"Ladies and Gentlemen, in just a minute we will begin boarding Valujet flight 451 service to Pittsburgh," the ceiling announces at 3:10. "This will be a pre-board only," it adds, and then, thinking better of it, chirps, "Now I would like to board rows 15 and higher please." Laminates shuffle in hands all around D-22 as eyes re-check numbers. A number of forms begin stalking a door to the longhair's right, and several, handing over their blue passes, trundle through the opening.

Steve's writing blends a self-portrait identified under the generic handle (the longhair) and a scene within an airline departure gate. Under a sustained zoom with pans, he lets us experience the sights and sounds that anchor and confirm longhair's thoughts.

Although writers maximize the scenic effect by leaving their perspective implicit, there are, as one might imagine, powerful blends of scenic writing with portraiture. Such blends allow a writer to expose how the surrounding environment both impacts and is impacted by the development of her own or another person's thinking.

Spaulding, faced with the challenge of scenic writing, relied on this blend to describe the environment he chose for his fiction writing one summer.

> I had already resigned to writing by hand all summer, at least, the writing I had to do. I often slept on the couch, looking out my window. I'd peel and eat an orange while I stood on my deck, rubbing the rind against my teeth, dislodging any extra food particles. I'd watch the people come and go, the boats drifting lazily across the glassy surface of the water, all the while jotting down notes, allowing myself to steal a glimpse into all these lives. I could feel the hot black top that fried their feet; I could feel it through the winces on the faces, and see it through the tap dance shuffle they did as they crossed the parking lot.

Just as Susan used mixed portraiture to describe self-discovery while investigating her Nana, Spaulding combines self-portraiture and scenic writing to reveal for himself and the reader the symbiotic relationship between his writing and the space within which he had hunkered down to write.

The Implicitness of the Reader's Role

Readers, too, have roles they must be invited to play in scenic writing, as well as roles they should be discouraged from playing. Scenic writing encourages the reader to feel and respond as an eyewitness on the scene. It invites readers to experience a physical space as closely as it can be experienced vicariously.

However, making the reader a character in the scene calls attention to the medium of interaction and interrupts the reader's pure experience as observer. The scenic writing in this case spills over into other kinds of writing, such as instructions and interactive gaming. In an otherwise fine scenic piece about a city bus ride, Peter plays up the reader's participation in the space when, in the interests of a pure "scenic" effect, he would have been better off downplaying it. Watch how he crafts an addressed second person reader (*you*) into his spatial story, giving the reader an explicit role to play:

The bus stops; the front door splits open, each half-retracting with the simultaneous motion of a closet door with a noisy track. You step up over three rubber-coated steps and ready this month's pass for the driver. Sitting at the wheel is a thin, balding man with long, wide, sideburns. He has thick arms; hands display black, leather, three-quarter driving gloves. One of his hands is on the steering wheel, the other is poised protectively over a button on the change machine. As the driver checks passes, he hits the token button on the change collector. Each hit emits a muted ding. The driver's eyes seem to drift off and settle at a point beyond the laminated PAT cards, as if he's staring through the side of the bus and into the street or sidewalk beyond it.

Walk past the driver; you hear a ring like a broken Pachinko machine and look for a seat. It is 9:30 AM but there are a few remaining places to sit. On the left side are all single seats, while the right is all double occupancy seating. Towards the rear wheel wells, past the back door, is bench seating only. Walking towards the rear of the bus, you spot a spare seat on your left; it's the last one before the back door. You sit and the blue, textured, vinyl, seat padding emits a brief sigh the moment you place your weight upon.

Peter's use of second person interrupts a pure scenic effect by making reference to the writing medium. If the scenic effect is to be kept pure, the reader's agency in the medium is best left off the marquee.

Summarizing the Writing Models in Relation to the Feel of Space

The scenic writer seeks to heighten immediacy as a dominant representational element and inhibit the reader's feeling of being displaced from the world of the writing. These representational actions are intended to give the reader a sense of physical presence as an observer on the scene of the writing.

The effect of scenic writing is compromised when writers fall into patterns that inhibit the reader's capacity to construct sustained images of physical spaces. Writers must learn to recognize and eliminate the textual patterns that inhibit imagery and to rewrite with the patterns that encourage it. Words that inhibit imagery are visually redundant, low in visual vividness and plausibility, exhibit unsmoothed boundaries between clauses, and insert the writer's mind between the world of the text and the reader's line of sight into that world.

Christina and Ann illustrate how visual metaphor can increase visual vividness, especially when describing shapes and movements that are easier to describe through resemblance than through geometry.

Tammy illustrates the relation between visual accuracy and the reader's feel of realism. Language can add to realism when it names what readers heretofore knew only through a wordless visual memory.

Christina shows how smoothing clause boundaries can facilitate the reader's constructing visual images by sustaining the image and postponing the reader's abstracting from it.

Alyce illustrates how revisions can help a writer get her mind out of the way of the world of the text.

Beyond representational immediacy, scenic writing relies on the capacity to tell spatial stories and to set up visual shots that are optimal for the stories one wants to tell. We have seen that writing accommodates various visual shots from zooms, pans, and scans.

Beth illustrates how zooms can add naturalism to writing. Susan illustrates how the careful back and forth movement from narrow zooms to wide pans can capture the ambiance of a busy and complex space.

Kerry illustrates how the writer can use visual writing to script the story of a space with textual shots (zooms, pans, and scans). Spatial stories may not have universal themes like major drama. They speak of the subtle motions and change that emerge out of a space, dynamics that readers often miss in day-to-day life unless they work hard to notice them.

Compared to self-portraiture, the scenic writer's subjective perspective remains muted. It nonetheless remains in control to guide the reader through spatial stories. These trade-offs are challenging for novices, who often dichotomize visual and subjective writing.

Randall's scenic writing shows the tendency to veer away from visual writing in the effort to keep it subjective.

Eric shows the reverse tendency, to veer from a single controlling perspective in the effort to keep the writing visual.

Andrew and Steve illustrate positive examples of balancing spatial detail and perspective. They tie their subjectivity to spatial detail so that, as readers, we experience their writing visually and from a point of view that always guides us, even if behind the scenes.

The reader's perspective in scenic writing, should remain implicit, like the writer's. Peter, by contrast, assigns the reader a visible role in the space. This action does not diminish the writings visual effect per se but it does transform the writing into instructions or gaming, writing that is more transactional or two-way than pure scenic writing. The pure scenic effect is heightened when the reader remains an unacknowledged onlooker into the world of the text.

Scenic Writing in Professional and Public Writing

In the age of multi-media and the flourishing of new visual professions, the representational elements used to construct motion and contiguity have become increasingly important in professional and public communication artifacts. The art of scenic writing plays a central role in this revolution as well. Scenic writing is important in the scenario-building that architects and city planners do with their clients and constituencies to plan out the utilization of interior and exterior spaces (Sanoff, 1990). Marketing and business writers also rely on rendering precise motion and contiguity in a text to design and test the atmospherics of retail space. Otnes (1998) used structured interviews with customers of a retail space to learn about their experience of it. Some of the most revealing writing she gathered reproduces the customer's moment-to-moment experience of the space. Investigating a bridal shop for example, Otnes found that customers expect, contrary to their expectations in an average clothing store, that the salespeople in a bridal shop will assist with a fitting from start to finish. She discovered this expectation when one of her informants, shopping with a bride-to-be named Belle, reported its violation.

> Belle was having trouble getting into this particular dress. The saleswoman was not around, so zipping the dress up from the back was a hard task for Belle. With her head out, she then looked outside of the dressing room door for the saleswoman and said, "I'm abandoned."
> (p. 246)

Prior to evaluating a retail space, scenic writing can be used as part of a marketing plan to propose a new space. Scenic writing is among the best, the fastest, and certainly the cheapest way to help investors and business partners visualize the spatial ambience the customer is supposed to feel. For her scenic writing assignment, Joy described the spatial ambience of a juice bar she was designing for a client:

The walls of the shop are orange. Shiny and bright, they're the shade of a freshly cut nectarine. Every inch of space is orange, including the ceiling. The brick wall behind the counter is painted, sacrificing its earth tone reds for a glossy, more modern look. The gray cash register looks more like a stone caught on the beach at sunset than a home for the day's earnings. Tunes flow from the stereo with long, soothing beats, as customers twist their heads left, right then back again trying to get their bearings. Smiles curl around the corners of their mouths as the high, clean scent of citrus tickles their noses, opens their eyes. The tan, athletic arm of the shopkeeper collects an assortment of fruits and vegetables from baskets hanging within reach. Plump strawberries and blueberries tumble into the open mouth of the blender. Sitting on the counter, muffins wrapped in cellophane, decorated with tiny bows bounce in sync to the pulse and vibration of the motor. Next, she turns on the juicer, juicing one large carrot at a time. The blade coming into contact with each carrot sounds like a table saw cutting through a 2x4. The relaxed feeling of an island oasis is maintained all day except for peak hours.

Scenic writing is becoming increasingly important in the depiction and navigation of virtual spaces. Writing in multi-user dimension object-oriented domains, or MOOs, is an increasingly popular form of textual interaction in social and educational settings over the Internet. MOOs are object-oriented environments that combine computer programming and scenic text to create the feel of participants sharing a contiguous space. They are, along with multi-user domains, or MUDs, what Sherry Turkle (1998, p. ix) calls "text-based, social virtual reality." *MOOs* represent a new form of writing where words name the objects, actions, emotions of the built world, even objects, actions, and emotions that only the novelist would normally describe—like flakes on hair, winks, facial tics and exasperation. Because a MOO world is built entirely from text, the world that exists *must be composed in its entirety.* Visual detail, small and large, must be texturally rendered along with the main characters, actions, and objects. Writing in these virtual spaces requires that writers create the illusion that they are sharing immediate space with their readers without displacement. This is precisely the illusion that makes scenic writing both representationally possible and effective.

4

The Feel of Elapsed Time

In the last chapter, we discussed displacement as a default of writing that makes the world of the text independent of the world of the writer or reader. It is a feature that scenic writing must override if the writing is to make the reader think she is experiencing immediate spatial reality. Yet, in the context of scenic writing, displacement has no direct relevance to representation. It is merely a default assumption that, if not actively inhibited, will diminish the reader's experience of spatial immediacy. In the examples considered in earlier chapters, even when the world in the writing was displaced, the displacement was an assumed default of the writing. It was not a representational element the writer tried, explicitly, to *show* the reader or to make the reader *feel*. In sum, displacement thus far has functioned only as an assumption of the writing medium rather than an element of representation.

In this chapter, we explore displacement as an element of representation in its own right. We describe studio students practicing representational displacement in an assignment we call narrative history writing. In this prototype, the writer must create a text that is displaced in time from the world of both the writer and the reader. Unlike scenic writing, narrative history relies on the regular defaults of writing. The writer makes no Herculean effort to override displacement to shape the reader's experience. Yet, unlike scenic writing, or any writing we have seen thus far, displacement is now a representational challenge over and above a medium default. The representational challenge, more specifically, is to *magnify* the reader's experience of displacement. The reader must be made to *feel* the temporal displacement of the world written about in comparison to the world at the time of reading.

Magnified displacement is a required element in a representation that makes the reader feel a world that has at least passed by and may now seem even out of date, anachronistic, yellowed with age, lost in the mists of time, and other clichés of obsolescence. All of these impressions are residues of a text that has successfully deployed displacement as a magnified element. Magnifying the reader's feel of displacement typically requires the writer's ability to take a historical and cultural perspective on the subject. This requirement alone poses a significant challenge for novice writers.

One of us regularly teaches a freshman seminar that has students practice the writer's voice in nonfiction writing. Students generally find it fun to practice the writer's voice of reminiscence. With that voice, students are asked to recall an earlier time or place in their autobiographical memory and to recall its significance to their current life, thinking, or outlook. With the voice of reminiscence, students are free to insert their subjectivity as a form of self-portraiture. They enjoy the freedom to write about memorable experiences from their personal past.

Students tend to be sobered, however, when they are then asked to move from reminiscence to reflection. The student's perspective must now embody a point of view that is removed in time and space from their own experience. They can no longer rely on the authority of their firsthand thought and experience as an exclusive resource for what they are trying to accomplish. Beyond their own experience, students must conduct outside reading and interviews to extend their eyes and ears to see and hear what others in the culture have seen and heard. In the end, they may need to return to their experience to complete the writing. Their reflection may reconnect with traces of autobiography or memoir. Yet for long phases of the writing, they must write by suspending their own experience in favor of the experiences of others. They must magnify the sense of displacement in their own expression in order to convince readers that their perceptions are collective and historically rooted rather than personal and immediate. This is the challenge of moving from personal reminiscence to cultural reflection. It is also a challenge behind our narrative history assignment. It is a challenge that students tend to find daunting.

Magnifying displacement is not the only representational challenge of narrative history writing. The writer must retain the scenic writer's heightening of representational element of immediacy. As we saw in self-portraiture and scenic writing, immediacy refers to the reader's perception that the writer's expression of thought follows closely on the heels of the writer's first formulating it. In narrative history, by contrast, immediacy is needed for the reader to feel the displacement of the past with the vividness of the present.

The writer must align displacement and immediacy in order for the reader to feel that what happened—happened then—though it remains vivid, as though it were yesterday. Often, the vividness of the past is enhanced by the implication that the events described in the past remain relevant to the reader's present. If the events of the past seem utterly cut off from the present, the displaced world may seem to the reader only quaint and antiquarian, like the blacksmith showing off his art at the country fair. Consequently, some histories seeking to compel readers develop worlds retaining threads of relevance to the reader's present. The past is felt not as something entirely over but as something that continues to condition the present and even the future. This feeling bridges narrative history and arguments of policy. Whether or not tied directly to the reader's present and future, however, an effective historical narrative assures the reader's engagement by describing the past with a feel of immediacy that the reader associates with her present.

Although narrative histories can and often do accommodate simultaneous events, the signature movement of the historical narrative is sequence. Chains of completed events (e.g., he *came*, he *saw*, he *conquered*) form the impression of sequence and, at times, causality. One event elapses just as another begins. Time moves, link by link, down a linear chain.

At its most conventional, as in the narrative of an encyclopedia entry, the history will string together event chains through the repeating simple past tense: "The north and south *began* the Civil War in 1861. The North and South *fought* for four years. The South *surrendered to* the North in 1865." The simple past tense expresses verbs of achievement that open and close the horizon of an event in one simple mention. Notice how the three-word chain *began*; *fought*; *surrendered* compresses the experience of a past war in the most economic expression possible.

Chaining events in the simple past tense is a good way to plot the temporal span of one's text, the ground it will cover in time and, implicitly, space. However, by themselves, simple-past event verbs produce only a stereotypical wireframe of the past. Notice that the chain *began, fought, surrendered* describes *any* war from a long distance lens and omits the intimate portraits, scenes, and spatial stories that give the past the concrete and particular interest it holds for contemporary readers.

In the earlier prototypes we surveyed, no clock exists to control the reader's experience of elapsed time. Compared to these earlier assignments, the narrative history elevates the reader's feeling of temporal displacement to an artistic imperative. The reader progressing through the text must experience progressing through a world whose sense of temporal displacement from the time of reading is palpable.

In our studio assignments, we motivate the narrative history by asking students to compose "worlds that have disappeared but that have stayed fresh in memory."

When student writers try their hand at historical narrative, they face a procedural challenge beyond the representational one. Procedurally, they need to work with external memories—sources. Professional historians invest much of their time making sure they have the best sources available. They travel to rich archives to find the people and documents best suited to characterizing the past they are interested in recovering. Students need to do the same when they write history from textual sources. Representationally, they need to shape these sources into a textual depiction of a past world that readers, displaced in time, will nonetheless experience in the vivid detail of immediate experience.

Because we are more interested in the representation of historical narrative than in the procedures of historical research, our studio focus dwells less on writers' gathering information from sources than on turning their sources into narratives balancing displacement and immediacy.

Balancing Immediacy and Displacement: Local Actions to Restore the Vividness of a Lost World

Without displacement, past worlds will seem to the reader not strikingly different in kind or degree from the world of the present. Without immediacy, past worlds collapse into the stereotypic flatness of the English past tense generic, *happened*. Rousing stories of human beings flatten into a limp "happened" that omits the compelling detail. Narrative history challenges writers to create representations of striking displacement punctuated by equally striking immediacy. How do writers coordinate these independent elements within a single text? We can best answer this question by first examining the local actions of writers working to create each effect on its own.

Local Actions for Composing Displacement

Writers achieve displacement by making sure to select details, situations, and cultural reasoning that will strike the reader as dated. Ann, for example, writing about family life in her grandparents' generation, is careful to include the sale price of homes so that we know how far they have risen in 50 years. "One rainy day, Al went to an auction and negotiated the bargain price of $3000 on a three-story, six bedroom, Victorian house at 612 Main Street in Mount Joy, Pennsylvania."

Writing about the world of the 1950s through the eyes of a female who was a teenager at the time, Joy made sure the detail included hairstyles, shoes, and skirts of the times. She could have told us that the skirts were long, bulky, and cumbersome to manage, but by stimulating our mind's eye to imagine a group of teenage girls sitting down in a circle on hardwood, she lets us visualize the detail so that its datedness strikes the the reader of today:

> Emerging from the kitchen, Jamie asked, "What did you say?" Her ponytail swinging side to side. Cathy responded, "Nothing yet." The sound of saddle shoes marching across the hardwood floor filled the house. It took a few minutes for everyone to adjust their skirts and find a comfortable sitting position on the floor.

Joy learned from her source about repressed and hypocritical attitudes toward sex and marriage that strike the contemporary reader as strange. She made sure these strange chords found their way into her narrative.

> "We went around the room and every girl's parents at the party, except for mine, had to get married because their mom got pregnant. Each girl experienced the same and relief of revealing their family secret to the group," she said. The only form of birth control that you could get were condoms and the pharmacist kept them behind the counter. You had to go through him and if you asked for them he would tell your parents. We all left Cathy's the next morning very confused. If you weren't supposed to have sex before you got married why were our parents doing it?

Writing about the life and times of women and schooling in 1950s America, Deborah was able to elicit from her source reasoning that does not resonate with the contemporary world.

"I went to school, but one day, when the teacher hit me, I ran away and never went back." It wasn't as important then, she shrugs. "The girls got married and had the children, took care of the farm. What did we need education for if we had a good husband?"

Tapping from the memories of her mother, Grace, a Taiwanese writer, recalls the historical prejudice against girls in Taiwanese culture. Two months before her mother was born, Grace's great grandfather had "prepared two big bags of grain for making rice cakes and polished glutinous rice in order to treat guests and celebrate her birth." Then Grace narrates from her mother's recollections of her grandmother's first person memories:

> When I was bearing you, your grandfather wandered about the outside of the window, being anxious to know your gender. Hearing the crying, he asked loudly, "Boy or girl?" "It's a girl!" the midwife answered. Grandfather walked toward the family room, commanding the workers to return the two bags of grain.

These examples of displacement recall the detail of the past with an eye on its contrast to the present. The writer guides the reader by selecting situations and details that seem dated, and by reproducing cultural reasoning that time seems to have passed by.

Yet another way of achieving displacement is for the writer to mention the contrast between the past and present up front. This is an effective strategy when the writer wants the time contrast to create a subjective attitude, a self-portrait, in the writing. The attitude may be of a progressive-minded optimist, indicating how much better things are now than then. The attitude may be of a nostalgic pessimist, complaining how much better things were then than now. The attitude may be that of a reflective time-traveller, marveling at the shifts in worlds caused by shifts in time.

In one of her passages, Ann uses nostalgic time shifting to emphasize how family life in earlier decades was typically more interactive than the silent couch potato syndrome of today's generation.

> Instead of watching television, people talked with each other. Fanny's husband, Jay, was a tenor in the church choir. Sometimes Jay would sing hymns for the family such as "How Great Thou Art," while Linda or Norma accompanied him on the piano.

The phrase "instead of watching television" is an explicitly marked present reference, spliced within an otherwise past account. We may have been able to infer Ann's nostalgic attitude without it. However, Ann wanted to make sure we could not miss it and so decided to signal it explicitly rather than to risk it to inference.

Normally, to achieve representational displacement in a narrative history, the focus is the past. The present, the vantage from which the displacement is felt, is left implicit. Effective time-shifting can also work with the past held in background as the lens of the source's implicit point of view. This is an effective style for creating a voice of an older source commenting how far and fast an unfamiliar present has evolved from a more familiar and comforting past.

Adopting the stance of a reflective time-traveller, Alyce used this explicit time-shifting to good effect when describing how birthday parties for 10-year-olds have evolved from her own 10th birthday party in the 1960s.

> My little niece was enthusiastic about her gift gremlin, with a computer chip that gave it thousands of words and a sophisticated database of sentences it could generate from them. The gremlin would be no more important to her than the Thumbelina soft dolls of the 1960's were to us, with the five canned sentences we'd hear them speak if we didn't break the string in their back.

While Ann had inserted bits of the present as contrast against a dominant past, Alyce inserts bits of the past (e.g. Thumbelina dolls) as contrast against a dominant present.

Spaulding also uses a dominant present to capture a nostalgic view of his grandfather, who grew up in a quiet seaside village and made a simple living as a fisherman. Holding his grandfather's prime as the temporal point of view, Spaulding captures his father commenting on the strangeness of the present from that past perspective:

> My father couldn't even make it as a fisherman now. "All the regulations they have, you know, you have a daily limit, you have a weight limit, you can only go out at certain times, you can't sell to certain restaurants cause they don't have certain permits, the list goes on and on." My father would never have made it these days as a fisherman. There would be no times for cookouts and the like. Large industry and tourism have overrun everything.

The starkness of death brings with it complex time-shifting elements. Grief for a life lost involves both a nostalgic looking back on a life and the projection of a future where the recurring sense of loss will routinely creep up on the grievers in gusts of immediate sorrow. Cori captures the temporal dynamics of grief through a dominant present tense, discussing the recent death of a favorite aunt and inspecting the small visual details that will continually haunt her uncle of his loss:

> I look down into the wastebasket. There is a pair of old pantyhose in the bottom with a few crumpled Kleenex on top. It gives me the shivers, and I turn around to take a good look at the rest of the room. The bathtub still has all the body lotions and soaps, back scrubbers and brushs, and that's when her death hits me as a reality. I think of my uncle having to come in here everyday and see these things, decide if he wants to remove them, and take action either way. It is a desperate feeling and I leave the room immediately.

From the standpoint of grammatical composition, Cori's writing is composed in the immediate present. Yet the dominant representational effect is future projection from a displaced past, the feeling of distance between a time when the bath items had an owner and the present time, when the items will, for a long time to come, recall for a widower a departed wife.

Local Actions for Composing Immediacy

Displacement helps the reader see how much has changed. Immediacy, by contrast, offers the reader a sense of vividness of what otherwise would be dim and faded memories. Writers create immediacy by probing their sources so that they can describe time past as much as possible from the way it looked and felt to the actors at the time. When the past is too distant to know vividly, we fall back on the stereotypes of the simple past tense.

In Ann's first draft history, she wrote that Al, her grandfather, had made ice cream for the family at one Sunday family gathering. Her first draft caught this event only from the distance of the simple past: "On a hot Sunday, Al *made* ice cream for the family." The sentence is accurate, but lacking the immediacy that would immerse her readers in the times of her grandparents.

Ann herself realized that this draft lacked the spirit and feeling of family closeness that her mother had remembered and that Ann was trying to recapture for her reader. Exploring opportunities to enhance the immediacy of her history, she questioned her mother further about the event. She was able, in a second draft, to get underneath the stereotyping of a distant simple past: "On a hot Sunday, Al decided to make ice cream. As we always did, the family formed a circle around the ice-cream maker, watching and laughing as each of us took a turn at the crank." Like the previous sentence, this sentence is accurate to her mother's memory. Unlike the last sentence, it is more immediate and involving, and more revealing of the spirit of family life past Ann was trying to capture. The revision shows Al's action to be intended as a participatory event. The event is now revealed as less important than the story it supported. Family love and participatory involvement are the point of her mother's memory, not dessert.

Ann's first draft had also mentioned, in the simple past, how her grandparents had moved from their home as they grew older. In her second draft, she is able to get underneath the simple past by describing simultaneous events (*watching, laughing*) that fill out the event and recapture its feeling. Even the simple past events that remain (*formed a circle; took a turn*) captures content that is more visually descriptive of the event, word choices vastly more immediate and revealing than the generic *made ice cream*. The simple past tense, Ann's writing makes apparent, does not by itself inhibit immediacy. It rather inhibits immediacy when it is used to describe generic action.

Ann's revision shows us not only more details about Ida and Al, but also about the pain aging brings and the forbearance it often requires.

> In 1995, Ida and Al sold their house on Main Street and moved into a small apartment a few blocks away. Moving was not easy for this couple that had grown to cherish their home and independence. However, Al was over eighty years old and maintaining the house had become too much for him. Feeding the coal-burning furnace three times a day strained his back, and shoveling snow off the balconies was too dangerous for someone his age. When her grandmother's doughboy sold for five dollars, Ida felt that she had been cheated out of her memories.

Ann's addition of immediacy to the paragraph also brings poignancy to the lives of Al and Ida. It also adds a feeling of displacement that reveals a past much larger than the lives of her grandparents. For it reminds older generations and teaches younger ones that heating a home was not so long ago manual labor and that a generation's most cherished keepsakes once lay in still-fresh memories of World War I. By bringing individuals and their lives in close-up, Ann brings us closer to the world that they knew.

Using Eyewitnesses to Capture the Displacement and Immediacy of the Past

Having considered displacement and immediacy on their own, let us now consider how these effects can be created in combination.

In our studio setting, we find the easiest way for students to practice this coordination is through oral histories. Through interviews of older people talking about the world of their youth or prime, students learn to draw out lost worlds from still fresh memories. Students interview their sources opportunistically, seeking out the then-now contrasts that the interview sources can recall in the richest detail and that their readers will find stark and interesting. A director of a period film works on the small details of interior scenes, from the home furnishings to the music, to make the film reflect its time. Similarly, we encourage students to tap an eyewitness source for the contrastive detail that keeps the contemporary reader engaged because of the depth of immediate detail that the source can elaborate and because of its contrast with the present.

Even with this advice, there is a significant gap between knowing the representational challenge and meeting it. Like all of our writing assignments, students seldom rise to the challenge on a first draft. We turn below to some common first draft problems.

The Danger of Turning the Eyewitness Source Into the Subject of an Observer Portrait

Eyewitness sources are invaluable for recovering a lost past. However, if the writer cannot get beyond the personal recollections of source memories, the narrative will slip into observer portraiture more than restore a lost world. Kenneth provides an instructive example of this problem when he writes about his great grandmother.

> "Just Before Dawn" is a book of poetry written by an African American, by the name of Izzy Curtis. She is my great grandmother, more then 80 years old and she published "Just Before Dawn" in 1976, the year of my birth. The poetry itself makes her book remarkable but even more so is the story of how she came to begin her writing. I interviewed her as she reflected on her past and as she explained to me a self-actualization that changed the course of her life.

Her book begins with the author's note: "I am a native of Pittsburgh, Pa., a mother and a grandmother—an occult student, a Theosophist, and one of the newest members of the Homewood Poetry Forum. I have lectured at the University of Pittsburgh, the Theosophical Society, and the Martin Luther King, Jr. Reading Center. My first poem, "I AM Soul," was written February 15, 1967. "Just Before Dawn" was published in the Pittsburgh Courier February 28, 1976. I have also been published in a magazine called "THE EYE. "I feel that another entity, outside my own intellect, has given me most of my poems, and I hope that you who read these poems will be able to relate to them in that we are all one in life, love, pain, happiness, hate, hurt and death."

In 1974, Izzy was admitted to the hospital for surgery. Something had stricken her ill and she had to have a large portion of her intestine removed. When she awoke from surgery, she found herself in intense pain. The pain left her in agony and despair. She decided that she could not endure the pain any longer and she tried to kill herself. She became clinically dead early that evening, marking the start of a cosmic experience. She felt her soul rise from her shell and looked down on her body. She recalls, "I then entered what seemed to be a tunnel. I felt a warmth and I could see a very bright light. It seemed as though I was heading—floating—toward this bright light. As it surrounded me I felt a deep love and an understanding of my life." Within the light Izzy heard a voice calling her. It said very clearly "This is not the time for you to enter there and you must go back. There is much for you to learn and teach in this life."

When she returned to her body she awoke with a great gift. She felt her self "very physic," and knew that her new gift had come from God. It was a tool for her. She knew that her purpose was to help people with her gift. To help fulfill her cause she entered the ministry. She felt that she must, "know and understand the human being and his counterpart to the universe."

The first—what she describes as—"experience" she had was an interaction with the entity that brought her to write very emotional poetry in a trance, sleep like state. This entity used her as a medium to put its words into print. Since then she has had many such experiences, dreams, and visions of enlightenment. However, she has never published any poetry before or since her first experience. She has developed herself, with the help of God, into an amazing individual. She soon began to study all religions and all cultures. She traveled all of Eastern Europe, 47

Mainland States and Hawaii. She ventured to distant lands across the globe in an effort to learn wisdom from every culture and race so that she might become "one with the person." That way she could help anyone suffering hardship and she could further share the wisdom she had gathered. Over the years she has become a reverend of the Baptist Church, a physic reader, counselor, and healer. She has helped countless students through mediation.

To this day, she occasionally reads through the poetry of "Just Before Dawn" and is reminded of her start. Each poem expresses great emotion, love and pain, each ends with a feeling of hope.

Kenneth's first draft offers an over-time portrait of a fascinating woman, Izzy Curtis. Yet, rather than open Izzy's memories to restore a lost world to us, Kenneth has us focus more on Izzy than her world. For a narrative history, Kenneth needed to take a wider lens to open up the world of his source.

Widening the Historical Lens on Eyewitness Sources

The next three examples illustrate writers working across drafts to move beyond profiling their sources and toward narratives of more encompassing past worlds.

Like Kenneth, Beth keeps her historical narrative close to the experiences of her source. She focuses on the life and times of her source, Shirley, a middle-aged woman who is a recovering alcoholic. Readers learn about Shirley's life as an alcoholic, but they learn about it through the historical world Shirley inhabited.

I was born fifty years ago in Cleveland, Ohio. Both my parents were immigrants. My father was Greek and my mother was Hungarian. They had met at an International Dance, and then dated for five years. My mother was pressuring my father to get married, but he didn't want to marry. Eventually, he went to his Greek priest and asked what he should do, and talked about things, and asked what he should do. The priest put his advice in a question of his own, "Well, how would you feel if someone had dated your sister for five years and then dumped her?" And so my father married my mother. I don't think he ever loved her. It turned out that the marriage was not very good, but they stayed together for "the sake of the children." They were very, very unhappy together.

Beth shares with readers memories of Shirley's generation and its shaming attitudes toward alcoholism.

> I have one older sister, ten years older. And then me. By the time I was aware of life and what was going on, my sister was already away at college. You see, both my parents were alcoholics. By the time I was a young teenager, I was old enough to realize this truth about my parents. In addition to their being well into their own addiction, we lived a very isolated family life. Our family life was complicated for reasons beyond alcoholism. My father had gotten into a fight with one of my mother's sisters, and they didn't speak for years, so my family was just this little threesome, estranged from relatives.
>
> Very isolated and very unhappy, my mother tried to kill herself, by hanging herself in the basement. It didn't work, and I was the one to find her. When we got to the hospital, my aunt, my mother's sister, pulled me aside and said to me, "Don't ever tell anybody that this happened because they'll take your mother and lock her away." Now, I know that my aunt had good intentions—she was trying to save my mother from being institutionalized—but the effect that had on me was that I started shutting down and not talking to people. I started to get—just—very fearful. I can remember my mother saying something about suspecting that my father was having an affair. Now that I look back on it, I think that he probably was. However, at any rate, we came home from the hospital, my mother, my aunt, and I, and it was never discussed.

Although her first draft penetrates aspects of Shirley's world and not just her biography, Beth realized there was more to do to move Shirley from a profile subject to a historical source. She had indicated that Shirley's family was in shambles, but she had not mentioned the subject of her parents' alcoholism. She made only a vague reference to "their addiction." Without pinning down this reference further, Beth's narration could not carry specific implications, either for Shirley's world or for Beth's readers trying to understand it.

In her revision, Beth not only mentions Shirley's alcoholic parents straightaway, but also mentions up front that Shirley too had been plagued by the same problem. As readers, we are immediately put on a trail of thinking that Beth's historical narrative might be leading to interesting contrasts between perceptions toward alcoholism in Shirley's generation and contemporary perceptions.

One of the things I know now, and probably only because I myself am a recovered alcoholic, the veteran of countless therapy sessions, is that it's really important to talk about things like that—to talk about your feelings—with people. And to ask for help when you need it. So, another sad thing to me about that incident is that my mother never got help. You know. It was just a very, very sad time.

Shirley went to college and married a black man. Her parents disowned her. In the first draft, Beth includes both events, but the narrative line does not assert a causal relation between them. The first draft, that is, does not clarify that her parents disowned her *because* her husband was black. The second draft makes the overt racism of Shirley's parents explicit. The filling in of missing inferences in Beth's second draft insures that the events appear within a tight story involving not only Shirley's life but also her world.

So anyway, then I went college, and that's when I had my first drink. For someone my age, the whole reason you went to college was to get a man. I mean, we didn't think of careers or anything. It was sort of, like you got an education as an insurance policy in case anything ever happened to your husband. Then you would go to work. So, I went to college, and fell in love with this guy. He was a senior and I was a freshman, but he was black. Minor detail. For some reason, I didn't think this would be a problem with my parents. So one day, I decided it was time to tell my parents about him. So I went home and told them I had met this guy, how wonderful he was and, in as much of an "as-a-matter-of-a-fact" way as I could manage, I mentioned that he was black. Well, with that revelation, my parents were absolutely livid. They hit the roof and tried to de-program me. They thought maybe I was on drugs. It was a crazy time. My father said that I had to stop seeing this guy or he would disown me.

Beth now ties the events of Shirley's marriage into the narrative by indicating how, in retrospect, Shirley must have started down the long road of alcoholism. Beth's first draft does not make this link explicitly. Her second draft does.

You can't just do it alone. So, looking back, I guess my very first drinks were with my husband, though long before I married him. I'd have a couple sips here and there at college parties. Nothing big. My first time really drinking, though, which was also in college, I got drunk. And I really got drunk. I mean I got drunk and really, really sick. I was living in an honor's dorm in college, and I literally could not sign in. I got reported to the Dean. I went to her the next day, and I guess I had leaned over something—I don't know what—to vomit in a building the night before. Whatever it was that I leaned on, I must have leaned pretty hard, because my forehead was all black and blue. I applied pancake makeup on my forehead before the appointment, and the Dean asked me, "Have you been drinking?" This was a campus where you could get expelled for drinking, so I told her I had one beer. This was a slight exaggeration of the extent of my drinking, Funny. Somewhere, out of nowhere, I just knew to lie.

Beth shows us the role that Shirley's husband played in her alcoholism. Unless we know that she saw her husband as part of her problem, we cannot understand why events related to the marriage play a part in her alcoholism and why only a life-changing realization could justify the decision to divorce. "Deep in my heart I knew that my marriage would end if I got sober, because my husband had no intention of quitting drinking."

From her first to second draft, Beth widens the lens of her story to include the world beyond Shirley's life. We see Shirley in a larger family and societal context. We learn about family and societal attitudes toward alcohol and race. We learn about the personal stigma and shame that may have played an underlying cause of her alcoholism. We learn about the overt racism of her parents and the family dynamics with her husband that brought on alcoholism. In sum, Beth brings her readers in view of Shirley against the landscape of a larger world. From the first to second drafts, Beth moves from a close portrait of Shirley to a story of the social forces that had swept Shirley up as a character.

Christine provides a second example of a writer who moves across drafts from the observer portraitist to true history writer. Christine's source is John Dunn, a personal acquaintance who had played a major role in the advancement of science education for the deaf at the postsecondary level. Christine teaches us not only about Dunn's life, but also about how, through his career choices, he participated in events that helped to shape the future.

Christine's first draft combined two themes from her interviews with Dunn. The first theme was that Dunn did not like to teach at large schools and so moved to a smaller school. The second theme was the more public story of his improving science education for the deaf.

Christine initially shows us Dunn in the context of his taking his first teaching job, at a large state university.

> At twenty-five, I finished my graduate work at a technology oriented Midwestern university. Bob Hawke, who hadn't graduated long before me, was at a large state university, and he sort of threw me a line: Would I like to work here? We were in the same field—not just biology; we both were interested in toxicology, too—and it was always nice to have someone in your department working on the same stuff. You could get together and talk about it.
>
> I didn't really want to work at a large university, but my advisor urged me to take the best job offer I could get, and to use that as a stepping stone later on. He told me it was best to build a career that way. Hawke's biology department was a step up for me, so when I got the job, off I went.

We then learn that the large school environment did not suit Dunn.

> The big university thing really drove me crazy, though. I remember faculty meetings where we'd talk for 55 minutes about graduate students and five minutes about undergraduates, when there were ten times as many undergraduates in the department. I was there primarily to teach, not to do research, so the graduate students weren't really of big interest to me. Also, I knew a total of two people outside of the department. It was just way too big a school to get anything cross-disciplinary going.

Christine now has Dunn describe the chain of events that brought him from a large to a small school.

> After a year as assistant professor, I had an accelerated general biology class for graduate students who had a weak theoretical background in their undergraduate program and who needed to get up to speed. There were about 30 students in the class.
>
> Before I started class every day, I would take roll so I could keep track of attendance. There were two guys on the list who never answered my call, but I didn't think much of it until a week or two into the class. Then one afternoon, these two guys show up in my office and write on a piece of paper that they've been in class every day but that they haven't known that I was calling role because they're deaf. Once they found out that I was taking attendance, they came by to let me know that they had been there the whole time.

At this point in the semester, I had developed the routine of going to the vending machine in the lounge before class every morning, to get a cup of coffee, and I started running into these two guys—Mark and Tom were their names—pretty much every morning. So we start writing to each other while we were standing around drinking coffee. I mostly asked them questions like Where did you go to undergraduate school? Did any of your teachers know sign language? and that sort of thing. It was mostly out of curiosity.

But as the weeks went on, the guys started to do pretty badly in my course, so I started to probe further. I asked them: What types of courses did you take? What books did you use? and so forth. Pretty soon I figured out that their undergraduate school had a curriculum that underestimated their potential. Combine that with the difficulty that their deafness posed for them in a class designed for hearing people, and it was absurd to think that they could do well. So after a few weeks, they both ended up dropping the course.

Christine reveals Dunn's thinking that a smaller school, more sensitive to the hearing impaired, would be a place to make his contribution.

But we all kept on drinking coffee, and it occurred to me after a while that maybe I could make a mark in a smaller school where there was a chance to challenge students in science better than Mark and Tom had been challenged. I was also intrigued by the challenge of teaching science at a school that better understood the potential of deaf students, like Mark and Tom. So when I saw an article about the establishment of a special group related to deaf science education at a nearby university, I wrote a letter just to kind of probe around.

The head of the newly formed group sent his assistant to talk to me, and his assistant told me that their students were not very advanced. He inquired whether I had discussed my interests with the college where I currently work. I hadn't, but I took his advice and they happened to have a position. Here, I found that they knew their students had the potential to achieve in science at the level of hearing students; but they felt they didn't have the biology curriculum in place to tap this potential, and that's why they wanted me, to develop that curriculum.

So I thought about it, and read Hans Firth's book on the psychology of how deaf people think—just to figure out whether I could work out a curriculum that could tap their potential. My wife and I also took an adult education course on sign language, to see if we could really learn it. It was neat. Once I realized that I could do it, the idea of teaching deaf students seemed worthwhile. So I took the job.

That was thirty years ago, and I'm still here today. Mark, one of the first two deaf guys that I met, is now a teacher at a state School for the Deaf. We offered him a position here once, but he wrote back that he was content to be where he was.

And Tom, the other deaf student from that accelerated class I taught thirty years ago? He finished his Ph.D. in biology and is now a respected science educator and I see him often—his office is the one right next to mine.

Although Christine's first draft provides an interesting glimpse of John Dunn's personal career choices, the larger public story of Dunn's life remained hidden behind the personal detail. Christine's first draft leaves the reader with a text more portrait-like than landscaped, more the résumé of a single man than a public blueprint of the world he inhabited and helped to change.

Looking to widen the lens of Dunn's world, Christine downplays in the second draft Dunn's personal reasons for moving to a smaller school. She inserts information to foreshadow the public role he would play, a role shaped by his growing awareness of the needs of the hearing impaired.

As the weeks went on, both guys [Mark and Tom] were obviously struggling in the course, so I started to probe further. I made copies of my lecture notes and distributed them to the class. I tried not to speak while I wrote on the board with my back to the class, so that Mark and Tom would have the best chance of reading my lips. At that time, interpreters were rare and expensive, and deaf students saw them as something of a stigma.

Dunn's preference for small over large schools survives into the second draft. However, Christine now links this preference to a public mission: Dunn prefers smaller schools *because* they are better equipped to diagnose and address the needs of hearing impaired students.

But in the end, even though I offered extra office hours, so that they could come in and get extra help, both guys ended up dropping the course. It was simply too demanding to keep up with all of their classes, even after I managed to get in touch with some of their professors and urged them to use some helpful tactics like distributing their lecture notes. In such a large university, though, Mark and Tom were a minute minority, their needs lost to the larger, hearing population.

Even after they dropped my class, though, Tom, Mark, and I all kept on drinking coffee, so we continued to write back and forth about the difficulties they were having. It amazed me how bad the science curricula was, and how little it accommodated the needs of the deaf, who were the equals with the hearing in science potential. Tom and Mark were bright and determined and it was hard for me to see them wasting so much time coping with just communication.

Just as Beth widens her second draft into a social story of addiction, Christine moves from an individual portrait to a public story. She widens the frame of the story beyond the dimensions of a single man to fit a broader horizon of historical reference.

As a third case of widening the lens of an eyewitness source, consider the writing of Laura. Laura draws on the life and experiences of her grandmother, Ginny, to present a story of the changing social and technological context of sewing in 20th century America. Like Beth and Christine, Laura's first draft clings too snugly to the personal details of Ginny's life. Like Beth and Christine, her revision turns an individual's personal recollections into public stories about a past displaced from the reader's present.

In her first draft, Laura offered many interesting facts about Grandmother Ginny's life, centered on Ginny's lifelong interest in sewing. Nonetheless, the details did little to support the telling of a larger story. Laura realized she could develop a better history by moving Ginny into the background and bringing to the foreground the profound changes in sewing that had taken place within Ginny's lifetime.

Her name is Lillian Virginia (Ginny) Franz. She was born in 1916 in Terra Haute Indiana, and will be eighty years old this October 24th. She is an active woman, volunteering her time for two churches in her city. Two of her many projects include making quilts that go to people in need, and sewing pillows for patients at a local hospital. It does not surprise me that she created three quilts last summer, or that she can turn out 12 pillows in three days if needed. To me, she is synonymous with sewing. I can remember sleeping in her sewing room when I would visit as a girl. She is my Grandma Ginny.

In her second draft, Laura continues to talk about Ginny's life. Yet, rather than focusing on a personal biography, Laura focuses only on events in Ginny's life that coincide with milestones in the technology of sewing. With this change of focus, Laura was able to move the text away from portraiture toward a wider angled, historical landscape. Ginny's changing experiences with sewing function as the lens through which Laura can chronicle the technological history of sewing.

Laura describes where Ginny learned to sew and the humorous mistakes she made while learning. These details serve the dual purpose of developing Ginny as a person and developing our understanding of the challenges (i.e., sewing by hand) and the institutional and gender expectations (e.g., it was taught in school to girls) associated with sewing in the early 20th century.

> As a child growing up in Indiana, and then in Detroit, her family didn't have a sewing machine. Everything was done by hand then. In fact, her mother didn't sew much—Grandma Ginny remembers her making only a few items. Grandma Ginny took an interest in sewing when she took a class in school. She can still remember laying out the material for the first time and cutting it incorrectly when the teacher wasn't looking (she laughs). They didn't baste the material and do a fitting in that class, so it wasn't until she had borrowed a neighbor's sewing machine and finished the dress that she realized the arm holes were in the chest and the back! But she didn't give up.

Laura goes on to chart societal trends relating sewing and class status in the 1930s. With rising income and the cost of manufacturing decreasing, the middle class could for the first time afford store-bought clothes. Sewing became an increasingly recreational activity for middle class woman, like Ginny.

> Grandma Ginny didn't have to sew her own clothes. In the late 1930s in Detroit, women only wore dresses and coats, and they were available in many department stores. Her family's middle income meant she could afford to purchase dresses and coats for everyday wear. It was the lure of pretty materials and unique dress styles that motivated my grandmother to start sewing her own clothes.

Luckily, when my grandmother decided to sew her own clothes, her mother-in-law owned a sewing machine that she could borrow. It was a Singer sewing machine. The machine was housed in a wooden cabinet, about table height, with four large drawers, and a secret drawer only 1-1/2 inches high. When in use, the hinged top would open on the left, and come to rest parallel to the floor to the right of the user, creating an extra working space.

Not a plastic electric sewing machine like the one she has today, the old metal sewing machine was operated by putting both feet on a big flat metal pedal on the floor, and rocking the pedal back and forth. This motion would cause a big leather belt attached to it to move, which would spin two wheels on the sewing machine, just like a bicycle chain works. One of the wheels was most likely up by her hand, where the machine was started with a little push. The other wheel was definitely down near the pedal. While she cannot remember exactly where the wheels were located, she can sure remember what a pain that leather belt was. When it would get worn out, it would break, and she'd have to go down to the store and pick another one up and replace it. Or sometimes it would just stretch out and slip off the wheels. It would have to be replaced then too.

She never had formal training as a seamstress. She learned by doing. She remembers trying to make a suit coat for her sister-in-law Nora, and having a heck of a time with the collar. It was 1939, and she hadn't yet started to take sewing classes. She couldn't understand the instructions and was starting to cry. Her mother-in-law, Mother Franz, thought my grandparents were having a spat. But when she realized my grandmother was crying over the collar, she came over to the machine and sewed it on in no time at all.

Laura now turns her attention to how sewing as a technology and as a social practice continued to undergo change into the 1950s. She relates how Ginny came into contact with her first electronic sewing machine in the late 1950s.

In 1957 my grandmother purchased her first electric sewing machine (a White), and began attending sewing classes offered through the PTA at my father's old school for $3.50/term. A few years later, the school millage didn't pass and her sewing classes were discontinued. So she and some other ladies started their own classes. The cost was $50/10 weeks, and they would take turns meeting at each other's house. They would meet once a week. Their instructor was Crystal, and she had a flair fashion! Grandma Ginny remembers choosing patterns and cutting out her size in muslin. Then, she would baste the muslin together as if she were actually making the article of clothing. Then, Crystal would "fit" her for it. Making sure that everything fit where it should. Crystal would make needed or creative changes to the muslin, then my grandmother would make the changes to the pattern. Then, she would cut it out again, this time in the desired material. The material would be once more basted, fitted one last time, and finally sewn together to make a perfectly fitting garment.

Except for the few years my grandfather was ill before he died in 1979, my grandmother continued to take sewing classes from Crystal until 1991 (Crystal died in 1992). Since then, she doesn't make her own clothes much anymore—it's hard to "fit" oneself. Mostly she just hems or takes in petite clothing she buys off the rack. Besides, sewing one's own clothes is no longer worth it.

Ginny's participation in sewing evolved from formal (school classes) to informal (self-supported and arranged classes) and, eventually, to a way of maintaining contacts with old friends.

A few years ago, Grandma Ginny bought 5 yards of 60" material. It was the loveliest red. She planned to make herself a suit coat and matching skirt and pants from a fitted pattern that Crystal had helped her with years earlier. She wasn't even done with any of the pieces yet, when her friend Georgetta came in one day to show off a new purchase—a three piece suit. She was wearing the jacket and pants and had the skirt draped over an arm, and it was exactly the same color of the suit my grandmother was making. Well, my grandmother never told Georgetta this, but she was just sick. Georgetta had gotten the suit on sale, it was ridiculously inexpensive, and my grandmother was working so hard on her suit which wasn't even done! Of course, after my grandmother finished her red suit, she had a suit equal to any $500 suit off the rack. It had a good quality lining, and she looked like a million in it!

In the first draft, Laura gives us a glimpse of her Grandma Ginny's life. In her revision, she widens the lens on Ginny to turn a portrait into a historical panorama of a specific evolving technology.

In the writings of Beth, Christine, and Laura, we can see a common challenge to widen the lens of the story so that it captures a displaced world rather than individual portraits of the sources who provided windows into it.

Remembering a Space:
Historical Flashbulbs with Minimal Scene-Shifting

Some writers in our studio opt to resurrect historical scenes. Such scenes, like history writing in general, rely on the combination of displaced writing with immediacy. The difference is that in scenic histories, the representational elements rely on minimal scene-shifting. The distance and immediacy of the past are consolidated into a single flashbulb memory. The writing shares the spatial immediacy and vividness of scenic writing. Like the first motion pictures of 1900, the writing depicts a moving photograph rather than a narrative spliced across multiple scenes. Yet, the scene retains the element of temporal displacement by including detail that signals the passage of time from the reader's present. The reader feels like a time traveler dropped into a scene from the past.

Don used this strategy to capture the reminiscences of his grandfather Neil. He found in Neil's recollections the opportunity to show his readers interesting scenic contrast between the conditions of public education in early 20th century America and the conditions today. Don realized he could also show certain continuities between schoolboy roughhousing in the early century and today. Finally, through Neil's memory, Don realized he could capture in vivid detail the early 20th century fascination for a still "fantasy" invention—the airplane.

Neil recalled a scene in the early 1920s, when he and his friends John and Pete were walking a dirt road to school. They attended a one-room schoolhouse where first graders sat in the front row and seventh graders in the back. The school had no plumbing and the teacher and students alike used an outhouse. Neil and John, in a spirit of coltish play, have just knocked Pete to the ground, when they are startled by a strange machine flying overhead:

> Pete was turning red, as he always did before he retaliated. Both of Pete's feet were wading in gallons of muddy water. Knowing he was armed, Pete lifted his foot back, ready to swing. Neil and John backed up. Mid-swing, Pete's face changed from anger to shock and then sur-

prise. Floating there, high up in the sky, was an airplane. Its silver sheen blinked brightly in the sunlight.

Wow, Pete gasped from behind.

In frozen silence, they watched the great silver bird until it disappeared from view. Pete splashed his way out of the puddle and jabbered, I'm gonna ride in one of those someday. They resumed their long walk to school. Seeing an airplane was a sign of good luck. It was going to be a good day, Neil decided.

In the 1920s, spotting an airplane overhead was still rare enough to be a sign of good luck. While the writing is scenic, the scene is meant to be historically rendered, crafted to magnify the reader's feeling of displacement rather than diminish it.

Mary relied on memories of her older aunts and uncles to recall the day, in the 1930s in Benton, Wisconsin, when the father of one of her relatives surprised his family by bringing home one of the first Bell + Howell movie cameras.

Our cooking was interrupted when Dad walked in the back door with a big brown box. As the paper ripped and the packing materials were thrown aside we saw a. movie camera. This was something entirely new. We had never heard of one before let alone seen one. In the past, we used the Kodak Brownie to take snapshots. But a movie camera? The camera, made by Bell + Howell, shone bright silver and was trimmed in black leather. It was oval, about the size of a flattened cantaloupe, and it was very heavy, especially for someone as the young as me. It probably weighed 10 pounds. It was beautiful. The sides of the camera were embossed with a pattern of scrolls, vines and swirls that reminded me of the white damask cloth covering our dining room table.

People are slow to learn the implications of new technologies and at first they understand them only through the technologies they know. Through the retrieved memories of the family members she interviewed, Mary saw how she could illustrate this cultural point about technological change while showing the details of a distant past. The father who brought home the Bell + Howell first used the movie camera as if it were a familiar still camera.

We waited excitedly as [father] read the instructions. He fiddled a bit with one knob and twisted another, mumbling as he went along. Then slowly, and with a deep sigh, my Dad stood so that his tall thin body towered above us. He raised the camera to one eye and said, "smile."

We were paralyzed. How do we act before a moving camera? The thought of waving, walking, or dancing never entered our minds. In the past, whenever we were set before a camera we were told repeatedly to sit still. So, we stood there like statues, despite my father's encouraging words.

Well, if that was all we were going to do, I guess Dad figured he may just as well record the furniture. We relaxed a bit, still watching intently, as he panned from the baby grand piano where we practiced our Principles, to the oak sofa with intricate carvings. He circled the room filming everything from the tiffany-style floor lamps to the ornate aquarium with the goldfish.

Little Bill, the kid of the family, is not hardened in the ways of the old technology and is most comfortable adapting to the new.

Little Bill was the least intimidated by the new contraption. He carried on his usual pranks in front of the lens. He stood on his head, made everyone laugh, and poked at the dog or at me. I don't think he stood still once that afternoon.

Like color televisions would become in the 1960s, the new Bell + Howell in the 1930s was a cause for formal celebration when it came to a neighborhood.

The filming of the interior tour complete, Dad brought the prized camera outside and before long neighbors stopped over. The women mingled in flowing dresses draped with large white collars. They wore dark, wideheeled shoes that laced up the front. Mrs. Mae exchanged hugs with my Mom when she came over; then chased after their children, Amy and Little Bill, who had started down the street with roller-skates strapped to their shoes.

Mary's historical narrative captures a family's slice of life that in turn captures a larger public story about technological change, adaptation, and generational contrasts.

Rick used a blend of scenic and more extended narrative writing to capture an older relative's childhood reminiscences of the Kansas dustbowl during the Great Depression.

I got to see a lot of Kansas back then. My dad was working for his uncle's bank. We moved from Chicago when his dad's company went bankrupt during the Depression. Kansas was a step down from Chicago, but we were just happy dad was working. I'd drive with him out to the farms. He wasn't foreclosing the farms like in Grapes of Wrath. His bank actually really tried to help the families save them. It was an interesting time, and I'll certainly never forget the dust.

They never should have plowed the buffalo grass. That was the big mistake. Of course, no one understood the implications until it was too late. The new wheat grew like crazy and the farms were flourishing. Even when it stopped raining the wheat kept growing. It must have seemed like a great decision at the time.

If you had to pick one word to describe Kansas, it'd have to be 'flat.' It's flatter than flat. The roads are all perfectly straight and stretch out for miles and miles like diagrams from geometry class. Each road runs due north and south, or east and west. They lay atop the land like a piece of giant drafting paper, perfect right angles at each intersection connecting with others to form hundreds of huge concrete squares. Every once in a while along those continuous roads the surveyors would have to put in a correction line.

You'd be driving along, shift over just a few yards, and then off you'd go again down that unwavering path. I found it fascinating when you'd see another car approaching from a connecting road. I'd squint hard and try to figure out how far away they were. Then I'd try to calculate when we might reach the intersection at the same time, and then if my dad would brake or speed up ever so slightly we'd be almost guaranteed never to meet. Just a slight adjustment either way made such a dramatic difference. And if you had a 55-mile trip and you didn't speed, you'd get there in almost exactly 55 minutes. The roads are that straight. The land is that flat. I remember one small rise between Dodge City and Garden City. It was barely a hill, but it was just big enough and the land was so perfectly horizontal you couldn't see the other side. Once you crested the hill, the sight was magnificent. You could see for five miles in every direction. The land, the wheat, and the farms created beautiful colored geometric shapes like a golden patchwork quilt.

Well, until the Dust Bowl, that is. Then you'd go along and just see ruin. The wind would come along and move everything. The tumbleweeds would be caught in the fences. Then the dust would blow and build up along the tumbleweeds. It ended up looking like a snow fence in July with huge drifts of topsoil lying along each rail.

It all started in 1931. The rainfall dropped way off that summer and stayed that way for several more years. There wasn't much snow either and that hurt them too. The farmers didn't know that most of Kansas has bedrock 20 feet down. The wheat just kept growing as if by magic during the awful drought. It took two years for the soil to dry up the whole way down and then came the trouble. The wheat stopped growing. Not only that, but then the roots became an issue. The wheat had long roots, but they didn't tangle up like the buffalo grass. It couldn't hold the soil down. Once the land was parched the wind just picked it all up and blew it away. The farmers tried different farming practices to combat the problem but nothing worked. They needed rain.

Dust was everywhere. Great black clouds moved along the ground to cover everything in fine, brown dust. It was just part of life. It got into everything, even the refrigerator. We tried to cool the house down in the day by putting these filters in the windows made of a fan, water, and wood shavings. They didn't work. On those hot summer nights when it might get down to 85 we'd open the windows back up. Once a storm came while we were asleep. The dust blew in through the open windows and covered everything in the house. Every lamp, every chair, every piece of clothing, everything. My Mom woke up the next day and put on her glasses. They were so covered, she thought she'd gone blind.

Through his relative's memory, Rick brings to readers vivid images of the devastation created by the dustbowl.

In the cases of Mary, Don, and Rick, scenic writing blends with representational displacement to capture a past through vivid scenic rendering. Mary, Don, and Rick each composed their scenes after studying the principles of scenic writing and after recognizing how the elements of such writing can bring the dim past to the reader's awareness with the vividness of the present. Each of these writers had to probe their informants carefully for details that would make stark and poignant contrasts with the world of their readers.

Achieving Immediacy and Displacement with Archival Sources

Thus far, we have considered historical narratives that rely on eyewitness sources. While we recommend oral sources for the narrative history assignment, we also permit textual sources. Many histories, of course, are written from archival records, news reports, and other documentary sources that readers are less likely to mistake with portraits of single interview sources.

Narrative histories depending upon documents still require the alignment of representational displacement and immediacy. However, histories from textual sources, especially secondary sources, are often presented as dry information, lacking the narrative plotting and immediacy required to stir the contemporary reader's interest and involvement. If the challenge of writing oral histories is to make the history larger than a portrait, the challenge of writing documentary history is to make readers care. When writers rely on individuals as sources, the source can furnish the human-interest eyes and ears on the past with which to invite the reader in. When the writer writes from impersonal sources, however, the sources are less likely to provide a human lure.

When students in our studio write histories from scattered textual sources, we require them to test their drafts for human interest with their peers. We expect student writers to be responsive enough to their peers to find in their secondary sources what their peers consider of immediate interest.

Eric's narrative history is illustrative. Eric's relied on his fellow students to help develop the human angle on an otherwise impersonal history. His subject was the Maccabiah Games and he relied on mostly impersonal sources. His challenge was to shape a human interest story from sources that were scattered and impersonal. He also had to winnow sources, for there was more to read than he could include.

In his first draft, Eric furnishes details about the events behind the Jewish Olympics—the who, when, and where of the past. He does not mention his specific sources by name. Yet, he provides specific enough detail in dates (e.g., 165 BCE, 1929, etc.), places (e.g., Constantinople, Czechoslovakia, etc.), and quantities (e.g., number of athletes, the number of countries, etc.) to create for the average reader the perception of credible source material.

> In 1992, I tried out for the United States men's fast-pitch softball delegation to the 14th World Maccabiah games. When I tell people about my tryouts, I find that many of them—Jewish or not—haven't heard of the Maccabiah Games. Those who've heard of them, sometimes call them the "Jewish Olympics," or the "Maccabees." What people don't realize is that the games have a symbolic historical narrative and almost didn't survive the Holocaust. And that some famous athletes have competed in these major games.

Why Maccabiah?

Judah Maccabee, a Hebrew religious zealot famous for his ability as a fighter, led a successful revolt against the Syrians in 165 B.C.E.—a victory that meant religious freedom for Jews living in the land of Canaan. In the nineteenth century, to better protect themselves from pogroms and religious oppression, Eastern European Jews established self-defense groups and gymnastic clubs. First appearing in Constantinople in 1895, these athletic clubs took Judah Maccabee as their role model and adopted the name Maccabee. By World War One, over 100 Maccabee clubs were scattered through Europe.

After the war, the European Maccabee movement organized international games, and in 1929 the first World Maccabiah Games took place in Czechoslovakia. The World Maccabee Congress met that same year and accepted the proposal to hold the next games in Palestine. In 1932, nearly 400 athletes from 22 countries participated in the Palestine Maccabiah Games. And in 1935, over 1,700 athletes from 27 nations competed. World War Two precluded any more games until 1950, following the devastation of the Holocaust and Israel's War of Independence. Jews had been scattered across the world. It was a miracle to even hold the games at all. But 500 athletes from 20 countries came to the new state of Israel and participated in the first Israeli Maccabiah Games. By 1981, over 3,500 athletes from 35 countries competed in the games. The games are now the third largest international athletic competition in the world, behind the Olympics and the Pan-Am games.

Eric now highlights the difference between the Maccabiah games and the Olympics.

The Maccabiah Games are similar to the Olympics, but not a replica. Modeled after the Olympics, the Maccabiah Games dared to vary the traditions of the Olympics. Basketball, for example, has been part of the games since their 1929 inception. The sport was not introduced to the Olympics until 1936. And the Maccabiah Games honored a woman torchbearer in 1965—three years before a woman was honored in the Olympics. Famous American delegates over the years have included Isaac Berger in weightlifting, Lillian Copeland in track, Ernie Grunfeld in basketball, and Mark Spitz in swimming.

In first draft, Eric concludes with a challenge to the reader and a personal story describing his experiences with the games.

> What about you? Over 150 men from across the country competed for one of fifteen spots on the team. The level of skill was very high. Star athletes scooped up hard grounders, made quick, perfect throws to bases, shot liners into the outfield. I played well. The coaches commended me. I felt I had a chance. Several weeks later, the four-sentence form letter from the coach dashed my hopes. I had been cut.

Reading this draft, Eric's peers felt that Eric had answered what the Maccabiah Games were, but not what they meant. Readers wanted him to explain the symbolism of the games. What did the founders want to achieve? More than just describing the history of the games, Eric needed to tell the symbolic story that shaped that history.

In his second draft, Eric took steps to achieve a better balance between the facts of the Maccabiah Games and the founders' intent for them.

> In 1992, I tried out for the United States men's fast-pitch softball delegation to the 14th World Maccabiah Games (pronounced maokaoBEEoah). Though unknown to many, the Maccabiah Games—sometimes called the Jewish Olympics—are the world's third-largest athletic competition—behind the Olympics and the Pan-Am Games. Like the Jewish people who throughout time have fought oppression and extinction, the Maccabiah Games are a story of resistance and survival. And though I didn't make the softball team, I came to understand the symbolism of the games.
>
> The Maccabiah Games are a story about overcoming religious persecution, which Jews have suffered throughout the ages. In the nineteenth century Jewish people in Eastern Europe suffered widespread pogroms and religious oppression at the hands of the Cossacks. In order to better protect and defend themselves, they established self-defense groups and gymnastic clubs. The first of these clubs appeared in 1895 in Constantinople. Claiming Judah Maccabee, a Hebrew religious zealot and warrior of two thousand years earlier, as their role model, these clubs adopted the name Maccabee. Just as Judah Maccabee had revolted against the Syrians—a victory that meant religious freedom for Jews living in the land of Canaan—so, too, would these Maccabee clubs serve as a means of strength and survival for the Jewish people. By

World War One, there were more than 100 Maccabee clubs throughout Europe. These clubs did not quash the pogroms, but they provided Jewish people with enough strength training and physical fitness to fight back.

TIME FOR A JEWISH OLYMPICS

In 1929, members of the Maccabee clubs established the Maccabee World Congress. The 1928 Amsterdam Olympics had impressed the Congress, and they thought the time was right for a "Jewish Olympics." Using the Olympics as a model, the Congress devised a plan for an international Jewish athletic festival—called the World Maccabiah Games—which would unite Jewish athletes from around the world. The games would feature Olympic events like swimming, track and field, weightlifting, tennis, and fencing. But they would also introduce basketball—a sport that the Olympics would not adopt for another seven years. The first Maccabiah Games were held in Europe, but the Congress voted to move the games to Palestine, the Jewish homeland. In 1932, the first Palestine games featured 390 athletes from 22 countries. By 1935, nearly two thousand competed.

PERSECUTION REVISITED

Nineteen thirty-eight was supposed to see the largest ever Maccabiah Games. But the shadows of another war descending on Europe forced the games' cancellation. During the next several years, the world's Jewish population was halved in the worst act of religious persecution, the Holocaust. Among the slain six million Jews were most of the European Maccabiah athletes. As in Judah Maccabee's time, as in nineteenth-century Europe, as in every age—the Jews had been devastated, but not crushed. After the camps were liberated, the State of Israel was born. Jews were free to be Jews again. And in 1950, a small contingency of Jewish athletes gathered in Tel Aviv to rekindle the Maccabiah Torch—and to compete in the first Israeli Maccabiah Games.

A NEW HOPE

Since the end of World War Two, the world's Jewish population has tripled. Russian and Ethiopian Jewry have found new homes in Israel.

And the Maccabiah Games have grown to five thousand Jewish athletes from more than 40 countries. The games, like the Jewish people, have survived—and thrived—in the wake of destruction. Even today, as peace wavers in Israel, Jewish athletes worldwide prepare to compete in next year's 15th World Maccabiah Games in Tel Aviv.

Eric's first attempt at a historical narrative missed some of the central concerns of his readers. He found he could rely on their comments to fill in the gaps. By integrating the "why" with the description of what occurred, he was able to create a link from the displaced events to his readers' immediate interests.

Defending a Past:
Using Displacement and Immediacy to Serve Argument

In some cases, the story about the past becomes a contested story. When this happens, narrative history blends with argument. The writer must not only tell a story about a world that is no more, but must also defend that story against competing stories.

Michelle's narrative writing reflects such a blending. She recounts the story of her distant and older relative, Susan, who was born in her mother's generation. Susan was a mathematics professor who grew up in a generation when women were discouraged from pursuing any kind of career, much less one in science. Going into her assignment, Michelle felt confident that she could use Susan to document the chilly climate that an aspiring career woman faced in the conservative 1950s. When Michelle interviewed Susan, she was surprised, for Susan had remembered a youth where she found plenty of family and collegial support for her career in science, not unlike a woman of the 1990s.

Michelle was happy for Susan but puzzled as a writer. Her prior expectations about the past had been undermined. The story she thought she would find was not there. Michelle had to devote much of her interview time to search out why, against all her previous conceptions, Susan had been supported in her career aspirations. Deliberately drawing on blends with mixed portraiture, Michelle decided to bring her surprise about Susan into the visible design of her narrative.

Born in 1934, Susan Friedman, a first cousin of my mother's, is one of the few women I know who has her Ph.D. in mathematics, a field considered to be a domain of men. When I thought of interviewing her I envisioned a conversation filled with accounts of difficulty, discrimination, and possibly harassment. Instead, what I got was a sweet and unusual story.

Susan remembers always being good in math as well as always being encouraged. I've always been in awe of Susan, my mother's first cousin. Imagine, a woman getting a Ph.D. in mathematics in the 50s. For a long time I wondered what it had been like, getting a degree and working in a field considered being a man's domain. I wondered if she had to fight to claim her ground; I couldn't imagine it coming easily, especially back in the 50s.

Susan remembers always being good in math and being encouraged by her parents. Unlike some females who had problems because people told them "Oh, girls aren't really interested in math and science," Susan fondly recalled a story of being in fifth grade and getting the commendation for the best arithmetic score on a citywide test when she was in the fifth grade. "I remember that commendation, my parents were very proud."

It's hard for me to imagine being a girl raised in the 30s and 40s and having had parents that offered encouragement for rigorous academics. But Susan was very clear of her parents about the support she received from them. "Yeah, they encouraged me, and my mother always said, I don't know if she was putting herself down.'Imagine me having a daughter interested in and good at mathematics and I could never do it.' She was very proud, and my father was as well."

Michelle keeps herself in the text, to the point of telling how she responds to Susan's answers as an on-scene character.

So I smiled when I learned of Susan's grandmother on her mother's side. Grandma Bessie had been a cashier back in the early 1900s. Whenever Susan did well in math her Grandmother used to say, "Ah ha, you got it from me!"

Michelle's first draft was so invested in mixed portraiture that the historical elements were barely visible. We learn less about Susan's past than about Michelle's surprise towards it. To strengthen the historical elements in a second draft, Michelle kept probing Susan to see if she could locate evidence that Susan's career path in the 1950s, however successful, may still have been limited compared to the paths open to women in the 1990s.

In effect, Michelle's story became an argument about the past that she was still seeking to support. Michelle returned to Susan to explore discrepancies between Susan's story and Michelle's expectations for the story she planned to write. Prompted by this exploration context, Susan was able to recall people in her life who had *not* been supportive of her career. Michelle's second draft included this newly discovered information:

> While Susan received much support at home, she had a mixed experience from her schoolteachers, who were not always supportive. In elementary school Susan related how she was considered one of the bright kids but never got any direct encouragement from a teacher until high school. "The greatest influence, I guess, was in high school. It was a music and art school but we took academic subjects as well. My facility at mathematics continued. I had a teacher named Mr. Friedman who encouraged me greatly." Mr. Friedman, Susan's high school math teacher—who later became her father-in-law—gave her encouragement but also warned her there was a ceiling on what she could accomplish. "He said to me, 'You're very good in math. I have to introduce you to my son.' So Stanley's father had the greatest influence in my life in total. He picked me out, I guess, and one thing lead to another and he finally did introduce us. And things happened from there." (Susan and Stanley married when Susan was 18.)

Finding contradictory pieces of evidence about whether Stanley's father was supportive of Susan, Michelle interrupts her narration to call attention to the discrepancy.

> There is a slight discrepancy in the support she received from Stanley's father. When she told him, in high school, that she was considering going into engineering he warned her off. Mr. Friedman senior cautioned Susan to avoid engineering when she mentioned she was considering it as a career. He said, "Look, you're a woman and a Jew and that's two strikes against you, maybe. Maybe you should rethink engineering." I was also surprised to hear that although Mr. Friedman senior thought that she was smart he warned her there is a certain time when she would be surpassed by the boys in intellectual ability. Susan remembers, "Well, that's fine, I'm smart. But, some of those dumb boys will be as smart as me." "But you know," Susan declared, "some of those dumb boys I went

to high school with wound up in college with me, but they never got smarter than me."

Michelle's writing became an investigative history. She sought to make sense of her own prior conceptions of the past, but in a way that still fit the complex facts of Susan's memories.

> This slight contradiction of support and discouragement didn't seem to faze Susan all that much. Perhaps it was because of all the other support she had in her life. My mother was very pro-girl and what was important to her and my father was that his kids were smart. "According to my father, 'Better to have smart girls than dumb boys'," was what she said.

Rather than accept Susan's original narration as the whole story, Michelle crafts her text to make Susan's answers responsive to her own prior beliefs about the status of women in the 1950s.

> I asked her if she was ever teased in any way. Apparently, she was fortunate in that she didn't meet any of those kinds of attitudes during her education. Support and mentoring also came from an award for the best math student she shared with a boy who is now a professor of mathematics at Arizona State University. Susan recalled doing a project for Westinghouse as a senior in high school. She was one of 300 honorable mentions nation-wide for the project. One reason Susan never thought it was odd for a female to be in engineering, science, or mathematics was because of an engineer friend of her mother's. "I had a friend of my mother's who was sort of my mentor in encouraging me and helping with the project. Actually, she had been a friend of my mother's from childhood. She became an engineer and in those days that was very unusual." As a senior in high school Susan did a project for a Westinghouse competition. Stella mentored her through the project and Susan was one of 300 students given honorable mention nation-wide. "Back in those days it was even more unusual for a woman to become an engineer than in my time. So, she was in mathematics and I never thought it was odd."

Michelle leads with the story she wants to defend rather than with the flow of Susan's spontaneous recollection.

> I was curious if she didn't think it odd, what did her peers think? Susan had a childhood friend who shared her interests. Thinking that it is

unusual to find one woman in this field, what was the likelihood of finding two who knew each other and mathematics. Again, my hypothesis was incorrect. Susan shared the story of an important childhood friend. "I had a friend who went back to the time when our mothers wheeled us side by side in our carriages. She got her Ph.D. in mathematics and has had a distinguished career as a professor at Rutgers University. She is still one of my closet friends."

Michelle then indicates how Susan's answers to her questions corrected her previous misimpressions.

Susan relayed the sequence of her college career. I was under the impression that completing her undergraduate work, master's, and Ph.D. had been a continuous sequence of events. Apparently not. I also inquired as to what kind of financial opportunity was offered her, here again thinking there may have been some inequality. Instead, she talked about the offers stemming from the Westinghouse competition and of her choice to stay in New York.

Preserving elements of mixed portraiture, Michelle includes her own reactions to Susan in the story.

"Because of the honorable mention from Westinghouse, I had about 40 offers from colleges all over the country. Many sent along scholarship information. At that time I made the decision to go to Queens College, which was free. I wanted to stay near Stanley. But we were engaged and married after my freshman year when I was 18.

"Anyway, there were certainly many opportunities if I had wanted it even at that time. This goes back to the 50's. I graduated in '51 from high school. I received my master's from the University of Maryland on a scholarship. I didn't finish my Ph.D. until after Stanley and I had our three children. Stanley said to me look, 'Look, you were Phi Beta Kappa, you were all honors. I'll put the kids to bed, go. Go back and get the your Ph.D.' He was the main influence really. That took another six years. But, I'm happy that I did it, and I don't think it affected our family negatively. I think it impacted positively in many ways. Stanley never went back to school because he wanted to continue his career as a producer of public television and it wasn't necessary at that time. But, it doesn't bother him that his wife has a Ph.D."

Michelle had revealed a number of interesting things about Susan's past. Yet, much of her inquiry, like that of Kenneth's, had stayed close to her source, focusing on Susan's life and not the larger context for women. Michelle thus shifts gears to explore Susan's relationship to the Feminist Movement during her early years.

> I was amazed by the support Susan received from those closest to her. That support continued both personally and financially throughout her education. I was particularly interested if she had enough scholarship offers or if there had been difficulty funding her education.

Michelle asks a question that allows Susan to go into a longer uninterrupted narrative about her past.

> Particularly when you consider how little cultural support there was in the 50s and early days of 60s for woman to develop their intellectual potential. Today, even with the feminist movement, there is more support for women to return to school and pursue their careers. It made me wonder if it had any influence on she considered herself a feminist and what her relationships with women had been like back then.
>
> "I had a good sense of myself but I didn't have a very high opinion of women in general when I was younger. Most of my friends were boys. I felt that there were a lot of girls that were very silly and I had very little in common with them. It was easier, then, to bond with boys. I wouldn't say I was a feminist from early on. I just had a good sense of myself.
>
> "When I started college it was a little bit before the Feminine Mystique came out. I remember reading it and saying, 'oh, oh!' I really thought Betty Friedan had put down in words a lot of the things that I felt. I can't really recapture exactly what my feelings were at the time except I've always had a fairly good sense of myself and so, it didn't bother me so much being a woman. Once I read the Feminine Mystique I sort of realized the extent women were discriminated against in many fields. It brought me a fuller awareness."

Susan's answers were informative, but also generic and nonspecific. Michelle decided to pin down Susan more concretely about her relationship with women.

> This made me wonder about Susan's relationships with other women in general. Her answers demonstrated her opinion back when she was growing up and in college. "I had a good sense of myself but I didn't

have a very high opinion of women in general. Most of the friends I had were boys. I felt that there were a lot of girls that were very silly and I had very little in common with them. It was easier then to bond with boys. I wouldn't say I was a feminist from early on. I just had a good sense of myself. I wanted five boys. When Debbie was born, there was initial disappointment, but it quickly past. And, then we had two boys."

Finally, Michelle pins down Susan's attitudes toward professional women.

Finally, I wanted to find out about Susan's career opportunities and if her feelings about women have changed. Here too, I am struck by the opportunities offered her. Her feelings about women have also evolved and I was impressed to hear her express support and interest in giving women the opportunities they have earned. "One of the first jobs I had was at Hunter College. The chair of the department was a woman who was not particularly encouraging and did not become one of my friends. But, there were several women in the department, one who has stayed a close friend and teaches at City College. I am a member of the CUNY (City University of New York) mathematics discussion group. It is composed of people who teach math throughout the City University. I am fairly active in this professional group and it is composed of both men and women. Now, there are a goodly number of women getting their Ph.D.'s—more than when I went to school. But, I wasn't aware of being put down when I was in school, maybe. Maybe it's just my own ego."

By this stage of her text, Michelle had presented a great deal of information about Susan but little, thus far, to indicate how the world for professional women had changed since Susan's youth. Michelle closes her historical narrative by letting Susan draw out, and so supporting, the then-now contrasts that form the core of Michelle's historical argument.

"However, there are many more opportunities for women now. In general, the climate is better for women than before. Women have a much better sense of themselves in intellectual endeavors. I think that "pre-Feminine Mystique" women were not brought up to have any career aspirations for themselves. The focus was on 'making a good marriage' and women were expected to bask in the glories of their husbands' accomplishments. Post-Feminine Mystique, women were encouraged to develop their potential, independently of any marital situation. The women's movement and affirmative action probably opened doors for many women in academia as well as in other fields. In all fields, I don't think women are as timid about entering and competing with men as they used to be. And my relationships with women have changed. I value the friendship of women. I think women are lucky that they can easily bond because men can't and are at a great disadvantage.

"I have a lot of women friends, single women and women in couples. Also, I have a lot of women friends who are professionals, not necessarily in mathematics but in a lot of other fields. I feel very strongly that in my college I am valued for a lot of qualities that I have—not only my intellectual qualities. I'm a member of the faculty senate, and I was just asked to be on the search committee for the new dean. I am on several other committees by invitation. I feel that my gender is a positive thing at this point in my life. I never felt it was terribly negative, but at this point it is certainly positive. If my department feels they need a woman on a committee, very often I am chosen. My 40's and 50's have been a very positive and rewarding time in my life."

Susan now works at Bernard Baruch College, City University of New York. It is primarily a business college, one of the largest in the country. She is the assistant department chair and, while the full time staff ratio is a 5 women to 22 men ratio, when it is time to hire adjunct faculty, Susan is very aware of giving qualified women equal opportunity.

Michelle found her source interesting as a profile subject, but initially unhelpful as a source for the historical narrative she was planning to write. She decided to enter her own text as a character to search out evidence for her version of the past. The historical narrative turned into a set of branching, often competing, stories. When the stories compete, and research must go into substantiating which story bears the weight of evidence, historical narrative becomes an argument about history.

Summarizing the Writing Models in Relation to the Feel of Historical Time

Narrative histories rely on the convergence of two independent representational elements: displacement and immediacy. Displacement sets the world of the text apart in time and space from the world of the reader. Immediacy makes that displaced world resonate with the vividness of the present. Ann, Joy, and Deborah illustrate ways of melding both displacement and immediacy into history writing.

History writing restores a world the writer did not know firsthand. The writer's memories cannot furnish the source of the writing. Only the memories of external sources can. Should the writer overdo the experience of eyewitness sources, efforts at history writing may lapse into a portrait of one's sources. Kenneth's historical narrative is a good example of this problem. Beth, Christine, and Laura worked on multiple drafts to widen the frame of their writing from portraits to panoramas of past worlds. Don, Mary, and Rick rely upon eyewitness memories to recreate historical scenes that feature sharp contrasts with the world of their readers.

Should a writer rely on archival material for sources, his narrative is more likely to be blended with exposition (see chap. 5) than with portraiture or scenic writing. The writer, as always, needs to tell some minimal story within or across scenes. Yet, documents drawn from the past will have neither a uniform story to tell nor a uniform point of view from which to tell it. The various sources become small bits of data that must fit together and constrain a story of the writer's design. Yet, it remains the writer's story to tell. Because the story must remain true to the past and of interest to contemporary readers, the writer can use her projected readers to help develop and test the story as the story evolves. Eric's historical narrative developed in this fashion.

The writer may sometimes find a clash between source memories and the story that he expected to tell. The contested nature of the past will surface, causing the writer to blend history with principles of argument (chap. 8). In this case, the writer will need not only to tell a story, but also to be prepared to seek evidence to decide which of the multiple competing stories to tell. Michelle found such a clash between her expectations and Susan, her source, in her narrative history. Using mixed portraiture, Michelle's drafts began to make visible the decision that she and Susan had to settle in order for her writing to proceed. As it happened, once Michelle made her point of view better known to Susan, Susan was able to confirm more of Michelle's impressions of the past. Michelle, as a result, got to write more of the historical story she originally wanted to write. Had Susan not been able to offer this confirmation, Michelle would have needed a new story, new sources, or both.

The historical narrative challenges the writer to maintain a delicate balance between telling the truth about the past and making the truth artful enough to entice readers to it. Truth and art are never far apart when the historical narrative works as it should.

Representational Displacement and Immediacy in Professional and Public Writing

Writing that reclaims a past from fresh memory is ubiquitous in professional genres, especially in blends with exposition and argument. Professional historians seek to reclaim lost worlds not only to chronicle what happened in as vivid detail as possible, but also to use that vividness for present and future policy. Business writers and politicians look to displacement and immediacy to justify a vision of the future from the perch of the past. The integration of displacement and immediacy forms substantial parts of corporate strategic plans, annual reports, and public policy arguments. Any attempt to step into the future requires anchors and precedents from a freshly recalled past. The vivid past furnishes not only specific narrative detail, but also analogies that can tie the past to the present and future.

Case studies within professions function as variants of Michelle's blend of history and argument. They play an important role in disciplines, like law and business, where professional knowledge is constituted by the generalizations (viz., precedents) that form over a vividly recalled past. Here, the immediacy and displacement of historical cases are used to serve the ends of generalization as well as representation. The case must have immediacy so that it can be recalled vividly. A constitutional expert for this reason knows the details of 19th century cases as if they happened yesterday. The displacement of the case, on the other hand, allows it to be manipulated from a professional distance and probed to explore its consequences for generalization and, hence, future action.

III. Invitations for Interaction

5
Invitations to Learn

Readers are an important consideration to the writer designing an interactive world. Writers must cue readers about their role within the reading experience. Just as a painting must define perspective to give viewers an orientation to look, texts must give readers a perspective from which to read.

In the previous chapters, the textual elements defining the reader perspective have been understated, even muted. The previous chapters have focused on building worlds for an off-scene reader. The reader is an invisible element in the world of the text, part of the offstage background with no addressed role to play.

The forthcoming chapters move to information writing. From the offstage background, the reader, as role identity, enters the visible representation of the world of the text. The reader becomes increasingly the customer of the writing rather than a patron of literary art. The textual elements defining the reader role and the writer-reader relationship are now more dominant in the overall composition. The world of the information text becomes not only a world of experience, a world asking the reader to sense and notice, but also a world of explicitly cued writer-reader transactions, asking the reader to learn, generalize and act on what is sensed and noticed.

Experiential worlds of portraits and landscapes continue to matter to information writing. Yet they matter less as an end than as a means to serve the reader's interest in generalization and action. The reader is explicitly cued to take from a textual world a durable commodity—information—meant to remain with the reader intact after she finishes reading.

The secret behind the reader's capacity to flip the switch from taking in "experience" to taking in "information" is to perceive the elements defining the world of writer-reader interaction as dominating the elements that contribute to the inner world of the text. Similarly, to move writers from designers of experience to designers of information is to mentor them in the techniques that allow the world of interaction to stand ahead and apart from the inner world of the text.

Information writing requires that these techniques be used visibly. However, our studio writers begin work on these techniques long before they come to full visibility in the information writing assignment. Each successive writing assignment asks writers gradually to strengthen the world of interaction against the world of inner representation. This gradual strengthening happens as a result of our asking students, in successive assignments, to achieve increasingly greater distance from the inner world of the writing.

In self-portraiture, all cues of this distance are suppressed. The writer and the world of the text are centrally aligned in thought, time, and space. In observer portraiture and scenic writing, the writer occupies the physical space depicted in the writing, but nonetheless stands, as an observer, outside the dominant focus of that space. In narrative history, the writer distanced herself from the temporal as well as the spatial anchor points of the world written about.

The transition from experiential to information writing marks a watershed where the inner world of the writing becomes not only a distal point for the writer, but also subordinate to the writer-reader relationship. *The world of the writing now exists for the sake of the reader's interactive learning.*

Elements of the text are now perceived as elements crafted to bring about reader outcomes. In experiential writing, the writer was not obliged to pin down exacting outcomes for the reader. To be sure, readers take generalizations away from written portraiture and landscapes. Still, the generalizations they take from an experiential text are too amorphously shaped for a reader to regard as stand-alone products. The writer of information, by way of contrast, contracts with the reader about reading outcomes. The information text subordinates the writer and reader's placement in time and space to less time- and space-bound generalizations. The text itself takes on commodity status, a product more than an experience. The world of the well-functioning information text serves whatever external purposes that readers bring to it.

Targeted reader outcomes are now dominant experiences to embed in the information text. Consequently, designing texts with the elements to support these outcomes takes on increased importance. The reader's journey through the text must be closely guided. Close guidance is achieved through hierarchical organization, where the reader can visit tiered categories of information on a tour the writer has plotted out in advance. Writers visualize the reader's tour through the convention of the outline. They signal points prominent in the information hierarchy with textual cues (e.g., topic sentences, sentence endings, or main clauses) that are designed to call attention to new information (i.e., information unfamiliar to the reader). They cue less prominent points through textual clues (e.g., non-topic sentences, sentence beginnings, or subordinate and relative clauses) that are designed to highlight familiar or more established information.

Writers who know how to provide these signals do so knowing that learners learn best when they are able to link the unfamiliar to the familiar. Readers who understand what writers are doing know to follow these signals in order to assume their role as learner.

While these observations record some of the shifts between experiential and information writing, they do not yet specify the representational challenges of information writing in terms of independent elements to coordinate. To appreciate these challenges and their contrast with challenges previously surveyed, it is useful briefly to review the earlier challenges. In every type of writing we have thus far surveyed, we have documented significant representational challenges facing the writer, each requiring the skillful alignment of independent representational elements. We saw that the writer of portraiture must skillfully align independent elements—disclosure and enactment in the case of self-portraiture; spatial, biographical, and quoted language in the case of observer portraiture. We saw that the writer of landscapes must also create a skillful combination of independent elements—immediacy and displacement—that do double duty both as default assumptions of communication and as representational elements. The scenic writer, seeking to use immediacy for representational purposes, foregrounds a heightened sense of immediacy against a muted sense of communicative displacement. Narrative history requires elevating displacement to representational prominence while keeping immediacy prominent as well. This causes the reader to experience a past that *feels* distant from the present, while at the same time capturing this feeling with the vividness of the present.

Informational writing brings new challenges of representational design. The writer must not only develop the world of the text in the writing but also develop as a dominant element the interactive ties of the reader to that world. The design of the text must encode what the reader is supposed to learn, do, or decide as a result of the reading experience. The text must specify and anticipate the cognitive actions and outcomes (e.g., generalization learning, experiential learning, the learning of guided action) on the reader's side as a way of directing the reader's learning.

The representational challenge of the information writer is to monitor the reader's side every step of the way. In informational writing, the content must be selected and elaborated in terms of the reader's ability to acquire it. The writer makes such selections and elaborations by aligning elements that include what the reader already knows with elements that the reader is targeted to learn.

The effective alignment of reader-familiar and reader-unfamiliar elements is fundamental to skilled information writing. The elements of the familiar and unfamiliar resemble the elements of similarity and difference that combine to make self-portraiture. However, in an information context, the elements of the similar and different no longer relate or differentiate human beings, but rather relate and differentiate groups of human beings according to their familiarity or unfamiliarity with externally referenced subject matters.

As one might guess, there are problems with placing students in the role of information writer that precede even the representational challenges. For information writing presupposes that the writer is in possession of exclusive knowledge the reader wants. The information writer must thus enter the writing transaction with some acknowledged expertise.

Student writers are often unsure of their expertise over subjects. They are accustomed to providing information as test takers but not as authors or authorities possessing exclusive knowledge. Challenged to provide information at the boundary of reader familiarity and unfamiliarity, they are often driven to soul-search about their authority over readers. They ask, "What do I know that others do not know and want to know?"

In our studio experience, we ask student writers to conduct personal inventories and external research to locate their expertise if they do not bring it to the writing assignment. We also rely on student peers, role modelling the average lay reader, to help their fellow students define the knowledge that can set them apart. Some of our studio writers are already deeply immersed in subject matters. They have taken on specialized jobs, experienced specialized training, acquired specialized lexicons, and entered specialized subcultures that set them apart. These writers tend to feel more immediately comfortable in the role of expert. They tend to worry little about where to find their subject matter authority.

Whether students' lack of knowledge per se is a problem for information writing, the problem is one of knowledge rather than representationproper. Beyond the knowledge hurdle, there are two additional representational hurdles to clear, both confronting the writer with expert knowledge to impart. The first hurdle is what we call the discrimination hurdle. The second hurdle is what we call the alignment hurdle. Clearing the discrimination hurdle requires the writer to step outside expert knowledge long enough to take a perspective on the target reader's horizon of the familiar and unfamiliar. Clearing the alignment hurdle requires the writer to position unfamiliar elements at the end of familiar elements so that the reader can learn new generalizations from familiar points of entry.

Without clearing all three hurdles, the writer cannot pull the sleight of hand that characterizes the world's best information writing—*leading* the reader through a subject matter by *following* her native curiosity for it. When this representational effect is achieved, the reader experiences reading as self-learning, experiences the text as the one the reader herself would have written had (contrary to fact) the reader known in advance exactly what she needed and wanted to learn. To move in the direction of this compelling illusion, the reader must be given prominence as an addressed and interactive presence whose interests and investments are directing the text.

It may seem odd to use the term *interactive* with reference to a static text. *Interactivity* calls to mind the newer, dynamic technologies such as the Internet, computer games, and virtual worlds. In these contexts, *interactivity* means that a medium can change in response to the user's choices and actions. The medium receives input from the user and the medium changes in response. The flow between the person and the medium thus moves both ways.

The word *user* in the digital age refers to persons who interact with media that permit two-way interaction. Increasingly, readers in the digital age are becoming users as well. They are able to read a text on a website and then point and click to move to another text. Reading has becoming increasingly hyper-textual in the age of the Internet. Yet, within the confines of a single linear text, our culture still differentiates *readers* from *users* on the assumption that reading remains a one-way process. Why do we make this assumption? The reason seems to have little to do with digitalization for even when digitized, linear texts are seen as a static medium. The reason seems more to do with our underlying assumptions about linear texts. We assume that texts cannot support true (two-way) interactivity, because, being fixed within and across lines, texts are not themselves changed, do not act dynamically, when readers interact with them.

These assumptions are unobjectionable as they go. What they leave out, however, is that through representational design, skilled writers have always had the ability to simulate two-way interactivity. Through anticipation of a reader's responses, a writer can design a text to simulate a text's responding, and so changing itself in mid-course, to a reader's anticipated interaction. The reader, at a certain passage, thinks to herself "Well, okay, but what about this or what about that?" The writer anticipates this reader response at composing time and inserts it into the linear flow. This is text design with two-way interactivity in mind, with the writer anticipating the responses of an interactive partner in absentia.

Learning to discriminate and align the reader's horizon of the familiar and unfamiliar is the pathway for simulating this two-way interactivity. With each new clause and sentence produced, the writer must appeal to her mental image of the reader to continue to ascertain: "What questions does the reader likely bring at this moment of interaction?" and "Given these questions, what is an effective way for the text to continue to remain timely and responsive?" The design of the text is driven forward by the writer's internal responses to these questions. The interactivity of the text, by design, adapts to the reader's learning purpose, allows the reader to see her internal questions externally addressed in the linear flow.

To give writers in our studio immersed practice in information writing, we rely on not one but two prototypes: exposition and popular explanation. Two prototypes are required because information writing can take place under two diametrically opposed contextual assumptions and we need a special prototype for each assumption.

Exposition has writers develop unfamiliar information in anticipation of a reader's wanting to acquire new generalizations in the context of the familiar. Exposition supports generalization learning. Popular explanation has writers develop familiar information in anticipation of a reader's wanting to acquire familiar experience in the context of a subject matter considered impenetrable. Popular explanation supports experiential learning.

To further illustrate the difference between exposition and popular exposition, let us map them as opposite poles. On one pole, the reader has been anticipated to find 100% of the information in a text familiar and 0% unfamiliar. This predicts a text that is so familiar that it will be perceived not worth reading. At the other extreme, the anticipated reader will find 100% of the information unfamiliar and 0% familiar. This predicts a text that will seem too inaccessible to read.

Skilled writers contextually activate exposition when they anticipate a reader closer to the familiarity pole. An information hierarchy giving prominence to elements of the unfamiliar is crucial in this context. Information that is new and unfamiliar is the target and focus and so positioned prominently in the information hierarchy. The new information is featured in titles, headings, and topic sentences in order to ease the reader's search for it. Information that is familiar and needed as background context for the new information is positioned less prominently in the hierarchy. Exposition lets the reader learn by imparting through the clarity of the hierarchy the unfamiliar generalizations that are the targets of the reader's learning.

Skilled writers contextually activate popular explanation when they anticipate a reader closer to the unfamiliarity pole. The writer is challenged to furnish a text that is, contrary to the reader's worst expectation, accessible. Unlike exposition, featuring the unfamiliar is neither the problem nor the point in popular explanation. The reader, after all, is already anticipated to feel overwhelmed by unfamiliarity. The writer must feature familiarity as a dominant element, must come across as a humane and patient guide encouraging the reader through. Popular explanation makes use of familiarizing elements in the service of giving the reader the experience of the subject matter without the technical generalizations that literally define it. These familiarizing elements are crafted through literary devices such as resemblance, analogy, metaphors, visual imagery, narrative, thought experiments and, in general, any renderings of experience that are close to the reader's access. The unfamiliar technical matter is stripped of its technical context and swaddled in the elements of the familiar. Popular explanations impart to readers the motivation to learn without trying to impart, or expecting the reader to achieve, technical mastery.

Exposition and popular explanation are not mutually exclusive genres. They are rather different prototypes from which to navigate a reader through an information space. They live in harmony within many natural genres of information. Whenever a writer informs a reader, both prototypes are serviceable for developing the text. One or both prototypes may remain in control for short or long stretches of the composing action. Control can shift, moreover, with variations in the subject and reader represented. When writers engage in information writing, therefore, they often blend expositional and popular explanation without knowing in advance how the blends will work. Our own studio practice is to ask students to "teach" a reader and let the writer's own path establish where on the dimensions of exposition and popular explanation it falls.

Although exposition and popular explanation are tightly linked prototypes in the practice of information writing, they are still analytically distinct. We have found from experience that students continue to collapse them if they are not first made to master them on their own terms. In our studio, we have found it best to discuss them on their own terms, as if they were intact genres, before considering the empirical reality of their living as prototypes in blended representations. We follow that practice here.

Exposition: Conveying Unfamiliarity in the Context of Familiarity

In exposition, the writer anticipates a reader who will find the subject familiar and who must be convinced there is enough unfamiliar to justify a reading commitment. What follows is a template for the expositional prototype were it to dominate, genre-like, the local action of a text from start to finish:

Introduction: Exposition
Attention Getter
Introduction of Topic
Motivation to Learn It
Stereotypic Views (Held by Readers)
How You Will Elaborate Stereotypic View
Division Into Points

Body: Exposition
Point 1
Point 2
Point 3

Conclusion:
Rehearse the Learning (Generalizations) That Has Been Offered
Tell the Reader How This Learning is Empowering
Tell the Reader About What Remains to Be Learned (and Further
    Reading and Experience on Which It Is Based)

In the introduction, the writer puts on the table what, if anything, the reader stereotypically knows about the subject. The writer tries to be general and inclusive to catch as many readers at the gate before the learning tour departs. The writer also uses the introduction to call attention to the new generalizations to be presented and how learning about them will be arranged through the text. The writer then proceeds (in the body) to impart these new generalizations from the information the reader already finds familiar. The information hierarchy plays a crucial role in helping readers discern the writer's best guess about how prior and new information sorts out for them. In the conclusion, the writer overviews the learning that she anticipates will have taken place if all goes well.

Like all our writing assignments, stating the representational challenge of exposition proves easier than meeting it on a first draft. It is thus relevant to review some first draft efforts and how they go awry.

Exposition That Collapses Into an Expert Journal: The Cost of Leaving Out the Reader's Perspective

A common confusion among information writers is to mistake information writing based in assumptions of representational composition—that is, creating an interactive world of text-based learning designed for a reader—with the psychological activity of retrieving information from memory or external sources. Writers embarking on exposition, searching for new things to say, understandably put top priority on searching, sifting, and recording on paper the information they believe a reader will find unfamiliar and interesting. These activities are cognitively preparatory to meeting the representational challenge of exposition. By themselves, they do not meet the challenge. Many students, furthermore, confuse the two activities. They dump generalizations on the page that are unfamiliar to readers and mistakenly think they are done. The result is to overwhelm and lose rather than enlighten their readers. The text functions as an expert's journal rather than a crafted vehicle to support the reader's learning.

Even when students do not mistake the expert journal for the exposition, moreover, virtually every first draft exposition resembles an expert journal. The information writer so invests in the cognitive effort of getting ideas on the page in a first draft that exposition barely has a chance to surface. The result, even for seasoned writers, is first drafts that leave out a satisfying interactive experience for the reader. Seasoned writers of exposition simply know that their first drafts are not their last.

Consider Andrew's first draft exposition. He wanted his readers to learn the history and influence of photography on the visual arts, how computers can be used to create deliberate photographic distortion, that photographers can make accidental distortions, and that photographs are never purely objective in any case. In his first draft, however, he leaves the reader in the dust with his skips from one to another topic. He starts by discussing deliberate photographic distortion through computer enhancement.

> The Simpson trial focused the entire nation on one media event, the trial of one man. Every news organization in the nation had to cover the trial, from the New York Times to the National Enquirer, or suffer the wrath of irate consumers yearning for their daily dose of courtroom drama. As part of their coverage of Simpson's arrest, Newsweek ran a cover featuring his mugshot. The mugshot had been darkened visibly, and controversy soon embroiled Newsweek about their choice to alter the image. The outrage that came afterwards focused on the perceived alteration of the image, but not on the process of the alteration.

He then shifts the topic to the idea of photographs as objective representations.

> Computer alteration of photographs became a bogeyman of the moment; people questioned whether they would ever be able to trust the rational truth of photojournalism again. In the wake of the mugshot though, while the death of objective photojournalism was being discussed, no one questioned whether it had ever been possible for photography to be objective. A cover story in Wired highlighted the problems, and questioned whether objectivity as a journalistic ideal was obsolete. Wired digitally altered a photo of O.J. Simpson, for a cover image, to make him look like he was white, right down to his straight blond hair. The article that the graphic accompanied questioned whether objectivity should be considered obsolete and if it had ever been a realistic goal.

He next moves to the effects of photography on the other arts of representation.

> Photography is a representational field. It captures the world in detail and allows it to be infinitely reproducible and preservable. After the advent of photography, it became possible for art to become a less

representational medium, and evolve into a form that is more abstract. While the camera was seen as the arbiter of absolute truth, it was soon shown that the photography was just as open to interpretation as any other form of expression. While the camera does capture a reasonably accurate representation of the real world, it is still a representation of the world, not the imperative truth.

He then turns to noncomputer distortions that arise in the normal course of photography.

Images captured by a camera have always been open to manipulation, so the ability of a computer to alter a photo is really a non-issue. Numerous distortions occur regularly, in addition to alterations that can be induced with the aid of digital processes.

And then classifies the routine distortions of the camera:

Many of the distortions that occur regularly are well known. Most casual photographers are familiar with red eye, which results from the retina not being adapted to flashes of bright light. To solve this problem a special flash sequence has been developed, consisting of a quick succession of small flashes that force the retina to shrink, eliminating the red eye effect from the resulting photo. In black and white, a photographer can also use a flash to turn day into night. When a flash is used on a person standing outside during the day, the sky will be exposed as black. The flash will define the person in the foreground, and the resulting image will appear to have been shot at night.

An easy way to change a photograph is to use a filter. You just pop it onto the lens, and you have effectively altered the reality that the camera will capture. Colored filters have straightforward effects. They add a tint to the negative or slide. Not all filters have such obvious effects though, such as polarizing filters. A polarizing filter can screen out excess light in a subtle way that would not necessarily be noticed by a casual reader. For instance, a polarizing filter can eliminate reflective glare from glass, allowing the photographer to get a clear shot at the interior of the window. The same filter can be used to reduce the intensity of very bright light sources, like the sun.

The type of lens can make an extreme difference. The various types of lenses will portray the same scene very differently, yet they are all photographs of the same scene. For instance, long focus lenses, now normally called telephoto lenses because they have been compressed into smaller size lenses, were originally called portrait lenses. They were called portrait lenses because they actually portray the human face with the correct proportions.

On the other hand, short lenses do not present the proper image. To fill the frame, when using a short lens, the photographer has to get very close to the subject. In addition to making the subject uncomfortable by penetrating their private space, it also portrays them improperly. At a close distance, the proportional distance from the lens to the subject's nose, and the distance to the subject's hairline and ears are very different. Consequently, using a short lens for portraiture causes the subject's hairline and ears to visibly recede, while their nose looms forward. This effect is not very pronounced with lenses of 50 mm and above, but anything shorter can induce cartoonish dimensions on the subject.

In the darkroom, the captured reality of the camera is developed and created in print form. After developing, which can effect the reality of the photo in many ways, the photograph must be printed. Most printing is automated these days, allowing the miraculous one-hour turn around that consumers value so highly.

A photograph can be altered through carelessness. Black and white photos are often exposed irregularly, as light sources can vary widely across the image. Consequently, it is often necessary to expose the paper with different levels of light to bring out detail that would be otherwise washed out in black or white. This is a process called dodging and burning. You dodge the area of the paper that you do not wish to be exposed anymore, at the same time allowing lighter areas of the negative to burn sharper detail into the paper.

I am not familiar with the particulars of developing and printing color photos, but I am aware of the limitations of color regarding exposure. Color is a fickle medium, much more so than black and white, and does not forgive little errors. In black and white, you can overexpose or underexpose by a few stops and still be able to get some type of usable image out of the negative. A color slide exposed incorrectly by more than a stop will be too dark or too light for use.

A key point in understanding the important aspects of exposure is the difference between the your eye and the camera. The camera needs much more light to see, and does not posses the ability to see across a wide range of light levels at the same time that the human eye possesses.

For instance, color film requires very specific settings for correct exposure, yet the human eye can see color across scenes of extreme light intensity.

After the film is developed and printed, then there is one final important alteration left, cropping the picture. When a picture is cropped, it is generally to add emphasis to the central object of the image, and cropping is usually done by removing parts of the image that are considered extraneous. Generally this does improve the image, focusing the power of the image. More importantly though, it can affect the meaning that a reader will extrapolate from the image.

Context is an important factor in your understanding of the image. While many images can stand alone, they do not appear that way in print; there is always text complementing the picture, and vice versa. The text will alter the meaning of the image, and the image will alter the meaning of the text.

In a recent Newsweek, which featured a cover story about the 1996 Republican primaries, a letter to the editor criticized the photos used in an article about Bob Dole. The writer believed that the black and white photography that complemented the article presented a false image of Dole. Black and white is very effective for capturing the texture of a subject, and the writer believed that the detailed wrinkles visible in the photographs portrayed Dole as a tired old man. While it is possible to dispute the energy levels of Bob Dole, he is over 70, and has the wrinkled face to prove it.

Having surveyed many sources of photographic distortion, Andrew concludes that photographic representation has never been objective.

The objectivity that people associate with photography has never really existed in my opinion, because different people will extrapolate different meanings from the same photograph. Photography is not a pure discipline, cut off or immune from the personal distortions that each person will bring to the viewing of a photograph.

Andrew's first draft is more typical than bad. The main uncertainty in whether the writer will write successful exposition is not whether she will leave the reader out on the first draft (she will) but whether she will ever reach a draft that lets the reader in? How does the writer of exposition learn to let the reader in?

There are two problems that need to be addressed to move beyond an expert journal. The first problem is *egocentric writing*. This is writing so close to the writer's idiosyncratic experience that readers cannot follow what she is talking about. The writer overcomes egocentrism by learning to recognize the symptoms of egocentric writing in a text and removing them in later drafts. The second problem is failing to take into account what the reader wants to learn. All information writing builds on an anticipation of the reader. Frequently, moreover, the writer's anticipated reader differs markedly from actual readers. The writer solves this second problem by testing drafts on actual readers to bring the responses anticipated in the text closer to the interests of actual readers. In the following sections, we explore these two problems and solutions to them in greater detail.

Identifying and Removing the Symptoms of Egocentric Writing

If the writer can identify her own egocentric writing, she can remove it, and remove an important barrier for the reader. We review three symptoms of egocentric writing that we tell our studio writers to be on watch for in early drafts.

First, egocentric writing tends to have immediacy. This is immediacy in the sense of Aaron's self-portrait (see chap. 2), where the writer is caught in a swelter of thought, not sure what will come next, and unable to take a distance on the ideas that is needed to make them comprehensible to others, if not oneself. Writing that is immediate sounds more spontaneous than planned, seems, like Aaron, to be expressing the idea at the same time it pops in his head. Such writing holds together through local association more than through an overall lesson plan for the reader. Note how Andrew's first draft language, because of the abruptly shifting topics, has a stream of consciousness feel.

> Images captured by a camera have always been open to manipulation. So the ability of a computer to alter a photo is really a non-issue. Numerous distortions occur regularly, in addition to alterations that can be induced with the aid of digital processes. Many of the distortions that occur regularly are well known. Most casual photographers are familiar with red eye, which results from the retina not being adapted to flashes of bright light.

Even though the topic sentence promises to stay with distortions that are "open to manipulation," Andrew transits in rapid association from deliberate to non-deliberate distortion (e.g., red eye). The writing shows an air of immediacy, changing course in midstream. While we have seen the appropriateness of immediacy in capturing suspense, scenes, and vivid memories, immediacy is a muted element in skilled information writing. The focus of such writing is not the writer, but the stable concepts developed for the reader's guided learning. The elements of emphasis need to seem sturdy and fixed in a well-structured hierarchy, not something the writer is making up as she goes. Done without care, immediacy can undercut the reader's expectation of a text that has been carefully designed to support stable learning.

Second, egocentric writing tends to be organized as islands of compressed information, lacking the summaries or transitions that creates a linguistic roadmap through an experience of guided learning. When the writer knows a subject very well, her knowledge is compressed like a ball of yarn. Readers get lost in such an intricate structure. They require simple lines to follow as they learn. To communicate with a reader, the writer needs to string out that ball of yarn into a single thread. First drafts seldom archive this singularity of movement, resulting in writing like the following:

> On the other hand, short lenses do not present the proper image. To fill the frame, when using a short lens, the photographer has to get very close to the subject. In addition to making the subject uncomfortable by penetrating their private space, it also portrays them improperly. At a close distance, the proportional distance from the lens to the subject's nose, and the distance to the subject's hairline and ears are very different. Consequently, using a short lens for portraiture causes the subject's hairline and ears to visibly recede, while their nose looms forward. This effect is not very pronounced with lenses of 50 mm and above, but anything shorter can induce cartoonish dimensions on the subject.

Andrew raises and drops technical concepts like the length of a lens (short, long) and proportional distance without defining them. The ideas are compressed islands of meaning rather than strings unfolding under the momentum of the reader's curiosity.

Third, egocentric writing is isolated from purposes and motivations. Readers are likely to ask, "So what? Why is this important? When would I ever run across this? What is the danger of not knowing this?" In information writing, the writer's ongoing transaction with the reader is the top-level element, dominating the various elements involving the inner world of the writing. The purposes and motivations of the writing are part of this dominant transactional layer. When these transactional elements disappear from visibly dominant positions, the reader feels that he is trapped in the writer's experiences rather than able to tie those experiences to overarching goals of learning.

In Andrew's first draft, we are left to guess why the concepts matter and how they relate to the things we already know. We do not quite understand what he thinks he is teaching and what he thinks his readers are supposed to be learning. When writers know their subjects well and have a focused learning purpose for readers, they will have ready answers to the reader's questions of significance. Yet, they will often need feedback on a first draft to know that the draft has failed to make their answers to these questions as explicit as readers require.

In sum, egocentric writing carries the feel of immediacy, compression, and diffuseness of purpose. This makes for an unsatisfying learning experience for the reader.

How much better can the writer do? Let us watch the improvement in Lois' drafts as she discovers and rids her drafts of egocentric writing. A practicing graphic designer, Lois had a long-standing knowledge about the recycling of commercial paper. She wrote on the Environmental Protection Agency's (EPA) misleading policy on recyclable paper, a topic she perceived to be unfamiliar and of interest to her reader. Lois had an appropriate subject for exposition. Nonetheless, her first draft so deeply tangled itself in her expert experience that readers couldn't find a way in.

> Paper with post consumer waste often has interesting fiber variations that give the paper a unique look. It's become so popular that virgin paper is now manufactured to simulate the look and feel of the recycled sheets. They do this because they can have a tighter control on the uniform look and quality of the finished sheet. Don't assume that seeing different colored fibers floating through a sheet of paper indicates that it has a bit of grandma's old recipe cards in the mix.

In her first draft, Lois did not integrate the roles of person and expert. Her role identities oscillated between layperson and expert, with no overlap between them. She was the expert ("interesting fiber variations") when she wanted to move ahead and hold her authority. She was the ordinary human being ("grandma's old recipe cards") when she wanted to give readers a sense of inclusion. Both local actions are well-considered, but in her first draft they are not integrated. The result is a jerkiness in role-shifting that keeps Lois' role as writer and ours as readers unstable and uncomfortable.

To reach her intended reader, Lois realized she would need to remove much of the egocentric writing. In her second draft, she adds a title and begins with an experience that is familiar to any reader who has ever worked in an office.

PAPER BLUES

I share office space with seven other people. Like me, they can often be found printing out drafts of work in progress on a shared laser printer. And while working off the printed piece can often be the only way to make a better revision, by the end of each month, we produce enough paper waste to bury a small child. I know this because our method of recycling this paper is so inefficient. Unlike other offices on the first floor that have custodians to dispose of this by-product, our office, on the third floor, has been left out of that loop. We wait until the mountain becomes an inconvenient office mate before one of us takes the mountain to Mohammed—the recycling bins downstairs.

One need not be a graphic designer to have experienced the explosion of paper in an office and the vague promise that recycling is a good thing to do. One also need not be fascinated with the subject of paper to be curious about how (or if) recycling really works:

Continually looking at this pile of paper has made me think more seriously about the issues of paper manufacturing and recycling. I wonder how much most of us really know about this process and the affect our ignorance may have on the quality of our lives.

Although readers may share Lois' curiosity, few are likely to have the knowledge to act on it. Lois creates an opening for an expert—herself. She shifts roles, from a curious office dweller, like any one of us, to an expert on paper who can provide specific information that we now want to know. By indicating that our current use of paper perpetuates a "toxic legacy," Lois implies that we pay a huge price for our ignorance and that reading what she has to say can help lower it.

As a designer of visual communication, I have always found paper an important decision for me. Choosing the textures, weights, coatings, colors, and archival quality of the stock is a time consuming process but also a labor of love. Unfortunately, each time I use a sheet of paper as it is now manufactured, I continue a toxic legacy that most of us are largely unaware of.

In the first draft, Lois conveyed that she was angry with the EPA but she had overlooked teaching her readers what they needed to know to grasp, much less share, her anger. Her later draft helps us grasp the context of the recycling problem and so allows us to share her emotional reaction.

> There are other ways that consumers can be fooled into believing that we are doing something good for our environment when we are not. Again, the Environmental Protection Agency can be held responsible. When the EPA established their guidelines, they also designed two versions of the recycled logo. In one version, the logo prints as an outline only, and in the other, the logo reverses out of a dark circular field. Most of us don't know that the two versions are used for different purposes. An outline logo indicates that the paper isn't recycled, but could be. It's a deceiving mark because, in this area at least, we are largely an uneducated public. Most paper can be recycled. The exceptions include foil stamped paper, laminated sheets, and envelopes with glassine windows. Heavy ink coverage also makes recycling difficult.
>
> Until the public understands the meaning of the outline logo, its value lies mainly in public relations strategies for paper companies, not in consumer awareness.

Removing egocentric writing from early drafts integrates the writer's expert perspective with the needs of the reader, creating the impression of the author as a literate expert. The literate expert comes across as both an expert and a human being, one who has learned how to stay ahead of readers without leaving them behind. The effect is to create an expert guide who shares the reader's surprise and sense of wonder at the twists and turns of the text—as if the text were just the experience of the writer and reader exploring the subject matter together on equal terms. The literate expert is well illustrated in Lois' final paragraph.

> Back in my office, the paper mound grows and even on this small scale, its size alarms me. But it's not just the amount that we use that is troublesome. We need to be aware of all the consequences caused by our obsession with paper. Even if every scrap found its way back to the paper mill, we'd still need to know about the related issues of manufacturing and printing in order to make responsible choices and changes.

By the time we reach this point in her text, Lois' voice seems, if anything, slow-witted. Many studio readers reported thinking they had beaten her to her own conclusion, paragraphs before. Yet, it was of course Lois who cultivated this level of reader comfort by playing to her reader's curiosity.

Testing to Include the Reader's Perspective

Eliminating egocentric writing makes the writer's ideas more comprehensible. Comprehensibility, however, is not a guarantee of success or effectiveness. The writer can share ideas with readers without connecting with them, without capturing and responding to the questions that they find important to address. Removing egocentrism is a sign that the writer has begun to solve the discrimination challenge, sorting the familiar from the unfamiliar. However, it is not yet a sign that the writer has solved the alignment challenge, has learned to juxtapose the unfamiliar elements that readers *want to know* with the familiar elements that move them there. A second problem can thus arise if writers are understandable without also being adaptive and responsive to their readers primary concerns and interests in a subject.

Jack's early draft problem was not so much egocentric writing, but writing that failed to be adaptive. Jack worked at a university creating class schedules for students. His exposition was intended to explain the process.

> After the Schedule of Classes is distributed every semester, I get a bunch of negative feedback. I directly control some of it, like concerns about font size or type choice. The rest, most of which has more to do with the information contained in the Schedule, has little to do with me because the Schedule is a collaborative effort between the Office of the Registrar and the academic Deans and departments. I (part of the Office of the Registrar) write and format the book. The Deans and departments provide the course information.

Jack goes on to describe all the problems that, from his perspective, make assembling the course schedule a difficult issue.

> Traditionally, the biggest concern is the lack of professors listed, denoted by TBA (To Be Announced). Often several hundred courses have the professor listed as TBA. Some students joke about the overworked "Professor TBA." Students are angry that they don't know who's teaching

a course, but the reason why is simple: when the Schedule is printed, departments haven't decided who's teaching what.

The second biggest concern is the number of changes made to courses (e.g., time, days, and professor) after the Schedule is printed. Students have to depend on correction lists that departments post inside their office or that the Office of the Registrar posts to its Andrew bboard, official.registrar-info. The reason, again, is that when the Schedule is printed, departments don't have a permanent schedule.

But it's not the departments' collective fault: they are ruled by the Schedule's production deadline. The Schedule has traditionally been timed so that it appeared on campus one month before registration week. This time is supposed to allow students to meet with their advisors. The downside is that the sooner the Schedule is printed, the less time departments have to plan offerings for the upcoming semester. In the case of fall classes, departments are planning for courses that won't be taught for five months.

In recent semesters, the one-month has been cut to three weeks in order to allow departments a little more time to plan things. But unless Registration Week is moved much closer to the beginning of the next semester (for example, in the beginning of August for the fall semester), or departments are locked into their choices, the printed Schedule will always end up out-of-date. The creation of the World Wide Web Schedule, which is updated weekly, has helped to eliminate this, but there is no way to inform students if a course they have registered for has changed or to compare the original printed Schedule with the up-to-date Web schedule.

Jack then highlights two recent changes in how the schedule is handled and he describes why, from his perspective, these changes were made.

There are two recent (within the last two years) concerns, which aren't related to the timeframe of the printed Schedule. The first is the removal of room assignments in the printed Schedule.

The Office of the Registrar decided to assign classrooms after Registration Week (which means that rooms aren't listed in the printed Schedule) because courses weren't being matched to classrooms very well. For example, a class with 5 students could often end up in a room that holds

50 students, which leaves a 50-student course without a room. By assigning classrooms after we know how many people have actually registered, instead of predicting how many would based on past semesters, class sizes have been better matched to rooms.

The downside is that students cannot plan classrooms near each other. This raised a big student outcry. We didn't know why at first: classes are designed to be 50 (or 80) minutes long so that students have 10 minutes to get to another class. And with the exception of Mellon Institute, it's less than a 10-minute walk between classrooms on campus. Then students began complaining to the Office of the Registrar that they couldn't get to classes because some professors were keeping them late. We informed departments of this problem, but we will not go back to a less efficient way of room assigning.

The second recent concern is the new distribution of the printed Schedule. In the past, we distributed boxes of Schedules to strategic points on campus: the hallways of Baker, Hamerschlag, Doherty, the CFA Dean's Office, and so on. For the last five semesters, we've mailed Schedules to undergraduates on campus, to graduate students at their department mailboxes, and told off-campus undergraduates to come to The HUB or the Office of the Registrar. We changed our distribution to prevent wasting schedules. Under the old system, we printed around 10,000 Schedules for around 5,000 students; we now print about 7,000, and the number will continue to drop each semester.

Jack thought his ideas would be valued by his intended readers (viz., students), but he turned out to be wrong. His readers could follow what he had to say perfectly well, but what he had to say was not responsive to what they were interested in learning. His readers told him that he came across too much like an officious bureaucrat, justifying a system that had caused too much anxiety for students. Jack had balanced his expert perspective with a human role, but he chose a role to which most of his readers could not relate—a person who showed no inclination to be responsive to the need of students. Taking the feedback seriously, Jack wrote a second draft to seem more responsive and sympathetic to his readers.

Don't you hate being the bearer of bad news? In my case, I'm that bearer for thousands of students each semester. I get complaints for months, usually until it's time for the next piece of bad news to come out.

This bad news is called the Schedule of Classes. If the Schedule frustrates you, you're not alone. We hear you. Unfortunately, the problems are here to stay, but we're trying to make them as painless as possible. Let me explain . . .

By labeling the schedule as "bad news," Jack adopts the perspective of his readers. He begs forgiveness and asks for time to justify himself. He then raises the questions that he knows are central to his readers.

Have you ever wondered why the Schedule of Classes has so many professors being listed as TBA? Or how much Professor TBA must get paid? The reason so many TBAs appear is that we produce the Schedule two-and-a-half to five months before the semester begins; departments just don't know which courses they're offering that early. As soon as departments inform us, we update those TBAs with real professors on our World Wide Web Schedule.

Ever notice that the Schedule is out of date pretty quickly? Which forces you to read the corrections lists taped to department walls. It's the same problem: when we produce the Schedule, departments haven't finalized what they're offering (or when). We update the Web Schedule weekly, and post changes to our Andrew bboard, official.registrar.

Jack anticipates that his readers have an obvious solution. As an adaptive response, he describes why their obvious solution is unworkable.

We can't do the obvious thing and move Registration Week closer to the beginning of the next semester. It's already as close to the end of the semester as possible without intruding on the last week of classes and finals. We can't move it between semesters because students and advisors couldn't meet. And we already tried the week before classes began. What a disaster!

Jack begins with yet another empathic question, couched in the terms (Isn't it a pain? How can you?) of his student readership.

Isn't it a pain that classrooms aren't listed in the Schedule? How can you make sure you only have to walk to Baker, not Scaife, at 8:30 in the morning? It comes down to those lists taped on the wall again. If we assign classrooms before Registration Week, like we did when we printed rooms in the Schedule, we have to make hundreds of changes afterwards. And we end up with some rooms half-empty and others crammed full. Assigning rooms after students register solves both problems. Do you have problems getting between classes? There are 10 minutes between class periods, enough to walk between any two classrooms on campus. If a professor keeps you late, let their department know.

Jack never eliminates the expert perspective. No information writing can or should. He remains the expert bureaucrat who knows all about the problems of assembling a university course schedule. However, by anticipating his reader's concerns with touches of empathic self-portraiture to show some sharing of perspectives, he was able to present the information needed in a way that was more accessible and acceptable to his readers.

Popular Explanation: Conveying Familiarity in a Context of Inaccessibility

Skilled writers activate popular explanation when they anticipate readers who expect inaccessibility rather than familiarity. In this context, there is no point stressing the unfamiliarity of the subject because readers already take that as the default. They doubt the subject can be made familiar and the writer must address this doubt.

We have noted in earlier chapters that notions like immediacy and displacement can do double duty both as assumed defaults of writing (the writing medium or context) and as representational elements in their own right. At this juncture, it is relevant to note that the same double duty applies to the notions of reader-familiar and reader-unfamiliar elements with respect to a subject matter. Both kinds of elements can be raised to the representational foreground, as active and working components of the writer's textual design. As a written prototype, we have seen how exposition brings the element of the unfamiliar (what in the text won't match the reader's prior knowledge and the reader can be made to perceive as a gap) to dominance against a default of familiarity (what the reader will find in the text that matches her prior knowledge).

In popular explanation, by contrast, it is the element of the familiar that is brought to dominance against the default of unfamiliarity and, especially, inaccessibility. As a written prototype, popular explanation features elements that readers already know, that they find familiar, and that they embrace as sources of comfortable understanding. Just as the scenic writer must feature immediacy against a muted sense of assumed displacement, the writer of popular explanation features familiarity against a muted sense of her exclusionary expertise. The reader of popular explanation knows the writer is an expert. Yet, she may know this more from the writer's credentials than from any dominant element in the written text itself. The text is less a communication of expert knowledge (like exposition) than an expert's way of allowing a novice to experience expert knowledge without the labor of actually coming to acquire it.

Below is a genre-like template of popular explanation, which shows the prototype were it to dominate the representational action of a whole text:

Introduction: Popular Explanation
Attention Getter
Introduction of Topic
Stereotypes Why Topic Has Caused Readers to Think It Inaccessible
How You Will Elaborate Topic to Make It Accessible
Division Into Experiences (Suggestive of Points)

Body: Popular Explanation
Experience 1
Experience 2
Experience 3

Conclusion:
Rehearse the Learning (Generalization-Based Experiences) That Has
    Been Offered.
Tell the Reader How This Learning is Empowering
Tell the Reader About What Remains to Be Learned (and Further Reading
    and Experience on Which It Is Based).

As with exposition, the introduction of a popular explanation must be general and inclusive to draw in as many readers as possible. Unlike exposition, what readers of popular explanation most immediately share is not so much an ignorance of the subject (though they do share that) as an apprehension about their capacity to learn it. Developing what the reader finds familiar, popular explanation addresses not the reader's learning but the reader's motivation to learn. While readers cannot become scientists solely by reading popularizations, they can, even through a single text, become motivated to support the science or even motivated to learn it on their own.

Aaron, with a background in physics, illustrates popular treatments of science when he motivates his lay reader to understand the physical principles underlying the steering of motorcycles. He knows that in a short text his reader cannot master the concepts of vectors and forces. He does know, however, that by appealing to their everyday experience and curiosity, he can, even within a short text, make these concepts comfortable and familiar. Consider the following notes Aaron wrote to his hypothetical reader about what he wanted to accomplish:

I want you [my reader] to read this and go—Wow, this is cool! I want you to start thinking about vectors and the forces acting on things around you. I can't teach vectors and forces directly but I can teach you about contexts where it affects you. For one, why don't bicycles steer like motorcycles? They both have two wheels and you lean to steer them both. But bicycles turn in the direction you turn the front wheel. And why do cars turn like they do? After all, the same forces are acting on the car. That's why, if you take a fast right-hand corner, the car tilts to the left (to the outside of the corner). Next, why do motor scooters steer like bicycles and cars, not like motorcycles, which they very closely resemble? Finally, and maybe worst of all, why can you steer a motorcycle like a bicycle up to about five miles per hour?

Aaron decided to keep his focus on the turning of motorcycles. He began by directing the readers' attention, and curiosity, to the phenomenon he was trying to explain.

THE PHYSICS OF THE MOTORCYCLE TURN

Motorcycles don't turn like cars. In a car, you turn the front tires right to turn right. On a motorcycle, you turn the front tire right to turn left. Isaac Newton explained how this is possible several hundred years before motorcycles were invented. His explanation is tricky, but very cool. If you don't ride, you need to know that you turn the front wheel of a motorcycle by pushing on the handlebars. Push the right side of the handlebars forward to turn the wheel left and the bike right; push the leftside forward to turn the front wheel right and the bike left. (The easy way to remember this is "push the side of the handlebar that matches the direction you want to go.") You also need to know that the bike actually turns because it's leaning.

Aaron now begins the physics lesson. We are introduced to concepts such as angular moment and torque.

Newton would say that motorcycles steer the way they do because their angular momentum vector wants to equal their torque vector. Then he would quickly explain—First, vectors are imaginary arrows that represent forces acting on something. If a barbell is dangling from a string, "weight" is a vector pointing down from the barbell caused by gravity. "Angular momentum" is a vector caused by something spinning, like wheels. "Torque" is a vector caused by something twisting, like handlebars.

Aaron introduces us to a personal experience that provides an alternative, less abstract representation, of these concepts. He asks us to conduct experiments with our own hands to enact in the concrete what he is talking about in the abstract.

Second, to make sense of vectors, we need the right-hand rule. The right-hand rule allows you to use the your right hand to "see" vectors. To use the rule correctly, lay your right palm flat on a table and make a backward L with your thumb and first finger. When your fingers imitate motion (for example, your fingers pointing forward when a motorcycle is moving forward), your thumb will imitate a vector created by that motion.

Aaron provides instructions to guide us, but unlike conventional instruction (see chap. 6), the movements he directs readers to make are not the primary end of the text. They are provided only to help us experience difficult concepts firsthand. Having instructed us on the correct position of our right hand to stand in for a physical model of motion and forces, he now encourages us to apply the concepts he is describing.

To see the vectors, you have to pretend you're on a motorcycle. So sit back, make "vroom-vroom" noises, and we'll hit the road. Since your motorcycle is going forward, the wheels are spinning. As I mentioned above, spinning wheels create angular momentum. To see angular momentum, use the right-hand rule. Put your right hand on top of the front wheel; your fingers curve down because the tire moves forward and down (remember, your fingers imitate motion). Your thumb now points left. Therefore, when a motorcycle is traveling forward, angular momentum points left from the wheels.

Next, let's turn right. Put your hands on the handlebars, rev the engine a few times for good effect, and push the right side of the handlebar forward. To turn, push the side of the handlebar that matches the direction you want to go, right. Seen from above, this push twists the handlebars counterclockwise. As I mentioned above, a handlebar twisting creates torque. To see torque, use the right-hand rule. Put your right hand on top of the imaginary handlebars, holding your hand like you're about to shake hands. Curl your fingers towards your palm; your fingers imitate the counterclockwise twisting. Your thumb now points up. Therefore, when the right side of the handlebars is pushed forward, torque points up from the handlebars.

Newton said that angular momentum always wants to equal torque. So, angular momentum at the wheels wants to move towards torque at the handlebars. But since the motorcycle can't bend, it does the next best thing; it leans in the direction angular momentum wants to go, up and over to the right. And since motorcycles turn by leaning, the motorcycle turns right.

To turn left, you push the left side of the handlebars forward, which twists the handlebars clockwise and makes torque point down. (You'll have to shake hands upside down to see it since your fingers won't bend backwards.) And since angular momentum always wants to equal torque, angular momentum will move down, which makes the motorcycle lean (and turn) left.

As Newton would say, that's why motorcycles turn like they do.

Aaron reduces the conceptual distance of his subject matter by turning it into experiences that the reader can physically enact. This allows him to create in his readers the feeling of familiarity even if they fail to grasp the technical details.

Lauren, a student intern in a robotics lab, draws from interviews with designers to explain Nomad, a robot designed for travel on Mars. Lauren tells us that the designers of Nomad chose to use a panospheric camera, which scans a scene at 360 degrees. Although the optics of a panospheric camera are unlikely to be familiar to her readers, Lauren shows us that the basic principles involved are no farther than our morning cereal.

The panospheric works differently from the cameras that we use when taking pictures of family and friends. Instead of pointing the camera at the object we want to see, the camera on Nomad is pointed upwards at a ball-shaped mirror. However, the reflection in the mirror gives a very warped view of the world around Nomad, which has to be de-warped. Actually, you keep a kind of panospheric camera in your own home—a spoon. If you look at the back of the spoon you'll be able to see all around, even though the image may be distorted.

Nomad judges the distance of an upcoming object by sending out pulses of light and calculating how long it takes for the light to return. If this sounds like an exotic way to judge distance, Lauren offers an analogy to convince us that this algorithm has been available for our notice from the time that we first threw a ball against a wall.

> Even if you don't have a laser you can test how the laser range finder works. First, get a tennis ball. Go outside, stand about five feet away from a wall and throw the ball towards it. What happens? If you experiment with different distances, you'll see that the further you are away from the wall, the longer it takes for the ball to return.
>
> Nomad uses two systems of antennae to relay information back to the scientists who control it: Omni-directional and actively pointed antennae. The distinctions between the two may seem difficult, but not if the reader knows the difference between sprinklers and water slides.
>
> An omni-directional antenna broadcasts in all directions, outward from the antenna. Thus, only one part of the signal reaches the receiver. The rest is just sent out into space. The concept is easy to understand if you use the idea of a twirling sprinkler as an example. This type of sprinkler sends water spraying in many different directions so it can cover a large area of grass. Up until Nomad, while a field robot was moving, it could only use an omni-directional antenna. While this isn't the optimal method of transmitting information, it sufficed for previous field robots because they weren't sending back panospheric images.
>
> However, to send back the millions of bits that the panospheric image requires, Nomad also sports a special directional or actively pointed antenna, which only broadcasts in one direction. Since it only uses power to send in the direction it wants to, it can send more information even further. Compare the actively pointed antenna to a waterslide. All of the water in the slide is falling in the same direction, so the stream of water is larger and stronger. As Nomad travels over bumps and rocks, its antenna stays precisely pointed to the receiver. This allows for the stronger signal, which is needed to transmit images from the panospheric camera.

Popular explanation makes the unfamiliar familiar by stripping it out of information hierarchies and inserting it within the reader's familiar experience. It pulls in the opposite direction of exposition, which moves the familiar *into* information hierarchies so that the familiar can guide the learning of the unfamiliar.

Blending Experiential and Generalization Learning

Thus far, we have gone over examples of exposition and popular explanation that are artificially isolated. These prototypes are frequently blended when writers can anticipate readers' oscillating between feeling both the impatience of the familiar and the remoteness of the unfamiliar. In these contexts, writers intermix prototypes opportunistically, developing unfamiliar generalizations when they anticipate the reader's feeling too little that is new; developing familiar experience when they anticipate the reader feeling too little that is accessible. The blends appear in various patterns but the most common pattern involves suspending (often early in the text) the writer's expertise. The writer delays generalization learning in favor of a friendly experiential learning that provides concrete examples of the generalizations to come. The experience of familiarity in this role does not substitute for generalization but serves as a foundation for it.

Peter uses the subjective experience of reading poetry to teach various technical concepts of poetry. He first confronts the reader with some stereotypes about poetry.

POETRY

What do you think of when you hear the word 'poetry'? Song lyrics? Rhyming, flowery language? Hallmark cards? Unfortunately, this is the very image many people have. The general notion of poetry as sugary language that rhymes is about as accurate as music being violin instrumentals of Barry Manilow's greatest hits. Not that there's anything necessarily wrong with favoring Hallmark cards and Barry Manilow violins; it's just that there's so much more to poetry, and music, than these select examples.

He then moves to an abstract definition.

At the core of poetry is the attempt succinctly and meaningfully to communicate the essence of an idea, experience, or expression according to the mind of a single individual. The medium used to communicate these meanings is words. While some forms of poetry might intrigue you more than others, for the uninitiated, it makes sense to start with the basics: formal or traditional verse. Though much modern day poetry often varies considerably from traditional forms, even the most esoteric contemporary poems use elements derived from traditional means. Therefore, in

order to meaningfully understand what is involved in writing poetry, it is
seems sensible to start with traditional, formal verse.

Peter now turns to an example. Rather than continuing to lay out
poetry in expository fashion, point-for-point, he leads us through the
experience of reading a poem, moment-to-moment.

So, without further adieu, I present you with the following poem by Leon
Stokesbury:

Luck is something I do not understand:
There were a lot of things I almost did Last night.
I almost went to hear a band Down at The Swinging Door.
I, almost, hid Out in my room all night and read a book,
the Sot-Weed Factor,
that I'd read before;
Almost, I drank a pint of Sunny Brook
I'd bought at the Dickson Street Liquor Store.
Instead I went to the Restaurant-On-The-Corner,
And tried to write, and did drink a beer or two.
Then coming back from getting rid of the beer,
I suddenly found I was looking straight at you.
Five months, my love, since I last touched your hand.
Luck is something I do not understand.

Finished reading? Great! First, let's define what the overall structure of a
traditional poem involves. A title is fairly obvious, and isn't worth redefin-
ing. What comes below the title is the body of the poem.

Notice the interactivity of this last paragraph. Peter offers himself as
our reading coach. His words become immediate with us and, like the
physical instructions of Aaron's explanation, Peter becomes our guide
through an interactive demonstration.

Take a look at the poem again. What did you notice first? For one thing,
the title and the body don't seem to match. The title sounds like medieval
or old-English prose while the body has a contemporary feel to it.
However, the subject matter in the title and the body do seem to match—
both are dealing with the general notion of human loss, desire and
remembrance. Also, there is another reason for the title sounding the
way it does. This particular poem has a specific form that is called an
English Sonnet. (This might be considered an acknowledgment of the old

form of the poem—Elizabethan—while respecting the content of the subject matter.)

Think of the form of a poem as a piece of writing that conforms to a number of rules and regulations. For a poem to be an English Sonnet, it must meet the following conditions:

Peter now offers a technical definition to help us distill our experience into a more focused understanding.

English Sonnet: A fourteen-line poem composed of three Sicilian quatrains and one heroic couplet written in iambic pentameter measures. It has a rhyme scheme of abab cdcd efef gg. Also called the Elizabethan or Shakespearean sonnet.

This definition, like much of the generalization used in exposition, is hard to grasp in the abstract, so Peter encourages us to return to our experience of the text to make better sense of it.

This is a lot easier to understand than it sounds. First of all, a sonnet is a fourteen-line poem consisting of seven couplets. Well, the fourteen-line part is easy enough. Counting each line of text reveals 14 lines. What about a couplet? A couplet is basically two lines of text within a poem whose end words rhyme. For example, going back to the model poem, the end words in the first and third lines rhyme with "band" and "understand." (It's subtle how the rhyming words work in this poem. In a sense, they aren't that noticeable unless you look for them.)

Peter points out things to us incidentally, while we are in the midst of looking at rhyming words.

As long as you're looking at rhyming words, consider the rhyme scheme. Basically, a rhyme scheme is how all the end rhymes in a poem are organized. By end rhymes I'm simply referring to the word at the end of each line that rhymes with another word at the end of another line. Thus, in the first four lines we have "understand," "did," "band," and "hid." Rhyme scheme assigns a letter to each of the end rhymes in the order that they appear. So, the corresponding rhyme scheme would be a - "understand," b -did," a - "band," b -hid."

Building on our new experience as readers, Peter helps us develop more abstract understandings of couplet, rhyme scheme, sonnet, quatrain, scansion, and iambic pentameter.

O.K. 14 lines, seven couplets, and a specific rhyme scheme. That's pretty straight forward, isn't it? Going back to the definition an English Sonnet, it appears there are Sicilian quatrains and a heroic couplet. A quatrain is any four-line stanza (or poem) that has a specific rhyme scheme. A Sicilian quatrain is a quatrain that rhymes abab and is written in iambic pentameter. Iambic pentameter? This is a type of scansion—a term that refers to the organization and number of accented and unaccented syllables for all the lines in a poem. "Iambic" refers to how the syllables in each word are stressed. An iambic word has its first syllable stressed and the second syllable unstressed. Pentameter refers to the number of iambic syllables per line.

Once again, Peter moves back to the context of our reading experience to help us see the patterns of stress that are needed for pentameter.

Look at it this way, most words or phrases you say are one part stressed, one part unstressed. For example you could say the words 'red book' as stressed 'red' and unstressed 'book' REDbook, emphasizing the red over book. Or you could do the opposite and emphasize book, redBOOK. In formal verse, or traditional, poetry the way a poem reads on a page, or sounds being read aloud, is largely dependent on organization and arrangement of the syllables for each line within a poem. Thus, iambic pentameter would be a poem with each line consisting of five (pentameter) pairings of unstressed then stressed syllables.

Peter also offers the following to help readers understand couplet:

A couplet is just two lines of text whose end words rhyme with each other. Take that fact and combine it with the aforementioned notion of iambic pentameter and you get a Heroic couplet. Two rhyming lines of iambic pentameter mean you have a Heroic couplet. There you have it. You now know what is technically involved in writing an English Sonnet. It has fourteen lines composed of three Sicilian quatrains and one heroic couplet written in iambic pentameter measures. The rhyme scheme is abab cdcd efef gg.

Yet, ultimately, he helps his readers appreciate poetry. "Next time you encounter poetry, consider what goes into the making of it. So many thoughts, so much work, for so few good words." Peter teaches technical generalizations by having us see, hear, and feel. Experience learning is used to reinforce and teach concept learning.

Susan, a visual designer, also puts experiential learning in the service of generalization learning. She teaches us sophisticated seeing by having us study a Vermeer painting (Fig. 5.1).

Vermeer, View of Delft, and the Jimmy Durante Effect: Understanding Three Aspects of Composition

Last January, I made an early morning pilgrimage to the National Gallery in Washington, D.C. to see an exhibition of Johannes Vermeer's painting. This event marked the first time the public could see an almost complete collection of his work. Vermeer was a seventeenth century Dutch painter who is known for the compelling way that he could portray ordinary daylight. He also carefully considered the way objects illuminated by that light should be composed on the canvas for maximal effect. Because little is known about the artist or how he viewed his own work, professional art historians offer these claims as the result of studying the paintings themselves.

Susan paints the scene of the hot ticket the Vermeer exhibition has proven to be. This writing sets the stage for the experience to come.

On that sub-zero morning, thousands of other crusaders lined up and waited to view the Dutch painter's masterpieces. The line curved around the National Gallery and back on itself. We waited at least two hours for the doors of the gallery to open, and more than that before we knew if we would get tickets. We finally arrived at the door, unsure if we would make it inside. We inched up the stairs to the second floor, worried. When we finally arrived at the ticket booth it was still morning, though we wouldn't be able to enter the show until 4:00pm. Given that late hour and the length of the line that was behind us, we knew that thousands of people would be turned away.

Now, only inches away from the master, Susan reflects on what she, a visual expert, can see in the composition of the painting that her many nonexpert readers cannot see so precisely.

But for us, Girl with a Pearl Earring, The Little Street, and View of Delft were just a few hours away. Being in the presence of the master—nose 3 inches from the canvas to see the paint; then a foot away to view the

FIG. 5.1. JAN VERMEER. *View of Delft*, c. 1660–1661. Oil on canvas. Approx. 38 x 45 9/16 in. Royal Cabinet of Paintings, Mauritshuis, The Hague. Reprinted with permission.

detail; now five feet to see the composition; now half-way across the room to compare one painting to the next—I couldn't help noticing that there were many pilgrims in the room. However, only a few of us had been trained to the priesthood. A painting can certainly be enjoyed when you are not aware of everything the artist did to make it successful, but it can only be relished when you learn more about what you are seeing. Most commented on Vermeer's ability to paint with such precise detail— no doubt an important skill. But few knew about composition. There was an exception. As I stood in front of the large painting View of Delft, a cityscape of a Dutch harbor town, I only heard one man say to his daughter: "Do you know why there are such long reflections of the city painted onto the river when the reflections he saw in fact weren't that long?" That is a compositional question.

By this time in the text, we understand that Susan is offering more than a diary of her trip to the Vermeer exhibition. Like a friend and companion, she will stand by our side as we view the painting. Like a museum docent, she will give us expert help on how to notice concepts of composition that only experts typically notice. As we view the Vermeer with her, she will teach us how to translate the unstructured experience of our seeing into structures that map onto expert elements of composition. Like Peter, she will also teach by having us see and feel. To provide a motivation for what she is about, Susan makes it clear that though our untutored viewing can lead to enjoyment, our enjoyment can be heightened when our viewing is informed. "A painting can certainly be enjoyed when you are not aware of everything the artist did to make it successful, but it can only be relished when you learn more about what you are seeing."

As Susan defines composition and indicates the implications of this definition on Vermeer's high-level choices, she stays with an expository, concept-based form of writing.

Composition refers to all of the elements an artist must consider and put together in order to create a unified work of art. In View of Delft, Vermeer has many compositional questions to answer before he can create a successful finished work. Where will he place the city on the canvas as opposed to the position of the clouds? How many women should be standing on the near shore? How important will the women be in relationship to other elements on the canvas? What time of day will reflect the mood that he wants to convey—what kind of weather?

She then offers some background about the work that goes into under-standing compositional choices.

> Looking at a painting in order to find its compositional elements takes patience, but it's exciting to discover what the piece has to offer besides a historic or symbolic meaning. It's also a good idea to read about the artist's work, so that you can take in the perspective of experts who have spent a substantial amount of time studying a particular painter or style. Among other things, you can learn how the artist manipulated the place-ment of objects, people or shapes to encourage your eye to quickly zoom into one area of the piece or meander throughout the canvas. That's not just a visual game. Like a composition created by Bach or Mozart, painterly compositional devices can influence the feelings you have as you look at the work.

Susan now describes three principles of artistic composition—emphasis, unity, and balance—that we can learn through the experience of our own direct viewing.

> Understanding the complexities of compositional analysis can take years of study. Nonetheless, there are some basic concepts that can be under-stood without much background. In particular, learning about emphasis, unity, and balance make for a good doorway into the priests' monastery.

EMPHASIS

> In order to get a visual picture of emphasis, imagine a line of kicking Rockettes at Radio City Music Hall. The Rockettes' line works because individual differences (contrasts) between dancers are minimized so that the whole line can be seen as one object and your eye can focus on the precision movement of that one working group. But, if in the middle of this line, you see Jimmy Durante, whom will you notice, and where will you focus? The old man stands out strikingly from the rest of the group. That Jimmy Durante effect of emphasis is a visual signal to the viewer to "look here first." The viewer settles into the area of dominant emphasis before moving around the work and comes back to it as often as he or she wants. If the artist doesn't provide that starting point, the work will often feel too confusing. Viewers may feel as if they're trying in vain to make sense of the space. Competing images outside of the canvas will take their attention instead.

The artist must make the dominant shape, whether woman, table, or rectangle different enough from the surrounding shapes to contrast or stand apart from the other elements that make up the complete painting. Depending on the painter's intention, this contrast can be subtle like a piccolo next to a flute or bold like a tuba next to a piccolo.

Taking this further, the artist then develops a second, less emphasized or sub-dominant area and a third sub-ordinate section to create a path that the eye will travel through in sequence.

Susan leaves Vermeer for the moment to give us other images and experiences to nail down the concept of emphasis for us. Rather than teaching by stepping us through concept and detail, Susan starts with an analogy (Jimmy Durante and the Rockettes at Radio City Music Hall) before alternating between concepts of composition and the expression of these concepts in Vermeer. In this way, she uses analogy to link concept to visual experience.

As Susan guides our eye through *View of Delft*, we can experience emphasis. The writing becomes spatially copresent and immediate. Susan is standing shoulder to shoulder with us in front of the painting. She is talking and we directly experience the visual implications of our understanding.

Where can you find areas of emphasis in View of Delft? How did Vermeer make one part of the canvas stand out in contrast to other parts of the composition?

The image on this canvas can be divided into three major areas that will allow us to take a closer look at the main compositional elements Vermeer uses to bring our eye into the picture and keep it there. These areas are the town with its reflected image, the sky above, and the sandy shore below. The large canvas portrays a cityscape. The sky with its wide dark cloud at the top and white cumulus giants underneath takes up about two thirds of the painting from the top of the canvas. The old Dutch port city of Delft lies in a mainly horizontal, darkly contrasting line below them. Small touches of red or bright blue can be seen in the roofs of the buildings. A boat juts out on the right hand side and a bend forms from the imaginary line that runs along the city shoreline and curves out as it approaches that docked boat. The river below passes by the city. In the water, you can see a reflection of the city and docked boats that are long enough to meet the small area of sandy shore that curves out from the left-hand side and down to the bottom right. That near shore's curve follows the curve of the city shore with its docked boats. Two village women in black stand by a small peer on the sand by the water, dwarfed by the city behind them. A few other villagers stand nearby blending in with the same small peer and its docked rowboat.

In this painting, the city with its boats and reflected image takes center stage. Why does this happen? The work displays at least four examples of emphasis employed by Vermeer.

First, the group of buildings and boats form a large dark shape—darker than anything else on the canvas. The dark reflection of the city in the water helps to increase the size of that area.

Second, except for the small peer, the geometric shapes of the city stand out in stark contrast to the organic forms of clouds and sandy shore in the rest of the painting. Vermeer must have worried about making one building too dominant because he painted that building's steeple shorter than the historical record shows it to be.

Third, the city also stands out from its surroundings because of its abundance of complicated shapes including the buildings, boats and trees. Nothing in the rest of the painting approaches this level of complexity. Imagine how tired your eye would get if every square inch of the canvas were filled with complicated detail.

Fourth, the rooftops hold areas of bright red on the left and bright gold on the right. These bright colors reinforce the your eye's decision to focus on the city first.

After looking at the town, you'll most likely travel upward to the large cloudy space. The size of that space makes it impossible to stay away from it for long. Finally, the small women will probably come into view. Their small size and simplified representation make them less dominant. But because we seem to be drawn to human images, your attention should eventually arrive there. Vermeer has done one other thing that will cause your eye to move to the women. In their very dark dresses, they stand out in contrast from the much lighter look of the sand and river. No reflection from the city touches this couple.

In order to keep the viewer in the compositional space, Vermeer also includes interesting areas that might not be noticed during the first viewing. Trees emerge from behind walls, and on the right-hand side, bright areas of lighter buildings are hidden behind the darker buildings and boats in front of them. The gathering of people on the near shore, who tend to blend in with the peer beside the two more dominant women, come into view. The thicker and thinner applications of paint and the brush strokes, which give different textural qualities to the objects in the space, become more apparent.

Vermeer establishes the Jimmy Durante effect of emphasis by playing on contrasts in size, darkness, color, and shape.

Susan now presents the concept of unity and does for that concept what she has just done for emphasis. Her description here can be shorter, in part, because we are now primed for experiencing new visual concepts.

UNITY

To understand unity, imagine Jimmy Durante standing in the line of dancers again, but this time that line has begun to break in places, large gaps forming at random spots between some of the dancers. The unity of the line is broken. Each area begins to look like a separate entity; Jimmy no longer has as much dominance. Confusion takes over.

Why do the three major areas, the town with its reflected image, the sky above, and the sandy shore below, in View of Delft hold together as one composition? How does the painter remove potential gaps that could make a choppy mess of his work? The artist unified his composition in two major ways.

Vermeer holds the three main areas in this work together by first echoing or repeating some aspect of one object in other areas. The quality of an echo brings the sound, or in this case sight, back to its source, out again and back as often as the viewer looks in that direction. In View of Delft, the city is very dark, in sharp contrast to the light clouds above it. That light area changes when your eye reaches the upper-most cloud expanse. This cloud covers the entire top of the canvas. It is much darker, very similar in color to the town itself. When your eye reaches that dark cloud, the echo comes back to the source and you move down to the city again. This quality of repeating or echoing is often called similarity. Were the top cloud lighter, no echo would be available to pull your eye back into the work, and you might just keep your head in the clouds. The same thing is true of the women in the foreground of the painting. Their dark color makes another echo, unifying the women to their city and the city to its environment. The black dresses he painted are not just a lucky use of the singular fashion of the day. Other Vermeer canvases show women dressed in greens, yellows, and browns.

Vermeer uses color similarity in other areas as well. The sandy near-side shore echoes the half-hidden sun-struck buildings on the right side. While on the left side a small area of red in the peer echoes the more dominant area of red in the city's rooftops.

One other similarity can be found in the curving line of the near shore. That bend resembles the curve made by an imaginary line that runs along the city shoreline and curves out as it approaches the docked boat on the right-hand side. This makes a visual link between what would otherwise be two contrasting kinds of shapes, geometric and organic.

Second, even with these echoes the completed canvas could easily become a series of stripes with its band of clouds, curving horizontal bands of city and river, and curving band of shoreline. The painter prevents this by using long reflections in the water that stretches from the edge of the city down to touch the shore. On the right hand side, the shape extends all the way off the edge of the canvas. The closeness or proximity of the reflection to both the town and the near shoreline unites the two bands. In order to integrate these two areas, Vermeer may have altered the reflection he actually saw.

Vermeer creates unity by using the similarity (the echo) of shared colors and shapes in his composition, while proximity can be seen in the shapes that touch and connect two bands of otherwise dissimilar visual information.

Finally, Susan describes balance in an artistic composition. Once again, Jimmy Durante provides an analogy for understanding this compositional device.

BALANCE

To illustrate balance, imagine Mr. Durante standing within the line of dancers one last time. Durante's emphasis gives him importance that equals heavier visual weight. However, the unifying feature of the line of dancers on both sides of the old song and dance man, as well as their larger number, offset his visual weight and ultimately gives the entire line your attention.

Balance results when the artist uses areas of emphasis and unity with skill, and pays careful attention to the placement of those areas within the picture plane. Emphasis and unity, working together combine to create balance that allows the viewer to move with ease across the entire image area. When the artist does not give enough thought to or have enough skill to place these elements effectively on the canvas, either chaos or boredom will most likely result.

When visual weight is not well distributed on the entire stage the result can look awkward. For example, too much emphasis could direct your eye to one place without giving you an area of secondary dominance to seek out. You might become bored with the single area of visual focus and move on before exploring the entire composition. On the other hand, if no areas direct your eye to "look here first," you might not have a desire to entire the picture space at all—there is no payoff for your time and attention. Further, enough attention has not been given to unifying the entire composition. While there might be interesting bits here and there, you probably won't want to explore the picture plane to find them. The overall chaos inherent in this kind of piece will most likely cause you to move quickly onto adjacent visual information which has been organized to convey the message in a more understandable tongue.

In the Jimmy Durante example, if the director pushes the line of dancers very closely together until they meet the curtain on the right while on the left, one eighth of the stage is empty. That empty space becomes an area of visual weight even though it is negative, not positive space. The unintended emphasis of empty space—that has been tacked on without any thought to unifying it with the rest of the dancing line—will distract the eye while at the same time the visual weight of the people in the line will seem too visually heavy on that side. Chaos results. In order to effectively use the space and restore the balance, the viewer wants desperately to move the line back to the left.

Artists can push emphasis to an understated hum or a loud crescendo, and unity to the point where it is barely visible or almost overwhelming. But once the artist violates the delicate balance between emphasis and unity, the successful qualities of the work, such as a beautiful application of paint or a lovely rendering of the figure, become overshadowed. The work fails to hold the viewer to the composition.

One last note about weight and placement on the picture plane. The picture is a two dimensional space that the viewer comes to from a three dimensional world. The viewer will usually still want his sense memory of gravity and weight to apply to this flat space. Depending on the artist's intent, painted images that have weight in the physical world usually need to be grounded or supported by their positioning on the canvas.

Susan now directs our eyes back to Vermeer.

In View of Delft, Vermeer maintains balance in four major ways. First, by placing the city, the area of first emphasis, below the midpoint of the canvas, he works with our sense of gravity. The visual weight of the city and its imagined physical weight are considered by placing the town low enough to feel as if it is seated in the space. Second, he supports that weight in another way by using long reflections which meet the bottom of the canvas and act like visual pillars supporting the weight of this mass. Without those dark visual supports, that are also unifying elements, the city might have a more surreal quality not in keeping with the artist's intent. Third, he offsets the heaviness of the bottom third with the secondary area of emphasis of the large expanse of clouds. A thinner area of clouds might not have enough pull to keep the area below from becoming too visually heavy. If that happened the viewer might not be able to get out of the city space easily enough to view the entire canvas. Finally, Vermeer balances the heaviness of the large boat on the right, an object that could easily push the bulk of the weight too far to the right, with the counterweight of the women on the shore. This placement completes the feel of visual balance and allows the viewer to move within the entire painting, concentrating on the work without being sidetracked by unintended distractions.

Balance, therefore, uses emphasis and unity to keep the eye moving with a certain rhythm across the entire visual field. If the artwork is without balance, you'll feel the loss, and you probably won't be able to enjoy the other aspects of the painting.

Susan leaves us with a warning not to substitute analysis for appreciation. She would rather we understand that analysis begins with appreciation.

A final word on all of this: Don't stop looking at paintings simply for the way they make you feel. The artist spent hours working out these problems of composition just to give you that emotional return. In other words, first let yourself simply love what you see for no other reason than it's there and you like it, but after that, stay with the painting until you begin to live in the compositional space as well.

Peter and Susan blended elements of experiential learning to support generalization learning. Another blend employs experience in the service of generalization, but this time the writer targets generalization learn in order to subvert the background assumptions of the reader. The new information to be learned is that the reader *has been mistaken* in her prior generalizations of the subject. The writer uses experiential text to show readers that the (stereotypical) generalizations they hold misdescribe deeper experiences that they must now confront. The writer guides readers to new generalizations based on the new experiences introduced.

This was Rick's approach to information writing. Rick wanted to show his readers that running a church youth group was not nearly the job that most people thought it to be. He penned the following notes to himself about what he wanted to get across to readers:

> Being a youth counselor requires a lot more than being a chaperone. It requires a deep and sensitive knowledge of teenagers. You must understand contemporary youth culture and relate the Bible to the teens and their issues. You need to supply more than good pizza. If you don't, then your just giving them an ancient religion and they ain't interested. They need it to be relevant.

Rick felt that he needed to wake up readers whom (he feared) falsely believed that the job of church youth counselor was nothing more than buying pizza for kids. Only by including experiences that would wean them off their simple understanding of the job, could he help wean them toward more accurate generalizations.

> Junior Highers are needy creatures. Few forces in this world can do as much damage in such little time as a pack of junior high boys. I know, I worked with them for ten years. They've invaded my house many times and left it a hollow, smoking husk. Someone needs to pay for the broken windows and for cleaning the stained carpet. Someone needs to purchase the curriculum material and Bibles. Someone needs to drive the kids from point A to B, and C, D, E, and F. Someone needs to pick up the tab for the pizza, Doritos, and Coke. Someone needs to unlock the

cabinet where the paper cups are kept. Someone needs to lock the cabinet where the paper cups are kept. Someone needs to fill up the van with gas.

Someone needs to spend time preparing the Bible study so the kids won't fall asleep, at least immediately, like kids usually do in church. Someone needs to recruit and train volunteers. Someone needs to make sure none of the volunteers are pedophiles. Someone needs to understand youth culture so that the church has something relevant to say. Someone needs to make the calendar so everybody knows what's going on. Someone needs to plan all the events so the calendar can be made so everyone can know what's going on. Someone needs to update the database so we have labels for the summer camp mailing. Someone needs to send the deposit forms and down payment to weekend camp in the fall.

Someone needs to know how to talk to the kid with the bad breath and the greasy hair. Someone needs to pick up the girl who lives fifteen miles away. Someone needs to deal with Josh who was caught smoking pot. Someone needs to deal with Robin who was beat up by her boyfriend. Someone needs to deal with Luke because he acts up every time we meet. Someone needs to take care of Kate because her mom is getting a divorce, again.

Moving from these experiences, Rick introduces his readers to the new generalizations that fit the experiences he has introduced.

Typically, teens don't get it on Sunday mornings. They might get dragged to church, but they don't GET church. They don't worship. They don't learn. They don't experience Christian community. They aren't challenged. They aren't supported. They don't grow. Studies show the average spiritual growth for members of mainline denominations in the US peaks right before 7th grade. The growth chart then heads straight down not to resurface again until age 70. Teens don't connect with Sunday church or Sunday School, and the ballads of our high school years effectively drown out the church choir.

Shifting back to experiential writing, Rick places us in the mind and experience of the average middleschooler with whom he worked.

To more fully understand the needs of the your typical junior higher I'd like you to take a walk back in time to when you were 14. Try real hard.

Now bring yourself back to the present day, complete with "Gangsta Rap," "Ellen," Monica Lewinsky, 9 Inch Nails, safe sex, Lollapalooza, and Howard Stern. OK? Now, your family has just moved. You had great friends back home, but your dad was transferred and you had to go. Your parents said, "they'll make it up to you"—whatever that means. You spend a lot of time on the phone with your old friends, but it just makes you miss them more. You hate your new school. You hate your home-room teacher. You're convinced he doesn't like you and he picks on you all the time. You don't have any good friends and you hate your parents for moving.

Mom's on the phone talking with Grandma. About me. "No, he doesn't seem very happy. No, he doesn't have any friends yet. There's this one boy Chris, but they don't really do anything together. No, we haven't found a church yet. It's been hard to find the time. Yeah, maybe that would help." I can't believe they're talking about me. The next day Mom announces that she wants everyone to go to church on Sunday. Dad's out of town on business and won't be there, but everyone else is going. Mrs. Jones down the street says it's a great church and lots of kids go there. We haven't gone to church in years, I mutter. Mom glares at me and I know to shut up. No sleeping-in Sunday. Groan.

The phone's for me. It's the guy from the church. I don't want to talk to him. No, no "Hi." He's talking to me like he wants to meet me. Yeah, I'm new in town. Yeah, I miss my friends. Yeah, I go to the middle school. Yeah, I like hockey. Yeah, Wednesday night. No, no, no, "Sure, that would be great. I'll see you." Darn. How did that happen? He sounded OK, I guess, and he said Chris is always there. He said they have some competition each week and this week its my favorite—hockey. Maybe I'll show up.

Mom drops me off down the street. No way I'm about to let anyone see her drive me there. I can't believe I have to do this. I thought Dad would let me out of it. I feel sick. What if they're all weird? What if they make me pray or something? As I walk up the sidewalk I notice how huge the place is. It's old. I hear some loud music. Oh, hey, I know that song. That's the cool one I hear on the radio. Some girls laughing over there. Oh, there's Laura. She's cute. Check my shirt, make sure it looks good. Hope no one can see the stuff I put on my face. I hate these zits! Basketball game going on over there. There's Tim and that's Matt I think. Oh great, there's John. He's such a jerk. Forget basketball. I don't wanna be anywhere near John. He might start something again. I'm hating this already. Maybe if I call mom and beg she'll come back. This is such a joke. Being a youth counselor for a Church is nothing what people think it to be.

Rick could have written a straight exposition, avoiding experiential writing altogether and interpreting his information assignment as generalizations to tell through direct exposition. Yet, as Rick saw it, to try to tell his readers what he wanted them to know within an assumption of familiarity would have defeated his message. Readers, Rick surmised, would have mistakenly thought they were hearing what they already knew, creating boredom. Before he *lived* the experience himself, he knew *he* would have made the same mistake. To change his readers' thinking, he reasoned, he first needed to share with his readers the very experiences that had changed his own.

Summarizing the Writing Models in Relation to Invitations to Learn

In this chapter, we have considered two writing prototypes cast in one information writing assignment, each dealing with the elements of the familiar and unfamiliar as they move a reader toward learning objectives.

Both prototypes rely on the writer's clearing three hurdles before settling successfully into the chair of information writer.

The knowledge hurdle requires that writers know something that their readers don't know and want to know.

The discrimination hurdle requires that writers be able to take enough distance on their exclusive knowledge to sort out the reader's sense of familiar from unfamiliar elements.

The alignment hurdle requires that writers be able to align the familiar with the unfamiliar in ways that promote reader learning.

The prototypes divide on the contextual assumptions underlying reader learning. Exposition becomes relevant when the reader's objectives are unfamiliar generalizations. The writer positions these generalizations at the end of familiar elements so that readers can move from what they know to what they don't know.

Exposition can fail for many reasons that are well-known. Through egocentric writing, a writer can forget to make the text a pleasing interactive experience for a reader. Egocentric writing is the common by-product of first-draft writing. Andrew's writing is a typical example of first draft egocentric writing. Lois illustrates how the writer can remove egocentrism in later drafts.

Texts that remove egocentrism can still remain unmotivating. Although they will not push the reader out, neither will they pull her in. To pull in the reader, writers need to make texts that are interactive with the reader's concerns and interests. Writers do this by testing their drafts against sample readers. Jack is an example of how testing the writer's drafts on actual readers can help the writer identify and include the perspectives and concerns that early drafts often miss. The result of such testing, as Jack learned, is not only information that readers want to know. It is also information that helps the writer learn how to fashion self-portraits that can carry greater empathy with readers.

Popular explanation becomes relevant when the reader's objectives are tying a remote subject to their sense of the familiar. The unfamiliar is an assumption of the communication rather than an element of the representation. The writer positions familiar elements throughout the text so that the reader finds the subject accessible, bathed in everyday understandings. Aaron and Lauren show how this composition scheme effectively works to make remote concepts accessible to readers.

Experiential and generalization learning can be effectively blended, especially when the writer sees a way to make experiential learning provide a foundation for generalization learning. To develop news generalizations from experience, Peter lets us experience poetry and Susan lets us experience painting as a prelude to learning technical generalizations about these arts. Blends of experiential and generalization learning can also be effective for exposing and subverting readers' background assumptions. The writer in this case, like Rick, can use experiential learning to show the inadequacies of his reader's current generalizations before trying to replace them with generalizations that are more adequate.

Information writing is stereotyped as part of the world of hard-hearted commerce. One secret we hoped to reveal in this chapter is how getting across hard information to readers so often depends on the soft artistry—the portraits and landscapes, imagery and analogy—that we tend to culturally identify more with our leisure than our work.

Information writing and the learning that results from it is already basic to the world of work. Consequently, we do not need a separate section to show how the principles of this chapter apply to real-world writing. We will observe, in closing, however, how we used these representational principles of information writing to design each chapter of the present volume.

Were this a "how-to" book, we would have made most prominent the principles of instruction, in the next chapter. As there are no exercises in this book, we obviously chose against that. Were this a standard academic book, we would have used exposition as our guide. We decided that we were somewhere in Rick's boat. Most readers reading our student examples, we thought, would find the writing familiar. Yet, we feared, they would miss our point entirely were they to classify the familiar examples into familiar categories, dealing with structure- and genre-based composition. After all, these were not the generalizations about representational composition that we were trying to make prominent. So we decided to begin each chapter with generalizations about representational composition straightaway, before showing the student examples. That way, we could confront our readers' prior generalizations about writing before they had a chance to apply them. Through the examples, moreover, we could introduce the sophisticated experiences our students had learned to render with texts, experiences that can't be explained within the categories of writing that are currently familiar.

6

Invitations to Do and Learn

In the last chapter, we considered writing where the end is the reader's learning new generalizations or new experiences that either substitute for or provide a foundation for generalization learning. In this and the next chapter, we consider examples where providing information is supplemented by an additional element, namely, providing direction. The direction of interest in this chapter is guided movement through a physical space. The prototype to be explored is written instructions. The writer of instructions guides readers through a task such as programming a VCR, assembling a swing set, or learning how to use a computer program. He combines experiential writing and the interactivity of information writing to guide a reader's movements.

Although instructions are widely regarded as a natural genre and are one of the most canonized forms of writing in the culture, orienting consumers to products, the challenges of instruction writing remain largely unexplored within a framework of representational composition. In our studio explorations, we have tried to distance ourselves from the collective wisdom about instructions as a genre and to step back to rethink the representational challenges that face a writer, generally, who is trying to manipulate the reader's hands to help the reader complete a task. Toward this end, we have simply asked students in our studio to invite the reader to "complete a task with his or her hands."

Learning through a text remains relevant in instruction writing, but learning now takes the form of learning by doing. The instruction writer brings scenic writing to bear, encouraging the reader to move and interact with a spatial world. But the element of space in scenic writing is non-identical to the element of space in instructions. In scenic writing, the element of space resides non-interactively in the world of the text. In instructions, the element of space betokens the writer and reader's two-way interactivity. Elements of interactivity permeate the inner world of text to guide the reader's actions in her physical surroundings. As scenic writing emphasizes space as a stimulus for mental imagery, instruction writing uses space to help the reader navigate her immediate surroundings. Instruction writers present cues that prompt the reader to press, grab, hold, drag, and a battery of other manual actions. Instructions focus on guiding this physical action, with the writing both establishing the preconditions of the actions and tracking their consequences.

As a form of representational composition, instruction requires the alignment of three independent elements tied to different learning outcomes. The best known of these elements, part of any generic description, is the imperative command to action. This element is directly tied to the writer's interest in having the reader learn guided action through a space. Through our studio observations, we have found that writers use textual elements both to direct the reader forward (act), but also to help the reader recover from mistaken action. These last elements we have come to call recoveries (elaborated below). Both types of elements support the reader's guided action.

In addition to guided action, instructions also involve elements that support the reader's experience in the task. The reader of instructions must learn not only to act but also to acquire the feel of verifiably correct action. Through our studio observations, we have found that writers use textual elements we have come to call confirmations, reassurances, and reinforcements (defined below) to support experiential learning.

Finally, in addition to action and experience, instructions involve the reader's generalization learning. The reader of instructions must learn not only how to act and the feel of verifying it as correct action; the reader must learn how to extend one's learning to contexts and situations he has not yet seen. Through our studio observations, we have found that writers compose textual elements defining generalizations underlying actions when they discover readers taking incorrect actions as a result of incorrect generalizations.

Thus far, we have overviewed in a preliminary way the learning outcomes associated with instructions and the textual elements that a writer must align to support them. Let us now elaborate this top-level picture in finer detail. We shall start by elaborating the learning outcomes and then work our back to the textual elements that contribute to them.

The Learning Outcomes of Written Instructions

These consist of guided action, experiential learning, and generalization learning. We address each in turn.

Guided Action. This outcome is the centerpiece of instructions. The reader is invited to learn a task through the experience of doing it. The reader is not simply using her hands to achieve a sense of familiarity with abstractions like torque and force vectors (see Aaron's writing in chap. 5). The reader is relying on a text as a guide for progressing through a spatial task in his immediate physical environment. Guided action through the reader's physical space relies on vocabularies of hand movement: *move, grip, hold, pull, push, drag,* and so on.

Experiential Learning. This outcome helps readers adjust action to verifiably correct action. Instructions involve complex motor motions or sequences of motion. When guided action is straightforward (e.g., take out the garbage, pick up your clothes), written instructions are not necessary. Instructions are written because guided action is insufficient to guarantee positive learning outcomes. Lacking written instructions, success would be hit and miss. The reader would sometimes be correct. Sometimes not. Instructions are written because being correct is not enough. The reader needs to have the correctness of action verified. Without such verification, success can be random. Without verification, actions won't be learned with the correct generalizations that are needed to transfer them successfully to new contexts.

Generalization Learning. This outcome is crucial for the learning that must take place if the reader is to apply instructions correctly later in a sequence or in different contexts. Instructions require adapting actions across experience, making adjustments in action that depend on conditions and context. Without understanding the instructions at the appropriate depth of generalization, the reader will not be able to take actions successfully as contexts and conditions change. The problem is exacerbated when, in the rush to act on instructions, readers try to act prior to learning the appropriate generalization needed to drive it.

Action as the dominant element. While the major outcomes of instruction move between action, experience, and generalization, the dominant outcome tends to be action. Readers routinely come to instructions for ruthlessly instrumental purposes. They seek out instructions until they think they no longer need them, and not a moment longer. This puts a premium on the instruction writer to move readers through the sequence of actions as efficiently as possible. In response, instruction writers after efficiency often cut corners on generalization to shorten the reader's line to action. "Don't give me a lecture, just tell me what to do!" is a common refrain of the reader frustrated by instructions. The dominance of action tends further to force trade-offs between the speed of performance and the accuracy and depth of the generalizations formed. The reader may get the next action right, but three actions down the line wrong because he has not yet understood the instruction in a sufficiently general way. In the short-term, the reader wants prompts to action, not generalization. Yet in the long-term, the reader needs to comprehend a set of generalizations in order to perform those actions reliably across conditions and contexts.

How the writer handles the trade-off between speed and depth of generalization depends on the context of the instruction, on the resources he has for providing it and the reader for taking it. If the writer aims for the casual readers who need only to push the right buttons without understanding why, he may properly focus on short-term action and avoid generalization. Should, however, the writer be producing a software manual for readers who need to master the software in their daily jobs, depth of generalization can be more important than the speed of learning isolated actions. Some research in fact suggests that, for robust learning, there is added value in blending generalizations, learned through inductive models, with action (Charney, Reder, & Kusbit, 1990; Cheng, Holyoak, Nisbett, & Oliver, 1986; Fong, Krantz, & Nisbett, 1986).

The Instructional Task

Exploring instruction in a writing studio poses a special challenge because it requires that writer and reader share the same task—even though, unlike a workplace or factory, the writing studio has no indigenous tasks within which instructions naturally arise. Because of this studio constraint, we created a uniform software documentation task for exploring instruction writing. The task was to write tutorial instructions for a virtual reality interface into which many three-dimensional worlds can be downloaded. Writers were told that the readers of the documentation needed to be able to handle the basic commands of the interface as an outcome of their reading. They were also told that readers would need to form correct generalizations so that they could take correct actions in contexts they had not yet seen.

The sample world was customized from free demonstration software and called the *Crime Scene world* (Fig. 6.1). This world is composed of a house with a raised living room. The carpeted room contains furniture common to an upscale living room or a den. It contains a couch, lamps, a coffee table, a fireplace, a television, and a billiard table. The room also contains two blood spots hidden at diagonal corners. We gave students the following guidelines for writing:

> To learn how to use this virtual reality software, we have created a Crime Scene tutorial. Imagine you are a chief detective who has been awoken in the middle of the night to be told a murder has taken place. You are told over the telephone that police on the scene have noticed two suspicious drops of blood at unusual places in the room. The police have since left the scene. You do not want to search randomly for the blood spots, so we will have to fax you directions about how to find them. Because this is virtual reality, you do not need to drive over to the crime scene before you test what you read over the fax. You can test out the directions as you read them. This exercise will show you where both blood spots are. More importantly, it will help you learn how to use this interface to navigate through any virtual world you care to load or build from scratch!

We told our students that the tutorials they wrote had to guide the reader until the reader was looking at each blood stain in close-up and at floor level. To illustrate this point, we told them that a reader had successfully located a blood stain only when the visual image looked like Fig. 6.3 (as opposed to Fig. 6.2). We also told them that the instructions had to be pitched with enough generality in mind so that, in working through the specific tutorial, the reader would essentially know how the commands worked in general. We made the virtual reality software available to each of our student writers. Each had to learn the interface thoroughly and then write tutorial instructions.

Setting Up Instructions

Instructions begin with a setup. While the setup has been embodied as part of many generic descriptions of instructions, we shall focus on aspects of the setup that remain relevant to representational issues, keeping an open mind about what is involved in approaching a human being from the distance of a text who is seeking manual guidance. From a representational point of view, the ordering of setup steps below is not fixed but this ordering appeared to be the one students in our studio adopted with the greatest regularity.

1. Welcome the Reader

Welcoming readers may send a hint of a positive self-portrait but has probably become automated into a genre convention. Self-portraiture is nonetheless important, as the writer can build empathy with the reader. We observed that instruction writers, like informational writers, can easily forget the uncertainty and anxiety a novice can experience when faced with learning a new task. Although perhaps inappropriate in some formal organizational cultures, writers of instruction, we found, can often help themselves by bringing elements of self-portraiture to the surface, by telling readers about some of the anxieties and concerns they had when they were in the readers' shoes.

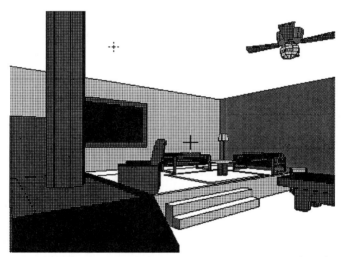

FIG. 6.1. The layout of the Crime Scene Instructional Task: The readers' assignment is to locate two blood droplets in the room. The writer's assignment is to teach readers the navigational skills needed to do that.

2. Overview the Learning Objectives

The writer needs to let the reader know the larger learning objectives to be reached from taking instruction. As as already been noted in the case of instructions, readers tend to focus on action more than generalization. However, writers can help even impatient action-minded readers when they help them monitor their own learning, and thus help them form the underlying generalizations that they need to become robust self-learners.

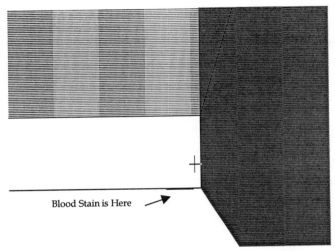

FIG. 6.2. A blood spot on the floor, in the corner, as it appears when viewed from a distance at normal eye level. Successfully identifying the spot in this fashion is a relatively straightforward task. Stopping the tutorial at this point is unlikely to result in an exercise that effectively demonstrates the challenges of working with the interface.

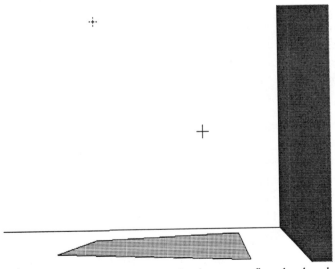

FIG. 6.3. The blood spot as seen in close-up at floor-level and at the reader's eye-level. Writers were asked to help readers navigate through virtual space so that the blood spot would be in this central foreground view.

It is important in instructional contexts that readers not confuse the tasks they undertake with the deeper learning objectives they should be pursuing. In the Crime Scene tutorial, the activity is finding blood spots in a virtual room. The learning objective, however, is to develop the knowledge of the basic interface commands that can support action in many virtual worlds, and not just in the Crime Scene world.

3. Tour the Space

Instruction depends on having the reader take action, often by moving objects in a space. To do this, the reader needs to be oriented within the scene. This orientation is largely focused on highlighting the objects and relationships that are key to the target task. The writer can achieve this orientation simply by pointing out the objects that will be manipulated in the lesson.

> The buttons you will be working with in this lesson are the navigation buttons located along the bottom of the window, where the house button is. The navigation buttons are the six buttons grouped together at the bottom of the window.

Unlike scenic writing, where the objects are referenced for an observer, the objects in an instructional setup are established for the reader to manipulate. Occasionally, the writer will find direct reference difficult because of ambiguities arising from the reader's lack of familiarity with the task. One reference may point to multiple objects. An effective way that writers deal with this is to acknowledge the potential ambiguity and proceed to disambiguate from there: "You will see two arrow buttons that point up, but one of them is much wider than the other. You want the wider one."

The text greets the reader where he is and then moves him to a firmer understanding. When the scene is complex and overwhelming, having the reader focus on particular elements and having him ignore others can also serve this purpose. "The only buttons on the toolbar you will need to know for this lesson are the six arrow buttons in the middle of the tool bar." Experts know what to focus on and ignore. Touring the space prior to acting on it helps novice readers narrow their attention on the relevant objects.

4. Preview the Conventions to Distinguish Generalization from Action

The writer relies on typographical conventions to help readers discern the boundary between guided action and generalization learning. Readers find it easier to read a text that clearly distinguishes what they are to do (action) from what they need to know. The typographical convention in the following text is typical. Many conventions can work as long as the writer remains consistent.

- <u>Typography for Information to Know</u>:
  Information you should know will appear in smaller type, like this.

- <u>Typography for Information to Do</u>:
  Information you should do will be in larger type and in bold-face, like this.

When he makes actions typographically distinct from exposition, the writer also makes it easier for readers to use the text as a quick reference to find instructional steps quickly. As Christine made explicit to her readers:

> For your convenience, each of the steps necessary in finding the blood-stains [in the Crime Scene task] is indented and underlined. This way, if you are interrupted, or if you forget what to do, you can find these steps easily when you consult these instructions again.

A danger with such conventions is that the writer encourages readers to separate action from the learning activities. Although this is not likely to be a problem for experienced readers who are returning to the text for a spot reference, it may result in impatient novices completing the actions without acquiring the underlying generalizations needed for self-sufficiency.

The four elements of an instructional setup that have been covered encourage readers to engage the text as active participants. By welcoming readers, providing an indication of the learning goals they are to pursue, now and over time, offering a spatial tour, and laying out conventions for separating knowing and acting, an instructional setup prepares readers for effective learning from a text.

Delivering the Instructions

With the actual delivery of instructions, the writer's challenge is to balance the reader's various learning outcomes by aligning the various elements that support them. We begin with the pacing of the writer's elements to guide reader action, through actions and steps.

Actions and Steps

Actions are the physical movements the reader must perform. Steps are the literary format through which the writer decomposes tasks into discrete actions. Actions and steps may be identical, but they need not be. In one instructional step, for example, the writer might expect the reader to take many actions. Generally, in the early phases of instruction, when the writer wants to hold the reader's hand, he will want to put single actions in each instructional step. Later, when the reader has more independence, the writer will be able to combine multiple actions in a single step.

In our studio experience, we found that one mistake writers frequently make is to forget the reader's need to identify *where* an action is to be performed before they can take the action. It is common, for example, for student instruction writers to write sentences like: "Move your cursor to the printer icon and click it twice. You can find this icon at the upper lefthand corner of your screen." Readers are asked to take a action in the first sentence before they know where to take it. The text is adequate to a point, but it forces the reader to return to the first sentence after the second is fully understood. Creating these backtracks, sentence after sentence, frustrates a reader, who expects to take action concurrent with reading. The following revision eliminates backtracking: "Locate the printer icon in the upper lefthand corner of your screen and click on it twice." This text maintains more of the on-line feel of a live tutor, who understands the importance of directing the student's noticing and visual attention (locate) before directing the student into physical action (click).

Anticipation of what the reader will need to know prior to acting can help a writer create the perception that the text is sensitive to the context and needs of the reader. Though the writer cannot see what the reader does, knowing the task well and testing early draft instructions on sample readers allows him to anticipate the kind of baseline knowledge that readers need at various steps.

Sequencing the Steps with Confirmation

Verbal confirmations are the primary textual element the instruction writer uses to simulates two-way interaction with the reader. It involves describing how the world looks—or should look—after a step has been correctly taken. Many professional instruction writers never encode confirmation in their text, leaving it, if anywhere, to visual diagrams. However, adding visual confirmation as an (experiential) element of the text can enhance its effectiveness and create an important resonance between verbal and visual information. Students who failed to see visual confirmation as part of the text requirement tended to confuse instructions with simple imperatives—"first do this, then do that . . . "—without thinking about instructions as verifiable correct action. Verification is required to give the reader the best chance of turning correct action into correct generalization.

There is no set sequence between textual steps and confirmation. The writer can tell the reader what to do and then describe what the environment will look like if the action has been performed correctly. An example of this alternative comes from Kerry. Steps are indicated in bold type.

1. Okay. First, take two steps toward the television.

Along the left wall on the raised platform, you should see a large television with speakers on each side and a large black leather chair in front of it.

2. Now, turn right.

You should see straight in front of you a large red picture. To the right of the picture is a couch, which is facing the front door, and in front of the couch is a coffee table. The right wall also has a couch facing the coffee table.

As a second alternative, the writer can preview both what to do and the visual consequences of doing it before releasing the reader to do it for herself.

I will show you how to travel along the left wall on the raised platform, where you will see a large television with speakers on each side and a large black leather chair in front of it.

1. Take two steps toward the television.

Next, you will be seeing straight in front of you a large red picture. To the right of the picture is a couch, which is facing the front door, and in front of the couch is a coffee table. The right wall also has a couch facing the coffee table.

2. Now, turn right.

Confirmation that precedes the instructional step often uses the future (*you will see*) or the future progressive tense (*you will be seeing*). This language gives the reader an anticipated taste of what the environment will look like once the action is taken and completed.

Placing the confirmation before the instruction can be helpful when the actions are hard to understand or mistakes are difficult to undo. If there are many possible interpretations of an action, knowing the correct endpoint makes testing alternatives more manageable. Knowing endpoints also means that readers are more likely to catch themselves as soon as something seems to be going wrong. On the other hand, if the actions are simple and mistakes are easy to recover from, the writer has reason to let the reader act and save the confirmation until the action is complete.

Continuous Forward Motion

The steps so far considered describe a discrete thing to do rather than a continuous activity sustained over time. For continuous activity, a reader is expected to keep doing something until he gets some signal to stop or is expected to refrain from some activity until he gets a signal to start. Instructional steps involving continuous action must provide signals for starting and stopping.

There is a small vocabulary of English words and phrases used to indicate continuous action in instruction writing. Such words and phrases include "Continue . . . until," "Until," and "When." These words and phrases all function in similar ways. Specifically, they combine action with confirmatory description. They provide readers with the information they need to act and then evaluate whether to continue with that action. Table 6.1 illustrates how these phrases combine reader action with description to create a text that seeks to be interactive with the reader's immediate context.

Entries into or exits from continuous action are often stated as simple declarative sentences (until you see) or imperatives (stop/start). The writer may also use an anticipatory future (you will see) tense, reflecting that it remains for the reader to take action to make the future true. "Then adjust your field of sight up or down a click—so that you will be able to see the place where the floor at the top of the steps meets the wall."

Recoveries: Giving the Reader Back-Ups When He Goes Astray

Thus far, we have discussed confirmations that tell the reader how a successful move will affect the task environment. This is fine as long as the reader keeps taking successful actions. What if the reader does not meet with success? Recoveries are a textual element that move the reader backward, to redo an action, just as successful action moves him forward. Unfortunately, actions that fail are common occurrences, particularly when dealing with novices or complex tasks in dynamic environments. In such contexts, the writer must anticipate the reader's failures as much as his successes:

> If you didn't find it, click on the back arrow once, then click once on the down arrow button, use the right or left arrow buttons to make sure that the corner where the walls meet is close to the middle of the screen.

> Did you miss the turnoff at the wall? No problem. If you want to get immediately into part of the house, the easiest thing to do is click on the "house" button on the far right side of the window

TABLE 6.1. Combining Reader Action With Description

Action Phrase	Example	Confirmation
"Continue . . . until"	"Continue stepping to your right until you see the television."	In this example, seeing the television is the anticipated outcome, which also serves as the signal to stop the action.
"Until"	"Don't move down until you see the projection screen."	Seeing the projection screen is the situation that grounds the instruction and is a signal to start the downward action.
"When"	"When you come to the end of the couch, stop (or start) moving."	Encountering the end of the couch is the anticipated signal for taking or stopping action.

The recoveries in these examples are context-specific, meaning that the recovery recommended is contingent on the particular situation of the reader. The context-specificity contributes to the reader's feel of the writer as a live presence.

Reassurances: Keeping the Reader Moving Forward When He May Mistake Noise For Error

Reassurances are an element used to tell a reader that things are okay, despite appearances to the contrary. Complex task environments contain noise that creates confusion for readers when it comes to confirming or disconfirming action. Readers of instruction in particular face the anxiety of false positives, thinking that they have done something wrong when they have not. Like a person walking an unfamiliar street with strange sights and sounds, the reader may feel that things are worse than they are, deciding there is a problem and retreating to an earlier point—when in fact there was no need to retreat! To guard against this type of error, the writer can include reassurances that keep the reader moving ahead when he is likely to hesitate.

Paul, for example, wrote actions that required readers to approach a yellow wall. Approaching the wall, however, involved readers' seeing a white patch off to the left. The yellow wall was connected with correct movement but the patch was not. Still, Paul found that in testing an early draft some readers worried when they saw the patch (which Paul had not mentioned in the instructions) and, as a result, retreated to an earlier instructional step. To prevent such mistaken retreats, Paul chose to reassure his readers, telling them they were on the right track and to ignore the white patch. "If you see a white patch on the far left, that's fine. You are getting closer to the yellow wall, dead ahead. Keep going straight. You'll be fine."

Reinforcements

Reinforcements are an element that provides positive feedback when a reader has passed an important milestone (e.g., "Fine, you are doing a great job. You are more than halfway done."). Used sparingly, they can help foster empathy between the writer and the reader. Used as small single-word comments, the writer can attain the voice of an impassioned coach shouting encouragement to an athlete (e.g., terrific, attaway, great, good, and okay). Michelle's instruction illustrates reinforcement.

> Great! Let your hand guide you along the couch. On your right is the coffee table. You will be moving between it and the couch so careful of your knees. When you come to the end of the couch stop. That's right. Terrific. Now take one more step straight ahead and then turn an eighth of a turn to your left. You're doing great! Take a small step straight ahead, careful. That's right. That lamp is in the corner between the couches. Use the lamp as a reference and step just to the left of it. That-a-way! Please take one small step forward and look down about 14 inches in front of you to the corner where the back wall and right side wall meet. I will take off your blind fold. Okay? What do you see? Another blood stain? Right! Great Work!

The writer must be careful when using reinforcements. Used judiciously, they can create the impression of an interested alert coach. Offered too often or in the wrong places, they ring hollow, like a "Have a nice day" greeting. Reinforcement should be restricted to the readers' passing hard milestones of the task.

Testing Instructions for Correct Generalization

We already discussed the trade-off in instruction between action and generalization. Instructions give priority to doing. Yet, readers can take correct actions without generalizing appropriately. They can form false generalizations from instructions that lead to wrong actions in future contexts. If they are to become self-sufficient, readers must learn not only the correct actions to take, but also the correct generalizations that underlie them.

In her testing of her early drafts, Lauren found a false generalization that she had inadvertently allowed her readers to form.

> Put the cursor about a half-inch over the lamp and then press down on the mouse. You will find yourself moving toward the lamp. Continue moving toward the lamp at eye level until you can no longer see its base.

Lauren's instructions invite readers to infer that placing the mouse above any object in the space will cause movement toward it—a generalization that many readers of her first draft made. Following this generalization, they then repeated the action with a coffee table, expecting that they would move toward it too. They were surprised to find that their action moved them steadily away from the coffee table, not closer.

The designers of the software had programmed forward movement to occur whenever the mouse was clicked in the top half of the screen. They had programmed backward movement to occur whenever the mouse was clicked in the bottom half of the screen. Coincidentally, the top of the lamp was in the top half of the scene, so clicking above it, as Lauren directed, caused forward movement. The top of the coffee table, on the other hand, was in the bottom half of the scene, so clicking above it caused backward movement. Although Lauren's first draft instructions worked for the immediate task, they led readers to form false generalizations about how navigation worked generally with the software. Lauren realized she had to revise to better align her instruction with generalization.

When evaluating instructions, it is important that the writer consider whether readers are forming the right underlying generalizations. If they are not, the appropriate generalizations need to become an explicit element of the text.

Making Actions Specific for Explicit Hand Motion

Another common problem arises when the writer leaves the action too vague for readers to act on correctly. This problem arises when instruction writers fail to specify what the hands or fingers are supposed to do. The spatial elements of the writing remain image-oriented rather than action-oriented. Stephanie's first draft illustrates this problem. Her confirmation statements direct the reader's eyes, but her action statements are not specific enough to direct the reader's fingers. She offers the reader the spatial immediacy of scenic writing without the precise hand or finger guidance to do the task.

> At the bottom of the view is a row of buttons. You can look around the room by using the arrow buttons. They allow you to move forward, backward, left, right, up ad down. As you look around you should see a wood stove, a television, some furniture, a red painting, a yellow lamp, steps, a ceiling fan, and a pool table.

After mentioning that the arrow buttons exist, Stephanie asks us to look around the room, assuming that the reader knows how to accomplish this task. The rest of her writing describes the scene, providing the confirmation a reader might need, but without reference to specific actions to be taken.

> To find the first blood stain, move so that you are in front of the steps with the pool table to your right. You should be able to see the red painting hanging on the wall. Next, turn to your right and move around the right side of the gray table. Now head towards the yellow lamp in the corner. Move to the right side of the lamp. Look up again and turn so that you are facing out of the corner and looking directly at the TV. Now move between the TV and chair so that you are next to the TV's left speaker facing the wall. Now look down at the floor. Along the edge of the platform and against the wall is the second blood stain. Congratulations, Detective.

Randall's first-draft instructions also subordinated specific action to description. In his instruction, he assumes that it is enough to describe how the on-screen view should change.

> During your exploration in the last section, you may have noticed a lamp. This lamp is in the far right corner of the room, on the raised platform and between two couches. The first blood stain is located behind this lamp, on the floor, in the very corner of the room. Navigate to this corner and find the bloodstain. Next to the TV, almost directly in front of you, at the edge of the raised section, you can already see the second blood stain on the floor. Move in and take a closer look! You found it.

Although some of Randall's readers were able to turn these descriptions into appropriate actions, many were not.

In both Stephanie and Randall's cases, the writers provided a context for learning, but provided too little guidance to make the reader an effective on-scene participant.

Tracking the Highlights of Effective Instruction

We now turn to an example of effective instructional writing. The text combines setup and delivery while keeping the two phases perceptually distinct. Beth's setup begins with a welcome and an overview. She explains the general learning goals, providing the reader with motivation and a framework in which to learn.

> Welcome to VR Player, a software application that allows you to navigate through a virtual house. With this tutorial, you will get a basic understanding of how 3D VR programs work. This will be of general help to you if you want to understand 3D design concepts in general.
>
> Though exploring a virtual space can take getting used to if you've never done so before, this program's instructions make it quite easy for you. Our simple, easy-to-follow instructions literally "walk" you through eight exercises, each designed to teach you a different VR navigational tool.

Beth introduces typographic conventions that will make it easy for the reader to distinguish setup information and confirmation from the literal actions to be taken. She also makes it clear to the reader why she thinks this information will be helpful.

For your convenience, each of the steps necessary in completing each of the exercises is numbered and put in larger type. This way, if you are interrupted or you want to look up what to do as a quick reference, it will be easy to locate the basic steps.

GETTING STARTED

To start, open the file called Family Room by double clicking on its icon.

Beth separates actions from exposition typographically. She also provides specific confirmation and continues to supply it as necessary.

Next, the Family Room window will appear on your screen, as shown below. As you will see, the name of the window, Family Room, appears on the bar at the top of the window. The window itself contains pink, white, and gray geometric shapes, as well as a cross hair in the middle of the window. Finally, notice the tool bar at the bottom of the window. It contains ten navigational buttons.

Beth returns to the goals of the specific task.

Now, you will use the arrow buttons in order to locate two virtual bloodstains. Once you have located both stains, you will have completed the first exercise of eight.

The entry into the task signals the delivery phase. Actions appear with more frequency than before. Notice the coupling of instruction and confirmation.

1. Move your cursor to the Move Backward button (the second arrow button of the six).

Check the lower, left-hand corner of your computer screen to make sure VR is telling you that you may press this button to move backward. When you see this message, you are ready to click.

2. Click the Move Backward button once and then release.

Did you hear that clicking sound when you clicked down your mouse? If not, listen for it next time you're instructed to click the next button. The sound is that of the virtual backward footstep you just took inside the virtual space. Before doing anything else, look at the Family Room window and make sure you see a diagonal, yellow bar near the center of the window. You should also see a darker pink object about one inch below—and about a quarter inch to the right—of the cross hair in the middle of the window. That is the first of two virtual bloodstains! You're halfway to identifying the two stains, and we're still only getting familiar with how to use the buttons! Keep up the good work.

Next,

3. Click the Move Backward button a second time.

I hope that you heard the second footstep, and after looking in your Family Room window again, you can see the base of a yellow floor lamp. Notice that the virtual bloodstain is still within sight, below and a little to the left of the cross hair. It looks farther away in virtual space because you just took another virtual step backwards.

Now that you've gotten the hang of using the backward button one step at a time,

4. Click on the Move Backwards button four times in a row.

Unless you have 20/20 vision, the virtual bloodstain is barely recognizable now because it is so far away in virtual space. We are now peering over a virtual gray table, and can see portions of two couches.

Next,

5. Move your cursor to the fifth of the six arrow buttons.

This is the Move Up button. Using this button allows you to get a view of the room from a higher point, as if you are taller than you were before. Click the Move Up button three times. You should now have a full view of the yellow floor lamp, including its yellowish-white lampshade.

After giving the reader detailed guidance early on, Beth assumes that her reader is gaining adeptness with the controls. With this assumption, she begins to combine multiple actions into a single instructional step.

In order to look to the left and right, you can use the Turn Left or Turn Right buttons, which are the third and fourth buttons on the toolbar, respectively.

6. Go ahead and start clicking on the Turn Right button.

7. Keep on clicking (or hold the mouse down) on the Turn Right button until you have seen the pool table, door, fireplace, gray chair, and a television.

8. Once you have seen the television, click on the Turn-Left button until the cross hair is in-between the fireplace and the gray table.

Beth also provides reassuring statements, in the midst of a recovery and personal reinforcement.

If you held your mouse down and scanned too far to the right, do not worry. Scanning too far to the right will simply take you back to the yellow lamp and bloodstain where you first started. Congratulations! You have successfully completed Exercise 1.

Doing Supported By Just-in-Time Learning

In the instructions reviewed thus far, the reader learns in the context of doing. If doing has high learning demands, the reader may feel compelled to learn and do as separate activities. The reader may want to learn in one sitting and do in another. This separation is nonoptimal, of course, for the impatient reader who wants to get through a set of instructions in minimal time. Because of their bias for action over generalization, readers of instruction often desire to strip down learning, even heavy-duty learning, to the bare demands of action. A motto is, "Let me learn what I need to learn just at the point in a task I need to learn it."

This is called just-in-time learning by doing. Just-in-time learning describes the design of any text that seeks to make information elements ready at hand within an overall action scheme. The reader is constantly poised to do. Yet, whenever the reader finds himself unable to do because of too few generalizations, he can immediately access those generalizations without leaving the action environment. In digital media, the close binding of exposition and instruction is achieved through context-sensitive, often hypertext, help systems. On paper, it can be achieved through featuring the action environment in close proximity to the context-sensitive help information, available on an as-needed basis.

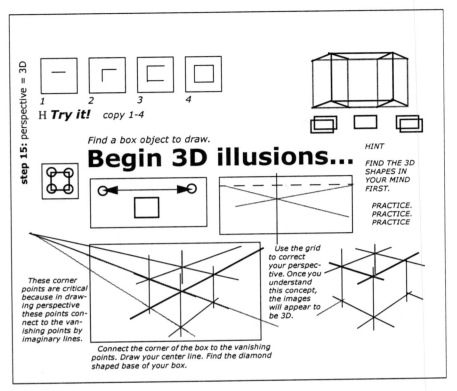

FIG. 6.4.

Alyce, a professional artist, used the studio environment to develop a just-in-time instructional document to teach three-dimensional perspective drawing. One page of the drawing environment she created for her readers appears above (Fig. 6.4). On each page of her document, she directs the reader's eyes to a star with an encouraging "Try it!" symbol next to it (Fig. 6.5). The star, along with the font, size, and weight of "Try it" is meant to catch the eye of the reader anxious to start drawing.

As a unifying element, Alyce uses imperative verbs that direct either eye or hand action (e.g., "copy," "find," "use," "practice"). These imperatives lead the reader's eye through the

Try it!

FIG. 6.5.

instructional sequence. As we have seen in the chapter on historical narrative, historical narrative, relying on simple past verbs, creates a displaced world with the reader as observer. Contrastively, instructional imperatives indicate an unfolding process with the reader as agent. At the periphery of some steps, Alyce includes background information designed to give the reader a boost should he need it. The perspective artist must understand corner points and vanishing lines as a conceptual underpinning to drawing perspective. Consequently, Alyce provides these concepts (bottom left margin) just at the time the reader needs to work with them.

Summarizing the Writing Models in Relation to Invitations to Do and Learn

Instructions invite readers both to do and learn. They involve guided action, experience, and generalization as learning outcomes, with guided action usually the dominant outcome. Outcomes that are dominant must be supported by corresponding elements in the text being assigned proportional dominance. Elements that support guided action are direct imperatives and recoveries. Elements that support the reader's experience in the task are confirmations, reassurances, and reinforcements. Elements that support the reader's generalization learning are statements whose scope covers not only the immediate context and task but additional contexts and tasks besides.

Kerry is an example of an instruction writer providing verbal confirmations in her instructions. Visual confirmations help the reader confirm that every action through the task is a correct one. Many instructional writers, in early drafts, overlook verbal confirmation or think it belongs only in visual diagrams. Instruction writers who overlook the need for text-supported visual confirmation tend to mistake verbal instructions for simple imperative statements. They overestimate the value of wordless, or lightly captioned, diagrams to teach a reader struggling to find his way. Even a captioned diagram can remain ambiguous about the state of the world it is trying to portray as feedback to the reader. Verbal confirmation, recoveries, and even reassurances can provide far more specific direction to a reader trying to make sense of a diagram.

Even with adequate verbal confirmations, Instruction writers also go astray when they write for the reader's eyes without providing enough specificity to direct her hands. Stephanie, Randall, and Steve illustrate how instructions can miss when the writer relies only on a scenic writer's sense of observed space rather than a sense of manipulable space.

Beyond verbal confirmations, instruction writers also rely on verbal recoveries, reassurances, and reinforcements to direct a reader through a task.

Beth illustrated built-in recoveries at places where she expected her readers to get lost.

Paul offered reassurance when he anticipated that the reader would mistake random noise for a genuine misstep.

Michelle used reinforcement when the reader reached a meaningful milestone and so, she felt, deserved motivation to reach the next.

Instruction writing is a trade-off between performing correctly in the short term and missing the deeper generalizations that are needed to perform correctly in the long term. Generalizations need to be made explicit when the writer anticipates readers' forming false generalizations. Lauren illustrated this point for us through her own hard experience with a first draft.

With the advent of dynamic text in electronic environments, the generalization learning underlying correct action can be presented just at the time the reader needs it to act. This is best illustrated in the many systems featuring context-sensitive help. Through creative spatial display, Alyse illustrates how concepts supporting instruction can be delivered "just in time" even on static paper. Digital texts make the possibility and prospects of just-in-time learning visible. Nonetheless, the foundations of these possibilities and prospects were firmly established in the layout and design options of ordinary print texts.

In all the cases we have considered, instructional texts illustrate the challenge of doing what writers find difficult to do—physically withdrawn from the scene and, through symbols alone, to have readers take verifiably correct motor actions, prompted by appropriate feedback and error recovery, and all from the correct underlying generalizations.

7
Invitations to Decide

In this last chapter, we consider written argument where, like instruction, the writer provides direction in addition to information. The direction provided is movement through a reader's internal deliberations, culminating in a decision. Our assignment to students in the studio was "direct a person to decide something."

In the tradition of structural composition, student writers are asked to envision a textual argument solely through the thesis-support format, often with some additional apparatus for annotating rebuttals. This format, best known in Toulmin's (1958) celebrated claims-data-warrant structure, has been the workhorse for the structural annotation of written argument. However, under representational assumptions, argument is better characterized as developing interactive worlds of decision-making into which a writer invites a reader.

As an object of representational design, written argument involves texts whose inner representation accommodates multiple worlds. Argument is not the first example of writing we have seen to involve a multiplicity of worlds. But it is the first prototype to require that the inner world of representation be splintered into alternative worlds.

Let us consider how multiple worlds have impacted previous prototypes. We will then be better able to understand how argument is unique in requiring multiplicity in a text's inner world of representation.

A multiplicity of worlds describes every prototype we have surveyed so far. This is the case because every prototype thus far has presumed an interactive world of the writer and reader and, nested within that, the inner world of the text. We have seen that the world of writer and reader interaction is usually implicit in written portraits and landscapes;

usually explicit in information writing, where writer-reader interactivity becomes a dominant element.

When we moved from information to instructional writing, we saw how two-way interactivity can penetrate the inner world of representation to guide the reader in her physical surroundings. The instruction writer constructs an inner world of spatial prompts and directional actions and recoveries that is permeable with and barely distinguishable from the outer world of interaction.

However, despite the differences across experiential, information and instruction writing, they nonetheless all share an inner world of representation that remains unified and intact. Written argument complicates this picture, for it splinters the inner world of representation into alternatives, branching paths that define a decision space. A *decision space* is an abstraction of the alternatives (i.e., paths) for a decision and the experience and information that recommend reasons for and against deciding to choose one or another path. Within the world of the argument text, the writer systematically explores these alternative paths, evaluates them, and either recommends an existing path or invents a new one to recommend.

Argument, thus, is not the first prototype to rely on a multiplicity of worlds. But it is the first prototype whose identity involves having this multiplicity penetrate the inner world of representation. The inner world of argument is one of a writer offering the reader the multiplicity of possible decisions while seeking to bring the reader to a singular one. The scholarly argument is strewn with the citations, elaborations, and evaluations of real and hypothetical paths and the voices who stand behind them. The writer signals her distance from cited voices by attributing the source from the third person (*e.g., according to John Smith*), from indefinite pronouns (e.g., *Some/many hold that*) or from situational states constructed by a generic and stereotypical mentality (e.g., *everyone believes that*). The writer signals the onset of her criticism of attributed sources through concessives (e.g., *although*) or contrastives (e.g., *but, however, yet*). Finally, she signals her affiliation with attributed sources by describing them from a first person afflictive pronoun (e.g., *we*).

To compose argument within a textual representation is to guide a reader through a decision space to a decision. This guidance can call upon every element of representation we have surveyed thus far. Take the element of self-portraiture as an example. The writer of argument relies on self-portraiture to assure readers of his ethos, that he is both caring as a person and credentialed as an expert to speak. Self-portraiture in argument extends beyond personal identity to the public identities that compel us to join political groups and fight for projects we cannot fight for alone. The writer of argument summons a public identity as a foundation for her decision-making and summons readers to one as a basis for theirs. A public identity invokes empathy and distance not between persons, but between persons and positions on issues. Writers seek to persuade readers to their recommended decisions by getting readers to see positive difference between their public identity and the identity of their opponents, producing empathy and admiration for themselves.

Beyond the elements of self-portraiture, there are also unmistakable elements of information writing in argument. The writer of argument must guide readers interactively, based on the alignment of the familiar and the unfamiliar. The arguer builds the unfamiliar from the familiar, the familiar for the arguer being what the reader does not contest; the unfamiliar, contested information. The arguer seeks to establish contested conclusions from uncontested premises. The more adaptive to the anticipated reader's thinking the writer can be, the more likely the reader will experience the writer's own recommendations as a self-directed tour. Just as the best information writing transforms a reading experience into a self-learning one, the best argument writing transforms an external recommendation into one that the reader can mistake for his own free deliberations.

While these examples show how self-portraiture and information writing are indigenous elements of argument, they are offered to illustrate the larger point that written argument builds on all previous representational elements that we have surveyed. The arguer often needs to give visibility to landscapes to show the experiences that condition or result from specific decisions; often needs to give visibility to observer portraits to acquaint readers with the persons affected by the decision or with previous writers whose recommendations are already a matter of record; often needs to teach the generalizations that are already known about the options to take; often needs to develop the confirmations, recoveries, reassurances, and reinforcements that can help readers orient themselves experientially in the decision space.

Given its multiple and inclusive representational dynamics, argument presupposes an utter fluency with all of the representational challenges we have previously visited. A seasoned argument writer will have mastered portraiture, landscapes, and perspective. Although she will need to combine a wide spectrum of elements to be effective, she will need to lapse only a little to destroy the overall, sought-after, effect of bringing a reader to a recommended decision.

In addition to drawing on all previous representational elements for its success, argument brings into play three contextual assumptions that are unique to it. First, written argument rests the power of choice with the reader. In portraiture and landscaping, the reader is not acknowledged and has no say in the world of the text. In exposition, popular explanation, and instruction, the writer enjoys a superior knowledge position and the flow of text, however adaptive to the reader, reflects this superiority. Only argument places the reader in an acknowledged position of power. The writer asks for a decision to be rendered that only the reader has the power to make.

Second, argument offers a new contextual wrinkle about perspective. Experiential writing presents the writer's perspective on a world. Exposition, popular explanation, and instruction bring both the writer and reader's perspective into the representational foreground of the text. Argument goes one step farther, bringing into visibility perspectives that compete with the writer's perspective. Perspectives are embedded within perspectives like Chinese boxes and the writer has unequal commitments to these perspectives. Argument is the single case of writing where the writer will include information that she does not stand behind. The writer not only asserts, but also characterizes opponents, mouthing perspectives that are not her own. Such posturing is necessary because the reader's purpose is to understand *whose* perspective to weight and *how much* to weight it when deciding on one's own. The writer wants her perspective to control the readers', but she can do this only by opening up and showing readers the superiority of her perspective over alternatives.

Third, in argument, there is no ultimate authority or expert. Unlike exposition, popular explanation, and instruction, where the writer is the expert, the writer of argument is not the sole or unquestioned expert. Argument becomes relevant in decision contexts where informed people disagree, where experts come to different conclusions, and where the issues remain open and unsettled. Processes and procedures must be defined to resolve open issues. Experts participate in these processes, but cannot determine their outcome based on their unilateral opinion. Abortion, capital punishment, and other headline-grabbing issues are obvious examples. The writer addressing capital punishment will find many experts on prisons, criminals, deterrence, and victims. However, she will not find the unquestioned expert on capital punishment, one to whom everyone is willing to defer as the final judge.

In previous chapters, we were able to identify representational effects that were locally tagged to one or another kind of world-building or interactive element or alignment. When we come to argument, we cannot isolate particular elements or alignments as distinctive because argument relies on a coordinative mastery of all the previous world-building and interactive elements. The writer of argument can succeed or fail in all the ways we have described success or failure in previous chapters. Consequently, unlike other chapters, we cannot localize on any discrete independent elements whose alignment captures the challenge of argument. Argument cannot be localized to any one kind of success nor can its failure be tied to any one kind of failure.

Relatedly, we find that student difficulties with argument have less to do with failing at any one kind of element or alignment than with letting slip any one of the many elements, alignments, and contextual assumptions that a writer of argument must juggle. Our studio observations attest to the daunting coordination challenge of structuring an authentic decision for a reader. In the sections to follow, we show how many small considerations can matter to the overall argument effect.

Presenting a Perspective in Support of Decision Making

When a writer designs an argument, she seeks to guide a reader's decision making toward her perspective. This requires the writer to develop an identifiable perspective. On early drafts, it is common for writers to create texts that do not carry such a perspective. Like the egocentric writing that is common in first-draft expositions, early draft arguments often meander from one topic to another. They often reflect the writer's introspective efforts to develop a position as much as to communicate one's settled views. The result is early drafts that look like fractured self-portraits.

Andrew's early draft argument about television is not an argument at all, but ruminations.

> The moral character of our country is in decline. Sex and violence are commodities sold over the airwaves on a daily basis. The politicians, both left and right, have embarked on a crusade to clear smut from the airwaves. The problem is that in the process of making television better, the government is also trying to sanitize it. The quality of television is a popular target of politicians and pundits alike. I agree—television is

crappy. The majority of television shows are insipid. They pander to the lowest common denominator in order to raise ratings. This is precisely why I only watch one or two hours of television a week. In general, time spent watching television is time badly spent.

As a technological means of control, the government has introduced the V-chip. The chip will be part of every television that is manufactured starting in 1997. The chip will allow parents to block out programs that are inappropriate, whether for sex or violence. The scale that the V-chip will employ to block out programs will be similar to the MPAA system used to rate movies, but the rating system and chip have their problems.

A couple hundred movies are released each year in the Unites States. Any movie intended to be released to mainstream theaters must be reviewed by the MPAA. There is roughly 2000 hours of television programming every day, much more than the relatively small output of the movie industry. The content of a show can also vary widely, complicating the process of rating any series.

The television industry is developing the new system from a flawed model, which has lead to unintended effects. In my experience, the MPAA ratings system make R movies taboo, they become more desirable to children. The MPAA ratings are rather vague in meaning also, since the standards used to rate movies are vague and open to interpretation. As with any regulatory policy, the intention and effects of the MPAA system are not the same thing.

Andrew's early thinking for his argument may be insightful as a collection of personal reflections, but it is not yet a perspective to decide for or against.

Presenting Perspectives that Compete

Lacking credible alternatives to a decision, there is no decision to make. Structuring a decision for readers involves providing clear alternatives to decide among. Writers often overlook this fact on early drafts. They leave out opponents and talk as if the truth of their position were settled. They lecture the reader as an expert instead of showing the unavailability of complete expertise and the need for deciding under uncertainty. When this happens, the writer backslides into information writing. The reader, in response, will either fail to recognize the need for a decision to be made or dismiss the writer as trivializing the issue.

Tim, a student in Electrical Engineering as well as English, did not include competing perspectives in his early draft arguments. He addresses a public issue, protecting children from violence and pornography on the Internet, by outlining a technical solution. He introduces the problem as follows.

> The World Wide Web is an amazing resource that is becoming increasing central to the world of communications. Freedom of expression has been one of the catalysts to its growth. Unfortunately, the lack of censoring such freedom also means that children who should not have access to certain parts, such as pornographic or violent web pages, do have access. To solve this problem, Congress has passed the Communications Decency Act (CDA), which prohibits web page producers from publishing ANY "indecent" material. CDA also holds Internet Service Providers (ISPs) responsible for willingly or unwillingly transmitting "indecent" material to minors. The CDA is a good idea but not the full solution. Unfortunately, the sheer breadth of the web prevents CDA from accomplishing what it should, which is the prohibition of electronic material to minors, without also censoring adults.

Tim now introduces his solution.

> I have another solution to this problem, which I call the "Interview" rating system. The Interview system has three components that will, in all cases, prohibit a child's unauthorized access to certain web pages in all cases.
>
> The first component of the Interview system is a plug-in for web browsers that detect a rating. Every web page is just a text document consisting of a text content and certain text "codes" which specify how the content should be displayed by a web browser. Content producers who design and publish web pages would embed early in their web pages a text rating. The viewer's web browser would read this rating, and if the viewer has access to the rating, the page would be displayed normally. If the viewer did not have access, the browser would produce an error message and would not display the web page.
>
> This first component is particularly easy to implement. For web browser providers, it would be simple to write a "plug-in," or helper application to facilitate the pre-reading of the rating, and a password function to determine a reader's reading privileges. As a computer scientist and engineer with extensive experience with programming and the

Internet, I know that a good programming team should be able to write it in a month or two. For content providers, embedding a text rating is also easy. The process is as simple as launching the document in a word processor, adding a rating, and then resaving the document. Since this rating is not displayed in the web browser, no redesigning of the web page is needed.

Tim sees a problem with web publishers doing their own ratings, a problem he addresses through the second component of his solution:

The problem with allowing content providers to rate their own pages is that they could simply rate a page incorrectly. A browser would think the page was appropriate for a viewer even if it were not. The solution to this problem, and the second component of the Interview system, are web "spiders." Spiders are specially written programs that traverse the web, scan a page, and then move on to linked web pages. The web pages which have the most links leading to them are most frequently scanned. Spiders cross-reference the text content of a scanned page in a huge database or catalog. (Carnegie Mellon University's Lycos Internet guide at http://www.lycos.com is an example of such a catalog.)

The Interview spider, like other spiders, would scan and cross-reference a page. The interview spider would also rate a page. The rating system would work like this: The spider would have a list of certain keywords.

The Interview spider would count the frequency of the keywords in a web page and catalogue a keyword's frequency. Any page containing keywords above a certain frequency would be given a certain rating. (The federal government would decide exactly how the ratings would be set.) At the same time, the Interview spider would compare this frequency to the page's embedded rating, and if an unacceptable discrepancy existed between the two, the federal government would begin investigating.

The Interview spider is a good choice to enforce a ratings system. Spiders are fast. Lycos is only half a year old and already has almost 30 million web pages cross-referenced. Because the database is continually updated, and spiders are so fast, no web page could be rated incorrectly for very long. The Interview has another plus: since web pages which are read most frequently by web browsers are most frequently reread by spiders, the most frequently occurring, most "damaging" pages are the ones which are checked the most often. Producers of special pages that might contain large frequencies of keywords, such as on-line encyclopedias, could lobby for a "safe" rating.

Tim now addresses a potential loophole in the spider solution and he proposes an additional fix, which is the third and final component of his solution.

There is a way around the spider system. Any child could download or "ftp" a new web browser, hide it somewhere in the computer, and then use this unrestricted browser to access the web. To solve this problem, I have developed the third component of the Interview system. Internet service providers who provide home access to the Internet would be required by law to accept Interview-compliant browsers only. They would also be required to accept only those browsers that have been registered by the person they bill, which would be the parent. This way, even if a child were to try to use a non-compliant or non-registered browser, the ISP would block access.

The Interview system is a very simple, elegant, and easily implementable solution to these large problems. Through spiders the Interview system facilitates the capture of those who knowingly allow access to damaging material in much more quickly than human web page-checking. The Interview system's three components close loopholes to those unauthorized at the producer, user, and provider level, without Internet censoring. The web, uncensored, will continue to grow and become increasingly useful.

Tim's solution appears elegant on its face. He acknowledges potential problems and shows how his proposal addresses those concerns. In this way, he is responsive to a reader. However, his writing does not move beyond informational writing because it does not consider alternatives. Readers reported they would feel more comfortable deciding his way had they known about other ways to decide. Perhaps there are alternative technical solutions that would have alternative social costs and benefits that we (or Tim) might examine. In argument, writers encourage the reader to decide based on the presented evidence. To make a decision based on Tim's writing is to render a verdict based on a single expert witness, without the benefit of cross-examination or alternative witnesses. For a second draft, Tim was advised to see if he could include a spectrum of opposing voices—both technical experts and child media advocates—in the course of presenting his proposal.

Peter found himself in a situation similar to Tim's. Although he hints that there are perspectives that compete with his own, his early draft arguments remained in the realm of informational writing, projecting an image of an opponent too faint for a reader to feel or know. Peter was writing in defense of the business mergers taking place in the mountain bike industry. He first makes us aware of these mergers and offers some short answers about their cause and value.

MOUNTAIN BIKE MANUFACTURER MERGERS:
NECESSARY AND BENEFICIAL

The sport of mountain biking has come a long way since its beginning in the early to mid 1970's. The sport started with a relatively few number of bike fetishists who created multi-speed bikes with fat tires and wide handlebars out of old Schwinn Excelsiors in their garages. Now the mountain bike is the single most popular type of bicycle sold in America and is a multi-million dollar industry. Recently, a curious event has been taking place among manufacturers of mountain bikes: mountain bike companies are merging with one another faster than conspiracy theories at a Lyndon Larouche speech. Why has this come about? Is this good or bad for those of us who [might choose to purchase and] ride a mountain bike? Is the UN New World Order secretly monopolizing all the corporations in Amerika? The answers: lawsuits, profitability, research and development, mostly good and I don't think so. Allow me to elaborate on the former two answers.

Peter now elaborates his answers about the value of mergers. Mergers protect manufacturers against high legal risk. The legal risk is high for mountain bike manufacturers because at least some mountain bikers try to live up to an image as risk-takers.

When considering why many mountain bike manufacturers are merging lately, one would do well to first consider what riding a mountain bike often involves: risk. People buy mountain bikes to ride over irregular surfaces, to take paths not paved or normally ridden with a road bicycle. Mountain bikes have an image: take me where no bike has gone before. Even if 80% of mountain bikes don't see dirt (Bike, Sept./Oct. 1994, p.17) many of these riders don't let their bikes live a genteel life. Riding stairs, jumping curbs, hopping over obstacles and other common antics often test both a rider's ability and a bike's durability—both of which have definite limits.

Most riders do not feel they must live up to this image, but there are always some bad apples, like Jumpin Joe.

The trouble starts when a rider does not stay within one's limits, attempting feats that are, more often than not, just plain stupid. To understand what I mean, maybe a little anecdotal story (probably more truthful than hypothetical) would help. Jumpin Joe just got a fancy new mountain bike. It has a big, thick looking frame and large knobby tires and even handle bars with those thingies (bar ends, that is) on the ends. Joe has been jumping curbs, riding in dirt lots, generally jumping anything he can use as a ramp or drop-off. He keeps improving and gets over-confident in himself and his bike. Joe never wears a helmet—he thinks they make him look like a "roadie-geek." And his bike is indestructible. After all, it has a "lifetime warranty" on the frame!

One day, Joe's feeling particularly Zen-master-stunt-man-like and gets an idea. He takes his Cannondale (foreshadowing hint: what word rhymes with crack-n-fail?) up to the roof of his garage. "With just enough speed and if I wheel off the edge and land just right, I can do this!" Joe thinks. Without going into the graphic details of the possibilities of idiocy, one can quickly imagine a disastrous result. Joe (helmetless, of course) misjudges things, flies off the edge wrong, lands, breaks his frame and ends up in the hospital. Question: who is at fault? A) The Bike Company for selling Joe a faulty bike with a lifetime warranty [after all, the logic goes, Joe would have made it safely if his frame had not snapped like a day-old pretzel upon landing], or B) Joe, for choosing to leap off his garage with his bike in the first place. If you asked Joe, it was probably answer "A."

There are many legal sharks out there waiting to help Jumpin Joe and run the bike companies into bankruptcy. Take this logic and add in lawsuit happy lawyers and legal precedent which seems too lenient towards product liability claims in favor of the plaintiff. What you end up with is every mountain bike manufacturer needing to be able to afford quality counsel, backing up suspicious warranty claims, and making more product recalls for fear of lawsuits.

In this early draft, Peter imagined an opponent insisting that a few people like Joe should not spoil the fun of mountain biking for everyone else. Readers told Peter his text would be strengthened by making his imagined opponent more visible. In his next draft, he granted this opponent more stage time so he could respond to him. He also invested more time coding the linguistic signals needed to help readers distinguish alternative paths from his own. His second draft inserted the paragraph:

> Now wait a minute. Most people probably aren't out to screw over a company. It seems reasonable that many people would adopt riding practices saner than Jumpin Joe. They would accept a certain amount of risk that is naturally involved with riding a bike. If a rider falls, and it's their fault, then it's their responsibility. But if someone crashes, and it's a direct result of a failure from a manufacturer, then the bike company should be to blame.

Peter signals the onset of the alternative representation with the phrase "it seems reasonable." He signals his rejection of this view with the opening conjunction "But." Peter agrees with his opponent that the individual bikers have rights. He insists, though, that only a few Jumpin Joes are needed to bring a highly profitable company to its knees.

In the following paragraphs, Peter shifts to the inclusive pronoun (viz., I), allowing us to feel the shift from the opponent's world to his own.

> I believe in the rights of the individual rider. If someone purchases a quality piece of equipment with a warranty, they should expect that equipment to perform to their satisfaction at least through the warranty period of the product. However, this expectation holds true only if that product is used within reasonable parameters of whatever purpose the product was created for. If I am riding my warranted mountain bike, and it fails—say my frame bends or cracks—as I'm riding along then I should expect the product manufacturer to honor its warranty. If I'm blazing down a hill, and smack myself and my bike into a tree or a big rock at 50 m.p.h., it is questionable that my bike was designed to take this kind of impact.
>
> My point it this. I would like to think that most people are reasonable and sane enough to know the difference between product liability and personal responsibility. However, it only takes a couple people like

Jumpin Joe to have a big impact on a bicycle manufacturer. Especially when you consider that most high-end mountain bike manufacturers are (or at least were) very small companies or businesses. Companies like Bontrager, Klein, or Yeti had only one manufacturing building. Each bike is assembled by hand, by a relatively few number of employees. They produce some of the finest quality bicycles on the planet. If just a couple Jumpin Joes sue a company like this, even if they are somewhat profitable, that company can only take so many lawsuits before profits, and the future of the company, start drying up.

Given that more people ride mountain bikes now than ever before, it's only natural that there are more Jumpin Joe lawsuit-happy riders than ever before. This has had a direct impact on how mountain bike companies do business. For example, in 1992 Cannondale recalled it's "Pepperoni" forks costing the company one million dollars (Mountain Bike, July 1995, p.46). Warning stickers and limited warranties are becoming the norm. For small manufacturers to deal with the legal risks of being in the bike business, they needed financial backing. Without financial backing, there is less money to afford decent legal counsel, less money for research, development, and innovation, and less profits. What is the solution?

Well, if you're like Bontrager, Klein, or Yeti, you allow your company to be purchased by a larger "parent" company that is able to provide the financial backing to remain competitive, profitable, and keep producing a better product. For example, in 1993-1995 Trek bicycle company purchased three smaller mountain bike specialty firms: Fisher, Klein, and Bontrager. The results? Fisher doubled its sales from 1993-1994 (Bike, April 1995, p.80). Its products continue to get good reviews by periodicals that test and review mountain bikes. Klein and Bontrager were both purchased in 1995. If the success of Fisher is any indication, Klein and Bontrager have nothing to fear.

Peter also anticipates another opponent, one who is loyal to the fiercely independent small company, and who fears the large anonymous corporation. Peter yields the floor to this opponent:

I can sense some of you may be skeptical. Especially those of you who may be familiar with the products and services of smaller bike companies. Often these companies had remarkable reputations for producing an excellent, unique product and for providing exceptional service for that product. What happens when the big company takes over the little one? It is the "big brother" syndrome, an Orwellian nightmare on two wheels? Since many of the mergers are in their early phase, it's hard to tell just how much control the parent company exercises over their new progeny.

Peter now retakes the floor to respond:

However, it seems reasonable that the parent companies will leave much of the control in the hands of those small companies. There are two good reasons for this.

First, changing an already proven product with a desirable customer base to something different and unknown will likely have a significant effect on those customers. When it comes to specialty mountain bike manufacturers, customers have come to expect certain things of a product. Things like a signature "feel" to the frame, a certain welding quality, and custom formed drop-outs (the part of a frame that holds a bike's wheel in place) are significant attributes associated with a certain bike. Changing any or all of these attributes risks losing that established customer base. For this reason, most, if not all, of the traditional features are retained.

Secondly, the special knowledge and abilities of the smaller, high quality bike manufacturers can be passed onto the parent company's product in the form of specific principles traditionally not present in a large bike company's manufacturing methods. Look at it this way: Some of the tricks and secrets of the world's best bikes (which are prohibitively expensive for many people to afford) can be passed onto the manufacturing methods for large volume bikes. This means that the affordable bike now gains the benefit of having high-end design and production attributes while remaining obtainable for a larger consumer population to enjoy. Better bikes for fewer bucks. A good example of this is Schwinn's purchase of legendary Yeti mountain bikes. Schwinn had the reputation for having some of the least desirable mountain bikes around. Now it is using principles learned from Yeti, and even some of they're manufacturing facilities, to produce a better quality product than ever before. The reviews of their new "Homegrown" series of bikes are

250/ INVITATIONS TO DECIDE

far more positive than many of their previous efforts (see most any February or March 1996 issue of Mountain Bike Action, Mountain Bike or Bike for specific details.)

I believe the future looks bright for current and potential mountain bike owners. Due to a great extent to a larger "lawsuit happy" consumer base, many smaller mountain bike companies have joined forces with larger parent companies out of necessity. I hope that the larger companies will retain the smaller manufacturer's traditional ways of doing things, while adopting some of their specialized manufacturing methods for less expensive, mass-produced bikes. In the future, one should be able to obtain a higher quality mountain bike for less money. Alternatively, a consumer may also purchase a specialized, high-end mountain bike without fear of that company closing.

Peter found himself arguing that a corporate merger is good for the company being merged. He realized that this perspective was bound to raise objections in light of the stereotypical thinking that mergers are bad. Consequently, he decided he needed to bring this common thinking into his text so he could respond to it. The following passage is an insert that Peter composed for his next draft. Notice how the insert both acknowledges the stereotyped thinking and overrides it.

First, it is often hard to imagine a merger as something good for the consumer. Usually mergers are associated with less choice of a product or service, higher prices, and sometimes monopolization of a market share. I cannot deny this has happened in other industries or that the aforementioned effects aren't real or haven't had a significant effect on consumers. They have happened and they do have an effect. However, the relatively new and rapidly growing industry of mountain biking is unique. I do not believe those negative aspects of mergers industries will happen in the industry of mountain biking. I believe that the merging of smaller companies with larger ones can and will be good for the consumer. In order to understand how this could be so, one must first ask "why" these mergers are occurring. You may well be asking yourself, "Why should I believe this merger is good for me, the consumer?" The mountain biking industry has good reason for not engaging in many of the practices of other industrial mergers.

Peter, in sum, provided images of an opponent in his early drafts, but the images are poorly signaled and elaborated and, consequently, not able to support positions concrete and credible enough to be included in a reader's decision making. In his subsequent drafts, Peter sharpened the portrait of the opponents so that his readers could experience the weight of legitimate alternatives as a foundation for their decision making.

Hyunjung, a student from Korea, also used a second draft to sharpen the portrait of an opponent. She is concerned with the practice of some Korean parents who send their elementary-school-age children to study in an English-speaking country. In her first draft, Hyunjung argued that this practice was wrong. Yet, she did so without portraying her opponent, a parent who would defend the practice. The parents in her first draft seemed odd in their attitudes about raising children, if not hard-hearted. Without a fuller and more human portrait of these parents, Hyunjung could not convince her readers that she was giving them alternatives to decide among reasonable persons. Her next draft corrected the problem by giving us a close-up of how these Korean parents think and the reasonableness of why they send their children abroad:

> Koreans have been emphasizing the importance of the English Language for quite some time. Now, Korean schools teach English in Elementary Schools. The parents want their children to stay ahead of their peers, so they try to teach English to their children at younger ages. Methods for teaching English vary. Some parents learn English themselves and teach their children. But the parents have realized that learning from a native English speaker is the only way to improve their kids' pronunciation and hearing ability. So, they buy English-learning videotapes made by native English speakers. However, the parents also find out that in order to improve the kids' speaking ability, the kids need to interact with the teacher and other English-speaking students. The parents finally decide to send their children to kindergartens or elementary schools in English speaking countries. For the last couple of years, the number of young children leaving for America, Australia, and Canada has visibly increased. This has all been caused by the parents' passion for making their kids do better than others.

Hyunjung's revision made her opponents more human, and so, worthier as opponents. It made readers feel the weight of an authentic decision context, which always includes reasonable alternatives.

Presenting a Decision for Whom?

To ask the reader for a decision, the writer needs to consider who is being asked to decide. As with instructional writing, providing a guided tour of a decision space requires that the text seem responsive, that it engage the reader interactively. Yet many argument writers we observed have no specific reader in mind, often resulting in unfortunate consequences. Without a reader in mind, the writer is unable to determine what decision needs to be made and what guidance needs to be given to make it. In the worst case, the writer will write only with herself as the implied reader. The decision path and guidance will fit a reader who thinks only like her. Only this ideal reader will feel the text as argument. Other readers will experience the text as a targetless instructional path toward a decision.

Lauren, a Hispanic student, was angry that the White culture had blurred the important distinctions between Latinos, Chicanos, and Hispanics. She wanted to convert this feeling into an argument, to ask a reader to make a decision in her favor. Yet, she had difficulty choosing the reader whom she wanted to decide in her favor. She first considered writing to the average middle-class white who had little interaction with Americans of nonEuropean descent. However, she soon realized that this reader had nothing to decide. That Latinos, Chicanos, and Hispanics are different groups is a fact. Writing to a person ignorant of this fact might be useful exposition, but not argument. After some exploratoin, she tried as her audience the Hollywood producers who often blur the distinction between Latinos, Chicanos, and Hispanics when they depict them in films. She found such producers culturally positioned to make a decision in her favor, having the power to back films that could clarify these ethnic distinctions for the film-going public. By locating the appropriate decision makers, Lauren found a way to turn her original emotion into a decision that could be decided in her favor.

When writers develop their image of the reader as a decision maker, they may find it helpful to scale down the reader to a proper name, to a person the writer knows. As part of this strategy, they may also find it useful to structure their text along lines that allow for a more personally targeted reader. Moving from an impersonal essay to a more personalized letter format is an example of this personalization strategy. Such a strategy focused Mary's alignment of the various elements required to bring a reader to a decision. After struggling in the abstract over a decision to recommend and a reader to decide in her favor, Mary found it useful to use a letter format to compose an argument to her husband about sending their biracial children to private or public schools.

Dear Sidney,

I know that you are a strong proponent of public school education and that diversity weighs heavily in your argument. Because we live in a primarily middle-income, white neighborhood, the public schools offer an easy way to provide the children with exposure to a blend of cultural, racial and economic diversity—in particular, real world exposure to African Americans.

The reasoning is that, daily contact with typical black children and their families via public schools will prepare Larissa to "hang" in that community with less effort. This is important since, as she gets older she will less and less be considered cute, and more and more be identified as black.

It is unlikely that she will fit comfortably into mainstream white culture or black culture without some effort. Since it is more difficult for blacks in America than whites, preparing Larissa for this label will give her the necessary skills for dealing with worst case situations. If she perceives herself as black she will be more conscious of stereotypes and work to dissuade them. The specific reasoning and clear emotion leading us to participate in Rodman Street Baptist Church (Southern Black Baptist) confirms for me that this is a key element in your decision making criteria.

I agree that Larissa, as a bi-racial/bi-cultural individual, needs to feel equally comfortable in both communities. I think that we both place significant emphasis on critical thinking, independence, curiosity and a sense of purpose and compassion too. Our role as parents is to build a world that helps her to develop these characteristics, in addition to cultural poise.

Mary invests her opening paragraphs establishing common ground with her husband.

My question today is: will a typical public school education providing diversity, hinder the development of the other qualities. Perhaps my concern, more specifically is: will a private or a public school more effectively foster all of these qualities?

She goes on to show her husband that his premises about schooling can lead to her conclusions. The advantages normally given to public schools can be found in private schools too.

Just because a public school is diverse, it won't necessarily provide maximum academic value. Similarly, just because a private school provides academic value, it won't necessarily lack diversity. In this sense, we cannot discuss the issue of public verses private until we know where we will live when Larissa starts school. We want to compare one specific school to another, rather than comparing one stereotype to another.

Neither public nor private schools have exclusive rights to warm and attentive teachers, appropriate class sizes, and a safe indoor and outdoor environment. Both should provide clean and healthy experiences.

Where private and public schools differ, the advantage goes to private.

So that being equal, we can look at the differences. Typically, in a public school a child can enjoy the camaraderie of neighborhood children. These relationships are reinforced by easy playtime in the evenings and weekends.

Among my concerns about public schools are the ability and willingness of parents to fully support their children through academic and emotional challenges. I could argue that public schools encourage self-discipline because the teachers are so busy with social counseling. But I find this a drawback. In private schools on the other hand, academic discipline is placed with teachers and administration, while parents assume top responsibility for social and psychological care. Because there are often less economic and social challenges for private school families, there is greater time and capability to devote to individualized learning. Research shows that minorities in particular benefit from individualized learning and virtually any female who has attended an all-girls school will tell you that the atmosphere provided significantly stronger support for girls to develop their voice as individuals.

Mary offers that for her and her husband to decide on private schools can break a bad stereotype:

I also believe that our family could have a positive impact on the stereotype of private school supporters. There is little doubt that Larissa would excel at an admissions test and interview. Both she as an individual and we as a family would challenge conventions. This is a worthy and responsible commitment to our children, the educational environment and to our peers.

She entertains the often-stated disadvantages of private schools and shows how they can be addressed:

> A noteworthy drawback to private school education is the potential for isolation within the neighborhood. Urban living promises proximity to many schools in our neighborhoods. Given the fact that no two families on our block send their children to the same schools, whether they are public or private, makes this a moot point in this case. Either way the neighborhood relationships will be separate from the school relationships.
>
> The financial commitment can be disregarded. I understand that it is a roadblock for many families, but I am grateful that we are in a position to choose. It is true that the money we will spend to provide a solid and reliable daily educational experience could also be used to create valuable single event opportunities. Foreign travel for example, can expand ones knowledge of the world and the variety of people, sites, and beliefs the world has to offer. While adults may benefit from one-time experiences, children, especially preschool and elementary age children, rely heavily on routines and consistency for reinforcement. A private school can offer solid role models, critical thinking, and a sense of purpose on a daily basis. Regardless, we as parents will always need to play the key role in creating a sense of compassion, curiosity and independence. These are characteristics established and reinforced most strongly in the home setting and supplemented in a school setting.

She concludes, summarizing her points:

> Sidney, I encourage you to think about this issue with an open mind. Reviewing this information, you'll see that private schools are preferable over public schools for these reasons. 1. Discipline issues are minimized allowing teachers to focus on teaching academics and allowing parents to focus on values and ethics. 2. There are other ways of exposing the children to diversity on a daily or weekly basis that will not hinder the development of independence, curiosity or sense of purpose. 3. Private schools are more economically affluent. Therefore changing a stereotype within that setting will have greater impact than fitting within it.

By narrowing her audience to a person she knew well, Mary was able to structure a decision for a reader, even if only one. There are trade-offs in this strategy, of course, as employing it may reduce the scope and applicability of the text. Mary, for example, wrote an argument to Sidney that was, more or less, a transcription of what she could, and had, spoken to him face to face. In order to pursue argument, creating a realistic and meaningful decision for a reader, Mary found she had to eliminate the distance and anonymity of writing. No writer of argument wants to limit argument to personal acquaintances only. But personal acquaintances are a good starting point for practicing the public identities that we need to acquire in order to argue to large, anonymous readerships. From childhood on, we learn argument strategies in our face-to-face world and only gradually do we learn to extend them through writing to more faceless readers. Lacking knowledge of a larger audience, writers are well advised to follow Mary's strategy: narrow the scope of the audience and narrow the decision making to known and familiar faces. In the culture at large, master arguers often are able to reach faceless audiences only because they have spent years honing public identities for listeners and readers whom they know by acquaintance. Like a dramatic play that performs in small theatres for years before making its bid for Broadway, argument requires testing a message and the public identity to back it with known audiences before taking it to unknown ones.

Balancing Experience, Generalization and Action

Like other information-based writing assignments, argument involves explicit invitations to the reader to engage in generalization learning, experiential learning, and the learning of guided action. As we have been describing since we started to examine information writing, each of the types of learning correspond with elements in the text that can advance these outcomes. Different elements dominate, furthermore, depending upon which learning outcome is dominant. In exposition, we saw, generalization learning dominates. In popular explanation, experiential learning dominates. In instruction, guided action dominates.

By way of contrast, argument requires that all three types of learning be used in balance, with no element that advances one dominating the elements that advance others. Perhaps this is because authentic decision-making, a guided mental action, depends on exploring across a space of rich experiences and generalizations over which any final decision must figure. Cut off from experience and generalization, the act of deciding turns into a content- and context-free imperative like "Buy!" or "Vote!"

The balance of generalization, experience, and action is an important consideration when understanding the representational challenge of argument. Unfortunately, it is an understanding that has yet fully to permeate our educational system. The American educational approach to argument, oscillating between structural composition and genre training, does its best to carve argument up into pieces that hide the overall representational challenge. Argument as action is taught (if at all) as "letters to the editor" to suggest social action. Such letters are long enough to propose action but usually too short to include the experience and generalization needed to justify that action. Argument as experience tends to flatten into expressive writing, a first-person self-portrait "with attitude." Argument as generalization tends toward implementation as the research or term paper associated with 3 x 5 notecards and library search.

This subjective-objective dichotomy reflects a chasm between so called expressive (experience) papers, where teachers want opinion and, on the other, so-called *research* (generalization) papers, where teachers want general facts. The *expressive paper* is typically written off the top of the head, without external sources. The *research paper*, by contrast, typically calls for library or web search, with little place for personal reflection, exploration, or guided decision making.

So well trained in the dichotomy between argument as experience and argument as generalization are students in the United States that by the time they reach the college freshman writing course, they ask the teacher as a matter of routine, "Do you want my opinions in this paper?" The question is asked seriously, as a way of finding out whether they are being asked to write with the "subjective" switch turned on, welcoming the personal pronoun, or the "objective" switch, forbidding all traces of the writer's mind.

Neither type of paper comprehends the representational challenge of composing argument. The expressive paper shares experience with the reader, but does not generalize that experience to cultural perspectives that compete. The research paper shares cultural generalizations with the reader, but leaves no trace of the personal experience that can make the stakes meaningful, either to the writer or the reader. Neither paper structures an authentic decision context for the reader.

It should not be surprising, then, to find some of our own studio students replicating the educational bifurcation of argument in their early argument drafts.

Jessica's early draft argument emphasizes personal opinion and experience. Her argument set out to counter the perspective of the person living outside the United States who stereotypes all Americans as "ugly Americans." Her writing focuses on her lived experience. When she was a student studying abroad in France, she fell victim to such a person. She introduces us to the stereotype at the beginning of her paper.

> There has long been the myth of the "Ugly American." He invades foreign countries shouting in English and makes a scene wherever he goes. He refuses to eat anything but Big Macs and criticizes the traditions of other cultures. Most Americans would probably assume other cultures have negative stereotypes about them. However, they have probably never heard a non-Americans view of the typical American.
>
> One day, my British professor enlightened my class with the facts of what it means to be an American out of America. He characterized the typical, American tourist for us. I was shocked to learn that some people believe the myth is true for all Americans. Not all Americans are Ugly Americans. Some of us do speak other languages and certainly appreciate other cultures.

Jessica then enters a personal narrative, telling us how she learned more about the stereotype.

> It was another cool, rainy day in South of France. Our "classroom" was a garage conveniently located next to a bakery. Only a few of the "young Americans," as we were always called, showed up for International Business. As usual, no one wanted to hear about direct foreign investments, joint ventures, or anything to do with business. We wanted to hear about European politics and how the English felt about the Germans and the French about the Swiss. How the French hated to bathe themselves and used lots of perfume to cover up body odors. The easiest way to get to Prague for the weekend. We were able to get Monsieur Boweren to discuss the relationship between the French and the West Africans in France until 8:45.
>
> He grabbed a fat marker and was about to write something on the board that begin with the words, "wholly owned." Oh, no. Not business. Not that stuff we could memorize from textbooks and learn in 500 person lecture halls back at our universities in the States. I raised my hand and blurted, "Wait, Monsieur Boweren. How do the Europeans see the Americans?"

He turned around and laughed. "The Americans," he said in an English accent and touched his Burberry's print scarf. For a second, I thought he was going to actually teach us business, but he set his marker down and sat up own the edge of his desk as he usually did. He crossed his arms and laughed again. "Well, people imagine the typical American as an overweight, white, middle-aged man in a bright flowered shirt and white shorts. You know, no Europeans even wear shorts and especially not white. He wears tall white socks pulled up to his knees and those huge running shoes you people seem to like so much. I know that all Americans are not like that, just as all Swedish are not blonde and all Germans not large, but that's the way they are seen. In addition, of course, they only know how to say, "Do you speak English?" You people should say, "Do you speak American?" because you do not speak English.

Although stereotypes can be unfortunate, they are not likely to disappear. To create an argument, Jessica must set up the terms of our decision making. What is the issue that we are supposed to be deciding in her favor? In her first draft, Jessica had yet to make this clear. Should we decide that stereotypes should go away? That would seem naive. Should we decide that the myth of the ugly American is not true for all? That point is already decided by her showing how she resisted the stereotype. Jessica's first draft had yet to define the decision she wanted her readers to make.

We laughed. I thought of Chevy Chase's European Vacation where even Hollywood showed what the American tourist was like. It is easy to find the "Ugly American" funny when we are not put on trial for being one ourselves. Not all Americans are ugly Americans, but we are all seen that way. We have our stereotypes and believe people from a certain country to be all the same way. We can be convinced that all people from a certain state, or region, or city are all the same way! "New York City people are rude and always in a rush. They only care about themselves and you wouldn't find the hospitality you would in a small town."

Keeping the writing on a personal level, Jessica contrasts the ugly American with other stereotypes she has experienced.

As a Southerner from Arkansas who has been educated in the North, I have always experienced Southern stereotypes. It was sometimes annoying to be stereotyped with the whole South. However, being stereotyped only as an "American" in a different country was another story.

Being stereotyped as an ugly American hit Jessica harder than being stereotyped as a Southerner.

The "American" stereotypes touched a nerve that the "Southerner" stereotypes never reached. For instance, the French family I was living with assumed I ate McDonald's all the time and loved fast food. They were shocked when I told them how my family really ate. My French friends were shocked that I actually dressed like them and didn't wear shorts and Nikes every day. They wanted to know why I didn't go running or to the gym. I didn't tell them that at home I used to work out religiously. They found it hysterical that Americans worked out and all the time, yet they were still fat.

As we traveled throughout Europe, everyone wanted to speak English to us. If someone in my group vaguely knew the language, they were still addressed in broken English. What disturbed me the most was that I would ask directions in French and everyone would answer in English.

During my first two or three weeks in France, it did not bother me as much. However, as my French improved, I told people that I was student and trying to become fluent in their language. So, please speak it to me! They seemed surprised and would then speak a mile a minute in French. I had to concentrate so hard that my head hurt, but it was worth it.

Jessica concludes her narrative by revealing her personal actions in response to the stereotype.

The final test for my French language and proving I could be French came when my French friend from boarding school, Nicole, invited me to her home in Le Vesinet, a suburb Paris. "Lots of Americans live in my neighborhood because the houses are much bigger than normal French homes," she said in the car ride to her home. I was very intimidated about meeting her parents. Her father and mother were both French, but had attended American universities. They were both fluent in English. Her father owned several plastic factories all over the U.S. and dealt with Americans every day. Not only did her family have titles, but chateaux all over Europe.

Apparently, Nicole saw my apprehension. "My sister, her fiance, and his family are going to be there too tonight. And they all speak English, so you don't have to worry." I told her I was prepared to spend the weekend speaking French. I was even more anxious about intruding in a family event. "Don't worry. We are having a tasting dinner for what to serve at the wedding." I wanted to let her know I didn't plan on making everyone speak English that night, let alone feel like they had to talk about America or my culture with me. "You mean you're having a degustation, Nicole." She was excited that I knew the word for it.

The evening began with everyone speaking English for me, so I would not feel left out. They had no accents whatsoever. However, I was in their country and did not want to give them the opportunity to practice English when I was there to learn French. I responded in French to everything they said to me. I ate their purple sea urchin and goose livers saying the dishes were "different" from anything I had ever had. Her parents were shocked that I continued to speak French to them, even though their English was better than my French. They joked that I was getting a "Provincial" French accent. How's that for an "Ugly American?"

Jessica's first draft is an able telling of her personal response to the stereotype of the ugly American. Nevertheless, her struggle in this opening draft remains personal and it is hard for us to fit it within larger concerns that can shape a decision context. Like a skilled self-portrait writer, she can make us empathize with her experience, but not until a later draft did Jessica place her readers in the role of decision maker, asking them to see that the stereotype of the Ugly American was much less widespread than many now thought.

If Jessica's early draft argument reflects the school-based understanding of argument as an expressive self-portrait, Michelle's first draft argument, against capital punishment, reflects the school-based understanding of argument as the reporting of objective research. Michelle starts with generalizations from the culture opposing capital punishment.

Who has the right to say when or why some one should die? As a culture, we profess to hold life sacred. Sacred unless someone pisses us off or offends our sensibilities. Then we, as a society, want to lash out-pointing a finger at the perpetrator. Vilifying him or her and acting as if we are blameless—our morality unvarnished by aggressive or violent behavior.

Michelle recalls the movie *Dead Man Walking* which, for many critics, offered a balanced view of the pros and cons of capital punishment.

> A couple of weeks ago my husband and I saw "Dead Man Walking," a powerful movie about a poor White young man put to death for violent crimes he had committed. It was also about a nun, drawn into counseling this young man, and the inner turmoil and struggles she experienced as their relationship evolved.
>
> Many issues emerge from this story. While efforts are made to transmute the death sentence to life imprisonment, the issue of the young man's accountability is brought into the foreground. Many people argued that putting him to death makes him accountable for the atrocities he committed. Using the Old Testament as justification—you know, "an eye for an eye." These are the voices that said the young man in the story deserved to die. They said that he was no good—that he was evil and should be disposed of, removed from this earth. As if we could (or even should) scour this world of all that is ugly, unpleasant, or disquieting. In this way can we live in a safer environment—a better place for our children to grow up free from fear.
>
> I say we live in a world filled with contradictions. As a society, we give lip service to valuing human life but we perpetrate socially condoned violence. We go into other countries, both overtly and covertly, and assassinate government leaders and citizens. Yet, when these stories come out about the actions of the CIA they can only be published in alternative newspapers (i.e., the destabilization of the Chilean government and the assignation of Salvador Allenda). Popular publications, for the most part, will not publish the reports or provide only a minimal amount of space in their publication. The general population is either apathetic, ignores, or finds a way to justify these actions.
>
> It seems ironic that voices rage (and rightly so) when an individual inflicts pain on another but the voices protesting undeclared wars in which we, as a nation, participate are not as loudly publicized. And, if we don't invade physically (Granada, Panama, Vietnam) then our government and or industry is often guilty of supplying the equipment needed to make weapons that are used for murder. (i.e., Iran-Contra, computer parts for weaponry that "found" its way to Iraq.) Are our hands not blood stained as a result of these actions?

Many innocent people die, often women and children in particular, from the consequences that ensue. Where is our accountability as a society?

How do we account for the fact that 80-90% of those on death row are men of color? Moreover, that 100% of these people are from poor backgrounds. Could at least some of the reasons for this situation result from growing up in poverty? The idea that the American Dream is available for everyone is fallacious. The notion that we have conquered racism is foolish if not downright arrogant. If this is true why would the majority of the population on Death Row be people of color?

Do not think I am saying that those found guilty of violent crime should be set free to walk—rather I am saying let's spend our resources so that there is 100% literacy in the U.S., spend our resources dealing with issues of poverty and racism, and spend our resources to work with other countries instead of dictating how they should live. How can we justify becoming outraged when an individual acts violently, but turn our backs when our money and resources are spent perpetrating cruelty on others?

The world has always contained elements of cruelty and violence. Although some may disagree, I doubt that there has been a kinder, gentler time in our society. But, what we can do as a culture, is to become honest with the contradictions, work to lift the veils of denial from our eyes, and deal with the paradoxes we create. Taking a life for a life is never the answer. We are not Gods. It is not in our capacity to truly decide who should live and who should die. But, we can have an affect on how we live and what our time and resources are used for. This is our responsibility, this is our accountability.

Michelle's early draft reflects a composite of many generalizations drawn from the external culture. Mimicking aspects of the high school research paper, she is reporting snippets of stock arguments she has read and overheard rather than fashioning an argument that bears her own stamp of experience.

In further drafts, Michelle began to find her own subjective investments around which to make, not simply report, argument. Her second draft inserts more self-portraying elements, grounding the generalized perspective she heard from the outside with the weight of her own firsthand experience. This makes her perspective on capital punishment more personal, credible, and less cliché-driven. She begins to fashion a public identity from a personal identity she has lived rather than from public stereotypes she has copied.

> I have worked as head of a trail crew for "at-risk youth." These youth have trouble in school and live on or near the poverty line. They really are at-risk. Most come from single parent homes, usually with only the mother present. These environments are often chaotic and abusive with caregivers struggling with addiction, alcoholism, or just a basic lack of survival skills. These youth were less than well cared for by society. They often walked around with an attitude of "I don't care," which mirrored back what they were given. It was heartbreaking to see the potential of these youth turn into self-destruction. I often wondered while working with them what life would hold in store as they reached adulthood.

By showing us her firsthand experience with at-risk youth, Michelle was able to submit the various external generalizations she heard to the scrutiny of her own personal authority. She found she could enter the issue of capital punishment from her direct experience with the kind of youths who often become candidates for death row. Her self-portrait went on to describe how the youth camps of the kind in which she worked are understaffed and underfunded. With better funding, she concluded, some of the problems people think they are solving with capital punishment could be alleviated.

The effect of Michelle's second draft was to make important connections between her intimate personal experience and a more generalized perspective on the cultural issue of capital punishment. She merged experience and generalization in her second draft to make her perspective more accessible and credible to readers. Yet, even in this draft, she has not set up enough competition across perspectives to induce her readers, without more information, to follow her to the same decision. In a third draft, she set up the competition between opposing positions so that readers could understand they had a decision to make.

Susan's argument, written across various drafts, illustrates how effective argument must balance experience, generalization, and action. A mother of a young son, she weighs the pros and cons of having him circumcised. She links experience and generalization to present both the pro and the con perspective. She lets these perspectives compete and then she judges the competition. As she weighs the reasoning on both sides and lets her mind follow the evidence, she shares her reasons for why her readers should walk down her decision path.

Four years ago my son was born. I remember watching his new eyes, while they roamed without focus, and being amazed at how he seemed so fragile he seemed to me. Never before had I felt that my decisions carried as much weight as I did during the first months of his life. I'm sure it's a universal experience. In these early years when we choose for our children, we can protect them. We can make the world exciting, and often, keep it from becoming painful. We can build a particular nest. Soon our children venture out into other worlds, the playground, friends' homes, and the school. In these places they will do some of their most important growing up. In these worlds, they will need to fit in with their peers.

This was on my mind as I faced a dilemma that centered on whether or not he should be circumcised.

In the next paragraph, we understand how carefully Susan has studied competing viewpoints on this subject.

I'd worried over this decision in the months proceeding his birth. Since I'm not a member of a religion that requires circumcision and my then husband had no strong feelings on the matter, the choice was solely my own. I read books, talked to doctors, nurses, and midwives, and asked my friends for their opinions on the subject. One day I found myself driving in my car, and trying to find some good music. As I moved the dial through the stations, I happened to hear a radio health care talk show dealing with circumcision. The doctor who hosted the show was talking about the increased sensation experienced by males who had managed to hold onto their foreskins. Well, my son would thank me for that, even if I'd never see it on a Hallmark card at Mother's Day.

Susan now lets the concerns of her imagined opponent take control of the writing. She uses a collaborative form—the question—to indicate how open-minded she is willing to be with that opponent.

But in avoiding circumcision would I make him different from many of the other boys in the neighborhood? Would he resent me for it? And if he was the subject of ridicule because of a choice that I made for him, how would we both feel?

Susan discloses some of her autobiography to let us in on what is behind some of her fears of the procedure.

In the years before my pregnancy, when the decision was academic, I could be studied and certain. During that time, a friend of mine, a photographer, scheduled work with a hospital to take pictures of newborns being circumcised. He told me later that he'd never seen anything so awful. The babies were strapped to a plastic support, isolated from any human touch, and with both arms held down, the cut was made. The screaming was awful and he could hardly bear to take the pictures. I knew then that when the time came, I would be more enlightened than other mothers. My child would never have to worry about that kind of experience.

Soon after I found out I was pregnant, this all became more personal, and I began to study the issue in more depth. I wanted to make sure that I clearly understood the position held by the advocates of this procedure. I needed to be sure that they didn't have facts in favor of circumcision that would make me change my point of view.

Her research suggests that circumcision might be overkill. Her image of the fingernail drives this fear home.

Were there medical reasons that would make circumcision a good choice? Some books pointed to the elimination of penile cancer for men who were circumcised at birth. But the incidence of that cancer is minimal to begin with that it's comparable to having your fingernails removed in infancy to prevent the possibility of fungal infections in later life—a pound of cure for an ounce of possibility.

Again, Susan lets herself be interrupted by the questions of her imagined opponent—so she can assure us that she has already thought through the answers.

The foreskin provides a warm, moist environment that bacteria love. Would he have to deal with infections that could have been prevented by the simple removal of unnecessary tissue? One of my goals is to keep him from having a lot of unnecessary aggravation, and I thought about this issue carefully. In the end, I couldn't make a choice for circumcision based on the possibility of an infection that can so easily be prevented. We live in a world with indoor plumbing, and in our grocery stores, entire aisles are devoted to soap displays. If he's lazy about hygiene, it will be necessary for me to impress upon him the importance of using soap and water as well as the correct way to take care of himself; just as I do when I show him how to brush his teeth. After all, I would never have his teeth removed just because he did not want to take care of them.

There are concerns of social conformity as well. Again, Susan lets the opponent interrupt so she can show she is responsive, with nothing to hide.

Since the medical issues did not compel me to change my mind, what about the social considerations. My son and I live in a conservative, provincial community. The people here do things the way they have always been done, and they do not like it much when someone acts differently than they do. Since circumcision is the norm here, how could I ask my son to be different from his friends, especially in this atmosphere where conformity has such value. This was my most difficult decision.

But the problem with conforming is that often refutes sound thinking. If I circumcise my son in order to help him fit in, why would not I, in a different time and place, bind my daughter's feet for the same reason. Maybe in another time and place, I'd have to do both those things, but not here. My son will not be shunned from his society based on his foreskin. At most he'll have to put up with some questions, and maybe some teasing. There's always something about us that's different. For me, it was my height. Growing up I was much taller than the other children my age. I would have done anything then to be the same height as my peers. Should my parents have found some way to stunt my growth so that I would not have to put up with the difficulties of being different? How could I let him be strapped to that board for such a thin thread of a reason. And what if I had him circumcised in order to be the same as other boys? And what if we then moved from this area to one where the majority of boys had not been circumcised? How would I soothe my conscience then? The only choice, given all the time I'd spent studying both the problem and my own heart, was to leave his body as I found it.

We all must conform somewhat to be part of the society, and most of us think that belonging is a good thing. Even so, we need to think carefully about how far we are willing to go in order to fit in. Will we someday look at circumcision, done in a clinical hospital setting, in the same way that we view the binding of feet or the practice of female circumcision which we ridicule when we see it in other cultures? If no religious necessity prevails, aren't we continuing the kind of burdensome legacy for our sons that we so disdain in other regions of the world; regions that we have the audacity to call more primitive than our own?

Combining generalization, experience, and action, Susan is able to present a complex decision making context and ultimately guide us through to the decision she favors. Combining these elements results in a text that is likely to engage readers, address concerns, and change perspectives.

The examples from this chapter illustrate how much art and practice are required to make argument effective and how little has to go wrong to diminish its effectiveness. More importantly, we think, the examples illustrate why the effort is worth it.

Summarizing the Writing Models in Relation to Invitations to Decide

Argument introduces the challenge of creating a multiplicity of inner worlds within the world of the text. These worlds form a decision space through which the writer guides the reader and recommends a decision. Guiding a reader through a decision space requires new challenges for the writer without letting the writer off the hook on any of the old ones. It requires holding experiential, generalization, and guided-action learning in balance, which entails a new mastery of the elements that need to be individually mastered in information and instruction as well as portrait and landscape writing. It also requires new contextual assumptions about the writer-reader relationship involving the reader's source of power, the reflexive nature of perspective, and the indeterminate locus of expertise.

So challenging is argument that it is easier to document all the small things that can diminish the overall effect than to pretend that novices are only near-misses from perfect success. In this chapter, we have used student models mainly to show the many small things that writers must overcome when they engage argument.

Andrew is an example of how the writer must first develop a perspective before asking a reader to share it. First drafts almost always show a perspective in the making, not one to offer to defend.

That an arguer must have a position before arguing may seem too obvious to point out. Unfortunately, it is less obvious than it should be. There is a tactical sense of argument that encourages verbal clashing for its own sake, using words to fight regardless of whether there is a developed perspective to fight for. In a culture like ours—a culture that Deborah Tannen has recently dubbed the "Argument Culture" (1998)—verbal fighting often replaces reasoned discussion. Argument is often confused with the fight rather than the stakes the fight is supposed to decide. In this highly charged and contentious atmosphere, writers too often try to persuade readers to a unilateral position that they themselves may have not worked through. The result is posturing, skirmishing, and smoke. Suffice it to say that we do not accept this image of argument. The image of argument we propose in this chapter is competitive and evaluative, but with the larger purpose of responsible change in the world.

Even when the writer has a developed perspective worth deciding for, she may overlook the reader's need to see alternative perspectives prior to a decision. Should the writer overlook credible alternatives, the reader may detect invitations to learn rather than to decide. Tim, Peter, and Hyunjung are examples of writers whose first drafts seemed more like exposition than argument. They required multiple drafts to develop credible opposing perspectives and credible portraits of the persons holding them.

Even with a seemingly developed perspective and reasonable alternatives, writers can overlook the identity of their readers. To whom are they bringing this decision? Lauren illustrates how the writer's sharpening sense of the reader can go hand in glove with sharpening the position she can develop. Mary illustrates how restricting the reader to known persons can help a writer who might otherwise be overwhelmed by the thought of structuring a decision for a faceless mass.

Argument requires that the writer balance experience, generalization, and action. This is a delicate balance and our educational system tends to cut the challenge up into less challenging pieces. The result is the bifurcation of argument as personal experience and as the generalized reporting of external sources. Jessica's first draft illustrates what happens when writers approach argument from subjective expression with little cultural generalization. Michelle's first draft illustrates what happens when they approach it from the side of a generalized cultural pastiche reflecting none of their own experience.

Susan's final draft illustrates the result of achieving an effective balance of all three elements. The writer ends up with a decision to recommend in a genuine controversy she has experienced firsthand, and to a group of decision makers who have been given reasonable motivation to judge in her favor.

Argument in Organizational Contexts

The occurrence of argument in professional contexts, spoken or written, is more difficult to pin down than one might think. Argument always involves ceding decision making power to audiences. In the purest cases, writers and their audiences agree that the context requires argument, but the contexts for argument in professional or political life are seldom pure. Writers may think the occasion requires argument, but their audiences may be apathetic and do not wish to make the investment to decide anything. On the other hand, audiences may think the occasion requires argument but the only people empowered to set decision making into motion do not want to share the decision making or do not even want to acknowledge that the context warrants a decision to be made managed, made, or shared.

Unlike other types of writing, the contexts for argument are themselves often hotly contested in the culture. In the professional world, the contexts where argument is least contested is communication from the less to the more powerful. By definition, those in positions of less power must share and justify their decisions with those who outrank them. This includes communication from subordinates to their bosses, corporate officials to stockholders, and professionals to the clients who employ them. In each case, the less powerful person must justify her decision making to those with greater power. Memos justifying action and annual reports justifying corporate performance are genres of argument that represent accountability to perceived superiors. Another type of document that fits this specification is the design rationale. In this form of communication, the designer reports to a paying client on the decision space that has gone into designing a house, a bridge, a website, or any other commodity that can be designed and paid for.

Both in organizational and cultural life, argument defines power relationships. The designer of argument invariably treats the audience (the targeted decision maker) as a potential peer. This is why, contrary to popular belief, people in power command and notify (through memos) more than they in fact argue. Indeed, people in power, with more subordinates than superiors, are accustomed to being argued *to* more than making arguments. Argument presupposes at least the appearance of equality between arguer and audience. Consequently, the experience of being argued to can be a disconcerting one to audiences who do not believe the arguer deserves a platform. For similar reasons, power holders who wish to protect their power at all costs do not wish to acknowledge their audience's right to argue with them. An organization, or a culture for that matter, that encourages argument at all levels distributes the power of decision making. This distribution of power is less efficient than in rigid hierarchical organizations that centralize decision making. But it often leads to employees who feel greater ownership over the conditions of the workplace. And in the larger society, it leads to citizens who feel greater ownership over their lives.

Epilogue: The Promise of Representational Theory in Writing Education

Were the mastery of grammar and usage the sufficient educational foundation for entry into specific textual genres, we would expect that, once students had the rules of structural composition down, their performance in different types of writing would be only a matter of preference. Words and syntax would be the basic and sole elements of composition and student performance in one or another genre would express itself only as a preference for the site or writing context in which a student wished to apply her compositional knowledge.

Significantly, from our studio observations, we find that one and the same writer varies markedly in her performance across the various examples covered in this book. Furthermore, these variations seem more than arbitrary preference. They seem rather to depend on a constellation of factors: aptitude, cognitive style, motivation, personality, and educational background as well as preference. For example, after years of observing writers work across the various writing assignments discussed in previous chapters, we identified, among others, the following writer profiles.

- Personal writers, for whom the self-portrait was the highlight.

- Diffident writers, who could not tolerate the self-portrait or the argument because both put the spotlight on their individual thinking.

- Imaginative writers, who could never imagine addressing the reader's perspective and wanted to hold the floor in monologue without interruption from an anticipated reader.

- Conversational writers, who thought of texts as pointed messages to an interactive reader rather than extended worlds that could hold the floor without interruption.

- Reflective writers, for whom scenic writing was an impossible assignment—because in trying to write what they saw, they could not help disclosing what they though.

- Visual writers, for whom scenic writing was the only writing worth doing.

- General interest writers, who did well with narrative but whose performance degraded with exposition or popular explanation when they were called upon to provide information from the role of expert.

- Expert writers, who did not do well until they could write from a specialized knowledge that set them apart from readers.

- Impractical writers, who could or would not write to the reader's hands.

- Manual writers, who never wanted to write to anything but the hands.

- Indecisive writers, who could never manage to complete the argument because they could not decide for themselves, much less ask a reader for a decision.

- Advocacy writers, who thought writing started and stopped with decision and action, and so, could barely conceive of writing apart from asking the reader for a decision.

Seeking to explain texts as constituted from myriad diverse compositional elements beyond homogeneous linguistic units, a representational theory of composing is poised to explain the variations we see expressed among individual writers. We have used the knowledge of these variations both for assessment and to train students in self-assessment. The knowledge of these variations has allowed us to isolate a individual student's strengths and weaknesses. Working on a student's strengths, we push her toward a professional focus. Working on a student's weaknesses, we push her to increase her range and to insure that her weaknesses do not hold her back.

Writers seeking admission into graduate programs or jobs requiring extensive writing help themselves by submitting professional portfolios. Students in our classrooms bundle their semester's writing into a professional portfolio. The portfolio is introduced by a cover letter that overviews the various written assignments and then proceeds into self-assessment. We typically find a relation among a student's self-assessment, her enjoyment of a writing assignment, and her writing background. English students, for example, schooled on the literary essay, tend already to find familiar the sequential logic of the self-portrait, narrative history, exposition, and argument. Visual design students, who often conceive of writing as solely logical and linear, are pleasantly surprised to discover in the observer portrait, scenic writing, popular explanation, and instruction opportunities to be profoundly visual, even lyrical.

By demonstrating their capacity to rise to the representational challenge posed by each writing assignment, students can show prospective advisors and employers both their strengths and limits, as well as evidence that they have the range required to design a variety of textual worlds and a variety of invitations to readers as to how to navigate through them.

The cover letter adds value to the writing portfolio in several ways. First, it gives students the opportunity to document their understanding of writing as a representational art involving single, blended, and cumulative effects. A second benefit is to provide room for self-assessment. Students can indicate which texts they believe are the strongest in represented effects and which are the weakest. These judgments, of course, must be tested against teachers and peers. A third benefit is to have the writer indicate which are the texts she most enjoyed writing and which she least enjoyed.

A fourth and, from our view, the most valued benefit of the cover letter is to deepen the students' understanding of writing as a unified body of representational principles. Not only students, but also professional writers sometimes mistakenly associate the whole of writing with only a limited subset of representations and effects. Students with a strong background in academic writing, for example, tend to think of writing in its most linear, logical, abstract, and hierarchal manifestations—prototypically expressed in exposition and argument. Students with a strong background in creative fiction and poetry tend to know writing best when tied to scene, spatial immediacy, and narrative. Students trained in science and science fiction raise popular explanation to the zenith of texts, where the inclusive and familiar puts a human face on the exclusive and unfamiliar. Students schooled in technical writing often find themselves more at home when the writer provides expert knowledge (e.g., exposition, popular explanation, and instruction) than when the writer meets the reader as an equal (e.g., argument).

Each concept of writing has value, but each is limited and utterly misleading when we mistake a single concept for the whole of the representational art. A systematic treatment of writing as representational composition makes it straightforward to see the whole without missing the legitimacy of the parts. It illumines how each writing assignment challenges the writer to make texts that are inherently hard to make, texts that align independent representational elements, and that bring into the writer's focus the central patterns that underlie and define these alignments.

Textual portraits challenge writers to add a third dimension to a person portrayed on the page. The self-portrait requires the alignment of disclosure and enactment needed to give a writer the feel of a third dimension. The observer portrait creates this third dimension through the alignment of spatial immediacy, over-time biographical knowledge, and quoted language.

Textual landscapes challenge writers to make environments that immerse readers within a world. In the case of scenic writing, this illusion is created by highlighting the reader's feel of immediacy while softening the feel of displacement. In the case of the narrative history, the writer must raise and align both displacement and immediacy so the world of the text feels gone, yet freshly vivid.

Texts emphasizing a transactional perspective challenge writers to guide the reader's learning within focused goals. In information writing, writers teach through experience or generalization. In exposition, they emphasize unfamiliar generalizations in an assumed context of the familiar. In popular explanation, they emphasize the readers' experience of the familiar either to replace or serve the reader's acquisition of generalizations. In instruction and argument, they use both generalization and experience to guide action, either through a physical task or a decision space.

Traditionally, the way we teach writing and to whom we teach it has been piecemeal and conceptually fragmented. We believe an approach to writing as representational composition can help systematize it. It can be especially useful as a middle layer bridging principles of mechanics and usage (structural composition) with situation-specific, or genre-based, writing (situational composition). Every complex situation of writing constitutes a blended effect of words used to represent interactive worlds. It takes a representational theory to map structures of words into unique and complex situations.

In this book, we have surveyed a spectrum of representational design principles underlying a wide range of effects on readers. These principles and effects cover both the design of virtual worlds and invitations encouraging readers to engage these worlds. More important, we have tried to bring enough specificity and cumulative unity to the principles discussed to indicate that, indeed, a systemic layer of coverage has been overlooked in most extant writing curricula.

After students know how to make sentences and before they tether themselves to one or another specific context of writing, they need to learn how to design interactive worlds through texts. They need a theory of learning that accommodates the fact that writing is a representational, as well as a syntactic art. Syntactic principles are needed for norm fitting and overall sentence clarity, but they do not scale to particular sites and contexts of writing. By contrast, the principles of flexible representation, discussed in this book, underlie a writer's ability to move across site and context with minimal retooling and can help a writer keep pace as sites and contexts shift. In a dynamic world coining new genres over new media at an ever-faster clip, the need for representational theories in writing theory and practice is already profoundly felt and will become even more so in the future.

Although we hope to have sparked interest in what can be taught to writers, our primary concern has been to call attention to the systematic and gaping hole between training in structure and in genre. We further hope that the body of principles brought forth here finds its way into the further development and implementation of writing curricula. Our vision is a tradition of composition where representational theory shares the stage with structural composition and the teaching of natural genres. It is a vision where composition for the writer converges more systematically with composition in the other arts of design, where the art of composition is more than workbook drill but a studio art, one practiced by any designer interested in building interactive worlds in the wondrous medium of words.

References

Bazerman, C. (1988). *Shaping written knowledge: The genre and activity of the experimental article in science.* Madison: University of Wisconsin Press.

Bazerman, C., & Paradis, J. (Eds.). (1991). *Textual dynamics of the professions: Historical and contemporary studies of writing in professional communities.* Madison: University of Wisconsin Press.

Berkenkotter, C., & Huckin, T. (1996). *Genre knowledge in disciplinary communication: Cognition/culture/power.* Mahwah, NJ: Lawrence Erlbaum Associates.

Bierwisch, M. (1996). How much space gets into language? In P. Bloom, M. Peterson, L. Nadel, & M. Garrett (Eds.), *Language and space.* Cambridge, MA: MIT Press, 31–76.

Booth, W. (1961). *The rhetoric of fiction.* Chicago: University of Chicago Press.

Brereton, J. (1995). *The origin of composition studies in America, 1875–1935.* Pittsburgh: University of Pittsburgh Press.

Chafe, W. (1994). *Discourse, consciousness, and time.* Chicago: University of Chicago Press.

Charney, D. H., Reder, L., & Kusbit, G. W. (1990). Goal setting and procedure selection in acquiring computer skills: A Comparison of tutorials, problem-solving, and learner exploration. *Cognition and Instruction, 7* (4), 323–42.

Cheng, P. W., Holyoak, K. J., Nisbett, R. E., & Oliver, L. M. (1986). Pragmatic versus syntactic approaches to training deductive reasoning. *Cognitive Psychology, 18,* 293–328.

Connors, R. J. (1997). *Composition-Rhetoric: Backgrounds, theory & pedagogy.* Pittsburgh: University of Pittsburgh Press.

Fong, G. T., Krantz, D. H., & Nisbett, R. E. (1986). The effects of statistical training on thinking about everyday problems. *Cognitive Psychology, 18,* 253–92.

Gardner, H. (1995). *Leading minds: An anatomy of leadership.* New York: Basic Books.

Geisler, C. (1994). Academic literacy and the nature of expertise: reading, writing, and knowing in academic philosophy. Mahwah, NJ: Lawrence Erlbaum Associates.

Gorgias (1993). *Encomium of Helen.* D.M. McDowell (Trans. and Ed.). London: Bristol Classic, p. 4.

Kaufer, D., & Butler, B. (1996). *Rhetoric and the arts of design.* Mahwah, NJ: Lawrence Erlbaum Associates.

Kaufer, D., & Carley, K. (1993). *Communication at a distance: The influence of print in socio-cultural organization and change.* Mahwah, NJ: Lawrence Erlbaum Associates.

Kershaw, I. (1998). *Hitler: 1889-1936 hubris.* New York: Norton.

Kosslyn, S. (1994). *Image and brain: The resolution of the imagery debate*. Cambridge, MA: MIT Press.

Leff, M. C. (1987). Modern sophistic and the unity of rhetoric. In J. S. Nelson, A. Megill, & D. N. McCloskey (Eds.), *The Rhetoric of the Human Sciences: Language and Argument in Scholarship and Public Affairs* (pp. 19–37). Madison: University of Wisconsin Press.

Miller, C. (1984). Genre as social action. *Quarterly Journal of Speech, 70*, 151–67.

Morton, O. (1999, May 17). In pursuit of infinity. *The New Yorker*, 84–9.

Murphy, J. J., & Jerone, J. (1982). *The rhetorical tradition and modern writing*. New York: Modern Languages Association Press.

Nietzsche, F. (1989). *On truth and lying in an extra-moral sense*. In S. Gilman, C. Blair & D. Parent (Trans. and Eds.), Friedrich Nietzsche on Rhetoric and Langauge. Oxford: Oxford University Press, p. 250.

Olsen, D. (1994). *The world on paper*. New York: Cambridge University Press.

Orkikowski, W., & Yates, J. (1994). Genre repertorie: The structuring of communicative practices in organizations. *Administrative Science Quarterly, 39*, 541–74.

Otnes, C. (1998). Friend of the Bride—and then some: Roles of the bridal salon during wedding planning. In J. F. Sherry (Ed.), *ServiceScapes: The concept of place in contemporary markets* (pp. 229-58). Chicago: NTC Business Books.

Petraglia, J. (1998). *Reality by design: The rhetoric and technology of authenticity in education*. Mahwah, NJ: Lawrence Erlbaum Associates.

Remnick, D. (1996). *The devil problem and other true stories*. New York: Random House.

Russell, D. (1997). Rethinking genre in school and society: An activity theory analysis. *Written Communication, 14*, 504–54.

Sanoff, H. (Ed.). (1990). *Participatory design: Theory & techniques*. Raleigh: North Carolina State.

Scott, F. N., & Denny, J. V. (1893). *Paragraph-Writing*. Boston: Allyn & Bacon.

Spirn, A. W. (1998). *The language of landscape*. New Haven, CT: Yale University Press.

Swales, J. M. (1990). *Genre analysis: English in academic and research settings*. Cambridge, England: Cambridge University Press.

Tannen, D. (1998). *The argument culture : Moving from debate to dialogue*. New York: Random House.

Toulmin, S. (1958). *The uses of argument*. Cambridge, England: Cambridge University Press.

Turkle, S. (1998). *High wired: On the design, use, and theory of educational MOOs*. In C. Haynes & J. R. Holmevik (Eds.), *Forward*. Ann Arbor: University of Michigan Press, ix–ixx.

Williams, J. (1994). *Style: Ten lessons in clarity and grace* (4th ed.). New York: Harper Collins.

Wilson, T. (1560). *The art of rhetoric*. University Park, PA: Penn State Press.

Yates, J., & Orlikowski, W. J. (1992). Genres of organizational communication: A structurational approach to studying communication and media. *Academy of Management Review, 12*(2), 299–326.

Author Index

Subject Index